D1174900

10/04

BYOSSET PUBLIC LIBRARY
225 SO. OYSTER BAY ROAD
SYOSSET, N.Y. 11791

BAKER & TAYLOR

JAN 2 9 2004

Race and Ethnicity
in America

Race and Ethnicity in America

A CONCISE HISTORY

Edited by
Ronald H. Bayor

Columbia University Press
New York

Columbia University Press

Publishers Since 1893

New York Chichester, West Sussex

© 2003 Columbia University Press

All rights reserved

Library of Congress Cataloging-in-Publication Data

Race and ethnicity in America : a concise history / edited by Ronald H. Bayor.

    p. cm.

    Includes bibliographical references and index.

    ISBN 0-231-12940-8 (alk. paper)

    1. United States—Race relations. 2. United States—Ethnic relations.

  3. Ethnicity—United States—History. 4. Minorities—United States—History.

  5. Immigrants—United States—History. 6. United States—Emigration and

  immigration—History. I. Bayor, Ronald H., 1944–

E184.A1R244 2003

305.8'00973—dc21   2003046164

∞

Columbia University Press books are printed on permanent

and durable acid-free paper.

Printed in the United States of America

10 9 8 7 6 5 4 3 2 1

4370039

In loving memory of my wife, Leslie

CONTENTS

ACKNOWLEDGMENTS

My thanks go first and foremost to James Warren, executive editor of Columbia University Press. He initially proposed this project to me and has offered consistent encouragement throughout its development.

The contributing authors deserve special thanks as well for their good work. They were amenable to revisions and considerate of time constraints and generally made my job as editor much easier.

LaDonna Bowen provided her usual excellent help in preparing the manuscript for the press, and I thank her for the close and valuable attention she paid to the project. Enid Pearsons as copyeditor improved the book considerably, and I appreciate her effort as well as that of Ronald Harris, Assistant Managing Editor.

My thanks go also to Jill, Robin, David, Ellie, and Logan for lifting my spirits and thereby helping me to finish this work during a particularly difficult time for all of us.

INTRODUCTION

"I thought to write a history of the immigrants in America. Then I discovered that the immigrants were American history." Historian Oscar Handlin's words convey some of the inspiration behind this book. To understand the development and complexity of contemporary American society, it is important to know the history of immigration, race, and ethnicity: voluntary and involuntary immigrants; different races, religions, and linguistic groups; conflicting nationalities; the development of a sense of ethnicity; initial interaction with Native Americans; the emergence of a dominant culture all shaped an American identity and society.

This book, then, seeks to explore that shaping, to get a sense of how the peopling of America took place. Written as a general history using race and ethnicity as its primary focus, this study is also intended as a research resource for students of this subject. It is divided into eight chronological chapters covering the following periods: 1600–1700, 1701–1788, 1789–1836, 1837–1877, 1878–1900, 1901–1929, 1930–1964, 1965–2000. Although any chronological division would present some problems with regard to overlap for some group histories, these dates were chosen with the intention of highlighting certain events and issues that are pertinent to an ethnic and racial history and avoiding repetition as much as possible. For example, 1965 marks the passage of a new immigration act that reversed earlier laws based on national-origins quotas; 1901–1929 covers the period of large-scale Eastern and Southern European migration, the main immigration restriction laws, southern African American migration north, and the rise of the Ku Klux Klan; 1837–1877 is the time of substantial Irish and German migration, expansion into Mexican territory, Civil War and Reconstruction, and the removal of the Cherokees on their "Trail of Tears."

Authors of the chapters were asked to write essays that would bring together the history of racial and ethnic groups and discuss the variety of experiences with migration, intergroup relations, nativism and racism, identity formation, etc., among a number of groups in different locales. Another focus of each essay was American society's views on immigration, race, and ethnicity during that period and what changes were evident. Authors ably wrote the essays and thereby provided a comprehensive effort to merge immigration and racial and ethnic history into one narrative. The authors were given some leeway on what they chose to emphasize in their narratives, but each provided an effective analysis of the main immigration, racial, and ethnic events and issues of their period. As with any book that encompasses the work of multiple authors, the emphasis and writing style in each is slightly different, depending on the focus of the author. The essays range from a narrative to a more theory-based work, and some stress foreign policy or culture more than others. However, certain themes stand out in all that together define American society: diversity, Americanization, ethnicization, the predominance of race as a national obsession, and the development of a sense of whiteness among European Americans. This last point is particularly revealing since the people in each group came with their own national or regional identities. Many of these people were vilified for their old-world traits yet eventually found commonality and protection in their whiteness. How this transpired and what it says about the development of American life is one of the important concerns of this book.

The essays that follow weave together the various strands of the American story. Carol Berkin (1600–1700) relates the contact between colonists and Indians and the effect each had on the other; intra-European rivalries for land and power; the multiculturalism evident early on in places such as New Amsterdam as English, Dutch, Danes, Norwegians, Africans, French, Germans, Jews, and Muslims intermingled; and the beginning of slavery. In the next essay, Graham Hodges (1701–1788) continues the themes raised in the earlier essay, discussing the relations between Indians, the English, and the French as well as interethnic/religious rivalries, but he extends his narrative to include Spanish colonists in New Spain in the present-day western United States. Slavery was by then a secure fixture in the colonies, although slave revolts occurred. Virginia's slave population soared from approximately 26,000 in 1730 to about 100,000 in 1750 and to over 287,000 in 1790. The American Revolution's impact on ethnicity and race relations is noted as well.

Marion Casey's third chapter (1789–1836) carries the story through the Jackson administration and thus deals with America's expansion westward, the Alien and Sedition Acts, anti-Catholicism and nativism, attitudes toward slavery and African Americans, ethnic colonization efforts, and Indian removal and reservation policies.

The absorption of new groups through expansion (Mexicans) and large-scale immigration (Irish, Germans, and Chinese), as well as the topics of slavery, abolitionism, the Civil War, Reconstruction, and the Indian Wars are the hallmarks of Michael Topp's chapter (1837–1877). In this era, nativism reached a high point and focused its wrath on the Irish and Chinese. The 1875 Page Law set the precedent for the soon-to-be-passed Chinese Exclusion Act. Who the excluded or included groups were took on sharper focus as nativist and racist activities increased.

Mae Ngai (1878–1900) takes us into the beginnings of Southern and Eastern European immigration as hundreds of thousands of Jews, Italians, and others left their *shtetl*, village, and city to come to America. From small towns in Galicia and Sicily and from such cities as Bialystok and Naples, a mass migration came to America's shores. Jim Crow laws, designed to institutionalize segregation, were passed throughout the South, and the *Plessy v. Ferguson* case established the separate but equal doctrine. Assimilation, cultural subordination, and the acceptance of "scientific" race theories affected the treatment of all minorities, whether black, Mexican, Indian, Chinese, or Southern and Eastern European. This factor was especially evident as the United States dealt with the territories gained after the Spanish-American War.

During Andrew Heinze's period (1901–1929) the foreign-born population increased to the highest level in the history of the country, representing 14.7 percent of the American people in 1910. U.S. cities reflected what was happening nationally: by 1910, New York's inhabitants were 41 percent foreign born; Chicago, 36 percent; San Francisco, 34 percent. Furthermore, a large migration of southern blacks to the North occurred. Reaction to the immigrant increase took the form of immigration-restriction laws, which culminated in the National Origins Act of 1924. There was considerable discussion, during these decades, of maintaining the country's racial balance and preventing the newer groups from controlling America's future. A sense of superior and inferior races continued to dominate the public consciousness. In addition to immigration-restriction laws, race riots revealed the public's hostile reaction to the changing demographics. In these riots, whites attacked blacks throughout a city, in black and white neighborhoods alike. Atlanta's 1906 riot reflected continued hostility toward southern African Americans, but riots became a national not just a southern event, taking place in Springfield, Illinois (1908), Chicago (1919), and elsewhere in the nation as well. The revival of the Ku Klux Klan in 1915, with its attacks on blacks, Jews, Catholics, and the foreign-born, further illustrated the tensions during this period. This was also the era of Sacco-Vanzetti, Henry Ford's anti-Semitic publications, and the anti-Catholicism evoked by Al Smith's campaign for president.

Thomas Guglielmo and Earl Lewis focus their chapter (1930–1964) on the issue of racial identity and whiteness. Picking up on discussions in earlier chapters of scientific race theories, and continuing on to look at changing racial identities as well, the authors analyze how various Americans came to terms with shifting racial definitions. While the immigrants of European origin and their descendants began to coalesce within the white racial category and thereby benefited from America's color line, blacks and others fought the social and political implications of their designations. World War II and the struggle against Nazism's racist hatred was an important factor in eventually helping to transform America's racial structure, although during the war, the incarceration of Japanese Americans revealed the extent to which excluded groups could be mistreated. Following the war, African Americans took the lead in confronting racial discrimination and pushed southern governments, through various court cases and mass on-the-street protests, to dismantle the segregation system. The end of this era brought the Civil Rights Act of 1964 and the soon-to-be-passed (1965) Voting Rights Act and Immigration Act.

In the concluding chapter (1965–2000), Timothy Meagher takes the story to the end of the twentieth century. He notes that during these thirty-five years "a new structure of thinking about ethnicity and race . . . emerged." Meagher moves us through the civil rights movement, Malcolm X's influence, Black Power, and the urban race riots of the 1960s. Largely inspired by the movement for black equality, Native Americans, Latinos, and Asian Americans responded with similar efforts to transform the American racial and ethnic political and cultural landscape.

"Red Power" protests led to recognition from the federal government in the form of favorable legislation such as the Indian Child Welfare Act of 1978. It also increased pride in Indian culture. "Brown Power" reflected the Latino efforts in regard to politics, cultural pride, and self-assertion. Mexican Americans, Puerto Ricans, Cuban Americans, and other Spanish-speaking groups pushed for their political and civil rights and for a pan-Hispanic identity. Asian Americans came together in a new pan-Asian movement during this time as well. As with the other groups, Asian Americans sought their civil rights, political empowerment, and cultural identity. "Yellow Power" became their slogan. Even white ethnics were drawn into the new focus and became part of an ethnic revival.

Changes in the immigration laws in 1965 and after resulted in an increasing number of immigrants from Asian and Latino nations as well as black Caribbean countries. This migration, and the ethnic movements triggered by the African American struggle for equality, began changing not only U.S. demographics but the power structure and conceptions of race and ethnicity. Meagher concludes by analyzing the significance of a "white ethnic" identity, multiculturalism, ongoing conflicts involving minorities, and the continued racial divide.

Readers will come away from this book with a clearer sense of the important role that immigration, race, and ethnicity have played in national events and development. The essays can help clarify who the American people are and what has shaped their identity and society. This is an ongoing story as the country continues to receive immigrants, discusses the incorporation of newcomers, debates the continuing role of race, and watches as ethnicization ebbs and flows. The complexity of this story is reflected in the differing opinions of the authors in regard to, for example, when a sense of whiteness began to develop, how persistent the ethnic divisions among European immigrant groups were, and whether those divisions are still relevant.

Readers are urged to go beyond the essays—to consider the suggested publications in order to reach their own conclusions about these and other questions related to America's ethnic and racial history.

Race and Ethnicity
in America

ETHNICITY IN SEVENTEENTH-CENTURY ENGLISH AMERICA, 1600–1700

Carol Berkin

The English colonies of the seventeenth century were notable for their diversity of population, religious institutions, and government struc-tures, a diversity arising in large part from the variety of purposes and methods that spurred their creation. Unlike the Spanish and French governments, the English Crown steadfastly refused to finance coloniza-tion, relying instead on private citizens to take the risks involved in establishing outposts in the Americas. The Crown was willing to grant charters to companies and bestow huge tracts of land on favorites in the Court, but it was not willing to deplete the royal treasury or provide military support for colonization. Few private citizens rose to the chal-lenge in the sixteenth century, for the dismal failure of Sir Walter Raleigh's efforts at Roanoke Island, and Raleigh's resulting bankruptcy dampened even the most patriotic zeal.

Dreams of an American empire did not entirely vanish, however. Indeed, they were enthusiastically revived in the early seventeenth century as English entrepreneurs learned to employ the principles of the joint-stock company to diminish individual risks. The Virginia Company's success in planting the Jamestown settlement in 1607, coupled with the Stuart kings' largesse in land grants, resulted in the creation of proprietary colonies, such as Maryland, Carolina, and Pennsylvania, and colonies chartered to joint-stock companies, such as Massachusetts. But what the Crown saved in expenses it lost in the ability to establish uniformity. Each pro-prietor or joint-stock company could declare its own purposes and goals and establish its own institutions and regulations as long as they did not run contrary to the laws, trade regulations, and diplomatic policies of England. By the end of the century, the crescent of colonies that hugged the Atlantic Ocean on the North American mainland reflected the variety of motives and methods of their founders: some colonies had been established by religious sects seeking refuge, others came into existence for profit, and still others emerged as offshoots from older communities, created by land-hungry settlers or exiled religious deviants.

The State's refusal to be responsible for the founding of the colonies also meant that key institutions were weak, or absent, in the formal and informal development of these communities. For example, the absence of Anglican church control or organized missionary activity contrasted sharply with the role the Catholic church played in both the French and Spanish colonial world. There was a noticeable lack of uniformity of religious practices, governmental structures, or Indian and land policies, and clearly there was no grand design for settlement. When, late in the century, the king attempted to rationalize and centralize the mainland empire, his efforts met with considerable resistance. The Dominion of New England, which united the colonies of New England, New York, and New Jersey under one governor, was the first American casualty of the Glorious Revolution. Before the debacle of the Dominion—and for several decades after—the English colonies continued to evolve in highly individualistic ways.

Regional distinctions did emerge, however, not only in economies and labor systems, but in patterns of ethnic and racial diversity. All regions were biracial in the early seventeenth century, for Indian populations remained within the borders of each colony. By the end of the century, small concentrations of African servants and slaves suggested a new pattern of triracial colonies, especially in the Chesapeake and Lower South. Throughout the century, the New England colonies remained ethnically more homogeneous than other regions. Massachusetts, for example, openly discouraged and even outlawed non-Puritan settlers, although by the end of the century, its transformation into a royal colony opened up settlement to Anglicans as well. The shortage of available land in New England, already a problem by the end of the century, would discourage the waves of immigrants from Ireland and Germany that would fill the backcountries of the middle and southern colonies in the next century. To the south, the Chesapeake was largely an English society, but one marked by the presence of Catholics as well as Protestants and by small communities of radical dissenting sects. The Lower South, still in its early phases of settlement in 1700, would not see its influx of Scots-Irish, Irish, and German settlers until the middle decades of the eighteenth century. The Middle Colonies of New York,

New Jersey, Delaware, and Pennsylvania were, by comparison, notably heterogeneous, in part because of the non-English origins of the first three and in part because of liberal immigration or land policies that did not discriminate based on religion or national origins. Thus, in the seventeenth century, the ethnic diversity of the middle colonies was the most striking regional anomaly.

ENGLISH COLONISTS AND INDIANS

Conquest, conflict, migration, and acculturation were historical realities among the peoples East of the Mississippi long before the arrival of European and English colonists. Indeed, the social and political map of Native American societies was no more static or stable than the map of Europe in the sixteenth and seventeenth centuries. In the Northeast, two massive alliances had, for centuries, shaped the realities of political and cultural life among local communities, pitting the Hurons, Algonquins, Abenakis, Micmacs, Ottawas, and several smaller tribes against the powerful Iroquois Confederacy that was based in New York. In what the English would call Virginia, a confederation of Algonquian-speaking tribes known as the Powhatans dominated local cultures, commanding tribute and military loyalties from a widening circle of villages. By the time John Smith arrived in Jamestown, the Powhatan had forced into its political sphere of control some thirty different Indian peoples. To the south, descendants of Siouan-speaking migrants, who had journeyed over the mountains centuries before Columbus journeyed to the Americas, created communities linked by a common culture but politically independent of one another. Like the Hurons to the north or the subjects of the Powhatans in the Chesapeake, these Siouan descendants had long experience with the aggression of would be conquerors, for Mississippians, intent on seizing territory and compelling political submission, had followed the Siouan groups eastward. Viewed from a global perspective, Europe and North America seemed to be experiencing similar patterns in the sixteenth and seventeenth centuries: shifting boundaries, migration prompted by aggression or by flight from aggression, refugee societies regrouping, and acculturation to the communities that gave them safe haven or to those who conquered them. For the Finns, for the Walloons, for the Irish, the tales of cultural conflict told by the Huron, the Mannahoacs, and the Stuckanocks would be familiar ones.

Many decades before English adventurers and their servants came to Jamestown or Separatist pilgrims arrived at Plymouth, Native Americans had felt the devastation that contact with Europeans would bring to their world. Not the sword, but disease proved the most effective weapon of destruction: an epidemiological disaster of immeasurable proportions swept away Native populations, as smallpox, measles, and other illnesses to which Indians enjoyed no immunities traveled rapidly throughout the Americas following contact with the Europeans. Historians now estimate that millions of Indians died in the centuries before English settlement began.

This catastrophic "exchange" between Europeans and Indians might best be personalized in the life of Squanto, the Wampanoag Indian who befriended the radical Separatist sect known as the Pilgrims and negotiated the treaty with his tribe that insured the survival of their refugee English community at Plymouth in the 1620s. Several years before the Pilgrims set sail for America aboard the *Mayflower,* Squanto had been taken prisoner by English fishermen sailing the coast of Massachusetts. He remained in English society, learning the language and absorbing the culture, for some three years before returning to his homeland. Here he discovered that his exile had protected him from an epidemic that destroyed his entire village at Patuxet. This outbreak had reached far beyond Patuxet, of course; of the twenty thousand Wampanoag Indians of Massachusetts, fewer than 10 percent remained when Squanto returned to America. Ironically, the Pilgrims' settlement of Plymouth was built upon the remains of Squanto's Patuxet.

Despite the devastation wrought by disease, the Indian societies of the Eastern coast did not immediately fall under the control of the European colonizers. Indeed, as historians now understand, negotiation and compromise marked the earliest years of contact between French, Dutch, and English authorities and the local Indians. A "middle ground," a cultural space contributed to by both Indian and white colonists, emerged, allowing the two worlds some possibility of understanding and cooperation. Although each society was interpreted through the prism of the observing culture, some genuine communication was nevertheless made possible; on the middle ground, a compromise of language, belief systems, political structures, and patterns of physical and emotional intimacy evolved. If the French were more flexible than the English or Dutch, even these more ethnocentric nationals made efforts to engage in commercial exchange, political alliance, and social interaction throughout the century.

The English brought to the "middle ground" a firm sense of their cultural superiority. Their assumptions about Indians varied greatly, with some seventeenth-century observers recording glowing accounts of the nobility and simplicity of tribal life and others detailing the heathen savagery of the indigenous population. The romantic notion of the "Noble Savage" thus existed side by side with the contemptuous judgment that Indians were uncivilized, without religion or culture. The assumed character of the Indian often depended on the English colonists' vision of themselves. Thus, among the Puritan colonists, who saw the hand of God directing their settlement, Indians appeared as Satanic obstacles to their mission rather than as proper objects for missionary zeal. The Quaker founders of Pennsylvania, committed to a belief that all people shared God's grace, demonstrated their religious convictions by efforts to treat Native Americans in an egalitarian fashion. In both cases, the prism through which the Indian was seen was self-referential.

No matter what their assumptions or stereotypes, most of the early settlers recognized that their survival depended upon a basic exchange of supplies and knowledge with local Indians. In Jamestown to the south and Plymouth to the north, the willingness of Native Americans to share corn and other foodstuffs as well as information on how to grow these crops made the difference between starvation and sustenance in the early years. In New Netherland, and later in New York, a thriving trade in beaver pelts and other furs secured most of the profits that Europeans wrested from their Hudson River colony. And, in alliances formed with Indian tribes, the English and Dutch found the safety from hostile attack by European rivals and their Indian allies critical to their communities' survival. To varying degrees, Indians who negotiated the "middle ground" acquired the fruits of European technology: weapons, iron and copper utensils, and woolens. Exchanges of a less concrete or tangible nature altered both white and Indian life as new theologies, modes of production, notions of property, and ideas of social organization passed between colonists and natives.

The creation of the middle ground did not, however, insure peace between Native Americans and European colonists. In the English colonies in particular, the settlers' relentless expansionist impulse eventually brought them into conflict with local Indians. As English populations grew, the willingness to negotiate and compromise diminished. Even when disputes arose between English communities, nearby Indians were likely to suffer the consequences. For example, in New England in the late 1630s, an intense rivalry between Massachusetts land developers and the expanding Connecticut settlements proved harmful to the nearby Pequots. Rather than initiating a damaging intra-Puritan conflict, the Massachusetts and Connecticut leadership agreed to turn their aggression outward. They decided to settle their differences by a contest, a winner take all for the colony that managed to conquer the Pequots first. By 1637, Pequot leader Sassacus and his men faced attack from two armies. The Pequot situation worsened when Massachusetts governor John Winthrop ordered Captain John Underhill to attack civilian rather than military targets. The resulting massacre at Mystic Village was recorded in all its gruesome details by Underhill, who noted with satisfaction that "Many [Pequots] were burnt in the fort, both men, women, and children." Villagers who attempted to surrender were brutally murdered. Soon afterward Indian resistance crumbled, and Massachusetts claimed victory over Connecticut in a contest that virtually eliminated the Pequots from New England. The few Indian survivors were rounded up and sold into slavery. The accounts, both private and public, of this brutal war of elimination waged against the Pequots reveal the Puritan certitude that God approved the destruction of heathen obstacles in the path of the faithful.

Thirty-eight years later, the long reign of peace enjoyed between Wampanoag Indians and the Plymouth colonists also came to an end, eroded by the land-hunger of the Pilgrim community. In 1675, Wampanoag leader, Metacomet, mounted a guerilla war against the English, raiding white settlements. Forging an alliance with other regional tribes, Metacomet (or King Philip, as the English called him) expanded the war. The English struck back, aided by Iroquois mercenaries sent by the governor of New York. King Philip's War ended in Metacomet's death and the total elimination of several of the tribes who had come to his aid. Those few who escaped death or enslavement scattered, seeking refuge with Indians to the north and the west. The English victory came at great cost to the colonists as well: over two thousand men, women, and children lost their lives in this short but brutal war.

To the south, a similar pattern could be detected. Alliances formed by struggling English colonists and native Powhatan Indians began to show strains before a decade of settlement had ended. In 1609, war broke out, marked by atrocities such as decapitation and torture on both sides. As the colony prospered and the desire for additional tobacco lands grew, aggressive policies replaced compromise and cooperation between the two races. In 1622, Powhatan leader Opechancanough mounted a surprise attack on Jamestown, killing one-fourth of the settlers in one day. Virginians retaliated, and the war continued sporadically for a decade. The Powhatan population was devastated; of forty thousand people, only five hundred remained by the 1630s.

Despite the steady collapse of cooperation between most English colonies and local Indians, the two races remained a presence in one another's lives. Accounts of predawn Indian raids on New England villages run like a leitmotif through the diaries of Puritan fathers and mothers and the sermons of their ministers. Captivity narratives, written by those who were ransomed from French-allied Indians or from French Canadian officials, recount grueling forced marches through snow and storm, injuries, unaccustomed work, and—in some cases— proselytizing efforts by Catholic priests or nuns. Yet these narratives also reveal the diversity of views on Indian life and culture: while some denounce their captors as heathen and savage, others show a growing respect for, and understanding of, a culture strikingly different from their own. Among those differences is the willingness of the Indian communities to accept white captives into their midst, to adopt them into their families fully and without any debilitating traces of racism. English colonists did not reciprocate: the limited efforts by Puritan ministers to convert Indians to Christianity, for example, never resulted in the integration of these "praying Indians" into the colonial community.

MAKING FOREIGN COLONIES INTO ENGLISH COLONIES

The contests for land and resources that erupted between Native Americans and the English were not the only conflicts in these early decades of settlement. Intra-European rivalries emerged as well, for the English did not initially monopolize the territory along the Atlantic coast from present-day Maine to Georgia. The Dutch, basing their claims upon Henry Hudson's 1609 voyage, created trading posts at Albany and Manhattan as early as 1614. Although Hudson had praised the area as a land of "Grasse & flowers," New Netherland attracted few settlers. Throughout the seventeenth century, Holland's Caribbean possessions held out the promise of quicker, and more extensive, riches. In 1621, a newly formed trading company, the Dutch West India

Company, took over the task of colonizing. To encourage settlement, the Company devised a *patroon* system, creating subcolonies within New Netherland made up of vast estates whose proprietors enjoyed manorial rights in law and were allowed to collect rents from their tenant farmers. Only one patroonship, Rensselaerwyck, proved successful. Using a sample taken from 1630–1644, historian Oliver Rink drew a portrait of the colonists who settled on Kiliaen van Rensselaer's million-acre holding. Most were single young men in their teens and twenties, drawn from the economically depressed area around Utrecht—immigrants similar in age and circumstances to the English indentured servants who flocked to the Chesapeake in the seventeenth century. Only 18 percent of the Rensselaerwyck tenants were married and had three or more children. Although most of van Rensselaer's tenants were farmers, a sizeable number were artisans—masons, carpenters, millwrights, and wheelwrights, along with cobblers, tailors, a baker, and a blacksmith.

Despite its efforts, the colony boasted only three hundred settlers in 1629, most of them Protestant Walloon refugees from the southernmost areas of the Spanish Netherlands. Slowly, because of the West India Company's liberal admission standards, a heterogeneous collection of adventurous, profit-hungry colonists trickled in. By 1673, there were somewhere between six thousand and nine thousand colonists in New Netherland, although few of them were Dutch. Nearly 40 percent were German, mostly from Aachen, Cleves, East Friesland, Westphalia, Bremen, Hamburg, and Oldenburg. This German emigration had been prompted by the devastation of war in southwest Germany, an experience of displacement they shared, although without acknowledgement or sympathy, with many of the Indian communities in the Hudson Valley. New Englanders accounted for much of the population on Long Island, while the multicultural atmosphere in New Amsterdam was intensified by the arrival of Danes and Norwegians, free and enslaved Africans, French Huguenots, a sprinkling of Muslims, and a small community of Jews.

The Jewish influx illustrates well the impact of the trading company's openness to diversity—and the resulting tensions within the colony. In 1654, twenty-three Jews had arrived from South America, most of them Iberians seeking asylum after Dutch rule ended in Brazil. Peter Stuyvesant, then governor of New Netherland, was outraged, and sought to banish these refugees from his colony. Writing to the directors of the Dutch West India Company, Stuyvesant insisted that they should not tolerate members of a "deceitful race—such hateful enemies and blasphemers of the name of Christ" who would "infect and trouble this colony." The directors ignored his advice and Stuyvesant had to be content with passing measures that restricted Jewish participation in the life of the larger community, limited their trading rights, and imposed special taxes upon them. Nevertheless, the Jewish population increased, and by the turn of the century, Jews constituted about 2.5 percent of Manhattan's population. While a small Jewish community also appeared in 1658 in Newport, Rhode Island, and four Jewish colonists settled in Charleston, South Carolina, in 1697, the Manhattan community remained the largest in mainland America.

Meanwhile, the Dutch faced what they considered to be Swedish interlopers along the Delaware River. Although the Netherlands claimed this area, in March 1638, two Swedish ships sailed up the river to present-day Wilmington. The Swedes and Finns aboard these ships— citizens of a single kingdom in the seventeenth century—named the site Paradise Point. Ironically, one of the moving forces behind this colonizing venture was a Dutchman familiar to residents of Manhattan: Peter Minuit. In 1626, Minuit had purchased Manhattan island from local Indians; now, in 1638, he repeated the process, this time buying lands for the New Sweden Company, the brainchild of the Finnish admiral Klas Fleming and Minuit himself.

Only a few hundred people ever settled in the colony, most of them Finns. By midcentury, these settlers lived in a half-dozen fortified areas— from Fort Christina in the south, to Fort New Korsholm on the Schuylkill in the north, to Fort Elfsborg on the eastern shore of the Delaware in New Jersey. Despite the meager size of this Swedish colony, the Dutch always viewed it as an incursion into their domain. In 1638, William Kieft, governor of New Netherland, warned Peter Minuit that the Netherlands considered the colony to be illegitimate, adding that he considered Minuit a traitor for accepting the post of governor of New Sweden. Insisting that Minuit had no authority to construct forts along the river, Kieft declared, "We do, therefore protest against all injury to property, and all the evil consequences of bloodshed, uproar, and wrong which our Trading Company may thus suffer." The letter ended with the threat that New Netherland would "protect our rights in such manner as we may find most advisable." Military action followed. By 1656, Dutch forces had seized the Swedish forts, meeting little resistance from the colonists. In 1664, however, control of the area again changed hands, as New Netherland fell, also without resistance, to the naval assault of the English

Duke of York. Surprisingly, the Duke of York pursued a liberal policy toward the Dutch citizens of what was now the colony of New York. The Dutch Reform Church was allowed to continue to serve the largely Calvinist population, Dutch property holdings were honored, and Dutch inheritance patterns, strikingly different from the English, remained legal. The Dutch tolerance of diversity within the colony also seemed to be acceptable to the new English proprietor. Indeed, between 1665 and 1685, the colony became a religious refuge for Scottish Presbyterians, English Quakers, and French Huguenots. By the time James ascended to the throne of England in 1685, New York was a thriving colony of fifteen thousand, representing the greatest variety of faiths, races, and ethnic backgrounds the English colonial world had yet seen.

If New York was multicultural, its colonists did not always live in harmony. English, Dutch, and German merchants engaged in some-times ruthless competition over control of the City's trade. The three ethnic groups were equally fierce in their rivalry to dominate the cultural life of the City. A similar struggle for dominance characterized life in Albany. The only thing that could possibly have united these quarreling factions was a shared threat to their prosperity and autonomy. That threat came in 1685, when James II decided to reorganize the northern mainland colonies, abolishing the separate governments of New England and New York and creating a single administrative unit called the Dominion of New England. New Englanders no less than New Yorkers chafed at the merger, and all came to loathe the profiteer-ing by the Dominion's leadership.

In 1689, news reached New York of the Glorious Revolution in England and the consequent end to James's rule. Four years of burning resentment burst into flame and revolts broke out in Boston, Long Island, and New York City. While Bostonians imprisoned Edmund Andros, the hated governor of the Dominion, Jacob Leisler, a German merchant, led the uprising against Dominion authorities in New York City. Leisler had personal reasons to resent Andros, whose favoritism toward English colonists had dealt a blow to the German immigrant's social and political ambitions. Thus when several towns on Long Island revolted against the Dominion, Leisler extended the revolt to New York City. He seized con-trol of the fort, imprisoned Andros's representatives—and then, for good measure, jailed some of his local non-German business rivals.

By the end of the summer, Leisler had declared himself commander in chief of the entire colony. Acting as head of a ten-man "committee of safety," he proceeded to imprison more opponents and drive others into exile. Insisting that he was the legitimate head of a constitutional government under William and Mary, Leisler looked for, and received, support from many of the less Anglicized Dutch colonists. Not all the Dutch citizens of the colony backed him, however. In fact, the Dutch community in Albany strongly opposed him, fearing his policies would do their city more damage than those of Andros. In the end, Leisler's Rebellion seemed to be an uprising of two distinct groups: New York City merchants and shopkeepers who were disadvantaged by the Dominion and Long Island communities of Puritan background

Despite Albany's refusal to acknowledge his authority, Leisler proceeded to establish a colonial government, create courts, and raise taxes. He believed he had initiated an era of home rule, but to his surprise, William and Mary did not support his efforts or reward them. Instead they sent a new governor from England. When Jacob Leisler refused to turn over the reins of power, the coalition that supported him dissolved, and he was eventually arrested, convicted of treason, and executed. Hanged, disemboweled while still alive, and then drawn and quartered, Leisler and his son-in-law now became local martyrs to the German community. For many years to come, New York's political life was marked by conflict between Leislerites and supporters of the royal governor and the Crown.

SERVANTS AND SLAVES IN THE CHESAPEAKE

While colonies like New York and Pennsylvania opened their doors to a wide variety of Protestant sects and European settlers, the colonies to the south were not without some pockets of diversity. Seventeenth-century Virginia's eastern shore contained immigrants from the Netherlands, Sweden, Portugal, Spain, Germany, and even Turkey. Maryland, founded as a Catholic refuge by the Calvert family, never attracted a majority of Catholic colonists. Settled largely by Protestants, the colony was frequently torn apart by its religious divisions. Protestants and Catholics were often as antagonistic as Dutch and English or Puritan and Indian, and over the course of the seventeenth century, despite the efforts of the Calverts to enforce and encourage religious toleration, violence erupted. When Oliver Cromwell's Puritan government repealed Cecil Calvert, Lord Baltimore's Act of Toleration and took he colony from its proprietor, civil war broke out in Maryland. The

Protestants triumphed, but Cromwell's government crumbled and, with the Restoration, the Calvert family became Maryland's proprietors once more. Anti-Catholic sentiment did not vanish, however; rebellions were attempted in 1659, 1676, and again in 1681. When William and Mary ascended the throne in 1688, Maryland's Protestants saw their chance. Led by Anglican minister John Coode, the Protestant Association defeated the Catholics and persuaded the new monarchs to make Maryland a royal colony. Coode was no hero, however, to many Maryland Protestants, and his abrasive personality, like Jacob Leisler's, soon generated strong opposition. When the Calverts converted to Anglicanism in the early eighteenth century, Maryland was returned to their keeping, much to the relief of many of the colonists.

Despite Maryland's origins as a Catholic haven, the majority of the immigrants to both Chesapeake colonies were young, single Englishmen, driven from their family farms by the economic dislocation of the era. Traveling from depressed areas of the English countryside into local market towns, then on to major port cities such as Bristol or London, these increasingly desperate young men agreed to bind, or indenture, themselves to ship captains or Chesapeake, contracting to work from 3 to 7 years in exchange for passage to America, meager sustenance during their term of servitude, and the promise of land ownership when their term of service ended. Even Maryland, originally conceived of as a Catholic refuge by its proprietors, the Calverts, was largely populated by young, impoverished English Protestants.

Tobacco was the magnet that drew both independent settlers and tens of thousands of indentured servants to the Chesapeake. Cultivation of this crop was time-consuming, tedious, and exhausting; more important, it was labor-intensive, for tools and machinery were in short supply in the colonial world. There seemed to be an insatiable need for field hands, as planters expanded their production to increase profits in boom times and to cover costs when prices fell. Most planters believed that indentured servitude was the most economical labor system, given the realities of the region. The disease-ridden environment of the Chesapeake resulted in high mortality rates, and only the small purchase cost for a bound servant compensated the planter for the loss of labor when malaria or dysentery claimed the worker's life. Few tobacco planters considered the preferred labor force of the Caribbean, the African slave, for supplies were limited on the mainland, prices were high, and the initial investment of capital would be lost if the slave fell victim to disease.

A shift to slave labor did begin by century's end, however. Several factors came into play: mortality rates dropped as colonists learned how to protect themselves within the disease environment; the supply of English indentured servants dried up as economic conditions—and employment possibilities—improved at home; and finally, the monopoly on the slave trade, once enjoyed by the Dutch, was wrested away by the English, thus increasing the supply of African workers to all English colonies and lowering the purchase price. The mass importation of enslaved workers and the rise of a slave society in the Chesapeake was still decades away, in the eighteenth century, but the process had begun before the close of the seventeenth century.

Before midcentury, most slaves in the mainland colonies came from Angola, a region that stretched along the Central African coast of the Atlantic from Cape Lopez to Benguela. While some of the wealthiest residents of Virginia's eastern shore could afford to purchase slaves directly from Africa from the Dutch shipmasters, most of the blacks transported to Virginia had, as historian Douglas Deal notes, endured years of service on the sugar plantations of British, Spanish, or Dutch Caribbean islands. Many of these "seasoned" servants could speak English well and were accustomed to English cultural patterns. But however these black colonists were acquired, they remained a rarity in the colonial tobacco world until the 1680s.

Laws and regulations based on race developed slowly and unevenly in the counties and parishes of the Chesapeake. In the early decades, white and black servants cooperated, feeling they had more in common with one another than with their masters. English servant James Revel, who left behind a remarkable poem recounting his arduous and dreary life in the tobacco fields, attested to the camaraderie felt among all servants, black and white. Court records demonstrate that blacks and whites drank, caroused, and fornicated together. More important, they occasionally plotted their escape from servitude together. In 1640, for example, seven African and English servants stole weapons and a small boat and attempted to reach Dutch-held territory by water. White men were willing to put their faith in black ones whose skill or daring might insure the success of an escape plan.

Although African workers did not sign indenture contracts, they were not always deemed servants for life before the eighteenth century. Records remain of black landowners who enjoyed most of the rights their white neighbors enjoyed, including legal recognition of their marriages, ownership of property, and the right to distribute that property in their wills. Marriages between free black men and free white women continued to occur throughout the 1650s and 1660s on the eastern shore, and African landowners purchased white indentured servants to help them work their lands.

By 1662, however, racial barriers began to be erected and the outlines of enslavement for life were drawn. In that year, for example, Virginia's legislature declared that a child's condition followed that of the mother rather than that of the father, thus condemning all children born to slave women to a lifetime of servitude. This law stood in stark contrast to the English assumptions that paternal rather than maternal status defined the status of offspring. Nonmarital sex between the races was punished more severely than fornication or adultery between whites, and by 1691, any white colonist who married an African, an Indian, or a mulatto was banished from Virginia forever.

The regulation of interracial contact and the distinctions between white and black conditions of service were, in part, the result of the slow increase in the number of African field hands. But other factors contributed to the growing number of distinctions based on race. In 1676, the violent and protracted revolt known as Bacon's Rebellion, pitting backcountry planters against the tidewater or coastal planter elite, proved to have deleterious consequences for black Virginians.

Nathaniel Bacon was a gentleman, not a former servant, but like many would-be planters after midcentury, he found the best of the coastal lands already claimed by a local elite. These tidewater planters dominated the tobacco economy and the legislature as well. Struggling to find prosperity on lands that bordered Indian territories, men like Bacon were caught between hostile enemies to the west and self-interested enemies in the House of Burgesses. Tidewater planters were willing to tax the backcountry colonists, but they were rarely willing to use that tax money to mount the military protection these western farmers believed was needed. When a new round of violence erupted between Indians and colonists in 1676, Nathaniel Bacon took the lead in demanding that the royal governor and his Tidewater supporters send military assistance. The governor refused—and Bacon and his followers took their revolt to the colonial capital. Along the way, the ranks of the rebellion swelled; servants rallied to Bacon's side, including roughly 10 percent of the black male population of the colony. Although the revolt was eventually suppressed, Virginia's political and economic elite feared the possibility of further cooperation between lower class whites and blacks. Many historians feel that Bacon's Rebellion marked a turning point in racial history in the colony, propelling the planter elite to a conscious policy of racial divisiveness.

By the late seventeenth century almost three-quarters of the Africans imported into the Chesapeake came primarily from two regions: Senegambia, at the mouth of the Gambia River, and the Bight of Biafra. Their numbers grew steadily: between 1670 and 1700, six thousand slaves arrived directly from Africa. The nature of the black population in the Chesapeake was thus changing: the new arrivals rarely spoke English and were unfamiliar with English customs, work patterns, or religion. In addition, although the sex ratio among the "seasoned" blacks had been equal, the slaves imported directly from Africa were almost exclusively young men and boys. Thus by the end of the century, the Chesapeake faced an influx of genuinely foreign colonists, Africans who had come not by choice but by force.

FIRST SETTLEMENTS IN THE LOWER SOUTH

To the south of the tobacco region lay Carolina, a vast area that included swamps and lowlands that King Charles had granted to eight of his wealthy supporters. Although these proprietors drafted an elaborate scheme for a feudal society in Carolina, the colony actually developed much as Virginia had by offering land to anyone willing to emigrate. After experimenting with several cash crops, including tobacco, sugar cane, and even olives, the Carolina planters soon focused their efforts on rice culti-vation. Although the significant development of the Lower South, as the Carolinas and Georgia were called, would lie in the eighteenth century, the biracial outlines of that society were already evident in the seven-teenth. The Barbadian planters who were among the earliest settlers of the Carolinas brought slaves with them to the mainland; unlike the Chesapeake tobacco farmers, these West Indian émigrés did not need to evolve a rationale or a legal structure for racial slavery.

IMPERIAL CONFLICTS IN
THE SEVENTEENTH CENTURY

The colonies were separated from their mother country by three thou-sand miles of ocean, but they did not escape the consequences of

England's aggressive foreign policy. England's slow rise to power during the seventeenth century made that nation a central player in the competition to control North America and its resources and to dominate the Atlantic trade. This competition influenced key aspects of colonial life, from settlement patterns to Indian alliances to militia activity and its funding. The mainland colonies, situated between the French North American empire to the north and the Spanish territories to the south and southwest, were quickly drawn into the four wars for empire among Spain, France, and England—and their allies and satellites—that began in earnest in the 1680s.

The succession to the throne of William and Mary in 1688 sparked the first major conflict between France and England. English allies included Holland, Sweden, and Spain, but for the colonists, the alliance between the French and the powerful Hurons was more important. Like their European counterparts, Indians of the Great Lakes and Northern New York regions were divided into competing camps of Huron and Iroquois. Their struggle for control of the richest fur regions was now joined to the European struggle known in America as King William's War as Hurons allied themselves with the French and the Iroquois with the English.

Few British or French military forces took part in the American theater of war. Instead, Canadian militias battled New England militia companies while Iroquois and Huron troops staged raids and incursions on enemy territories. New England colonies rushed to enforce militia laws that required service by all but ministers, magistrates, doctors, schoolmasters, fishermen, and students. In Massachusetts, each town was required to raise a band or company of militiamen, amateur soldiers led by elected officers. Canadians organized in a similar fashion, calling on tenants to do military service as a duty to their landlords. The first serious blow had been dealt even before war was officially declared, when Iroquois warriors attacked the French outpost at Lachine in July of 1689, killing somewhere between sixty and two hundred inhabitants and taking more than a hundred prisoners. The French Canadians were quick to retaliate. Well-planned raids in Maine and New Hampshire destroyed garrison houses and cost the lives of local militia leaders. The violence spread quickly from Canadian border towns like Dover, New Hampshire, to upstate New York. In February 1690, a force of Indians and French troops struck the village of Schenectady, leveling the town in only a few hours, and killing sixty residents.

Accounts of atrocities began to spread early in the war—many of them true: children's heads dashed against staircases or apple trees; women hacked to death by hatchets. When these murders were perpetrated by the Indian allies of the French, the colonists decried them as savagery, but when Hannah Duston, a matron from Haverhill, Massachusetts, killed ten of her captors while they slept, scalping them in the bargain, she was hailed as a Christian heroine, honored in sermons by such distinguished divines as Cotton Mather. When the war finally ended in 1697, at least 650 English colonists were dead, killed in battle, in raids, or in captivity. The Iroquois death toll was far greater, reaching somewhere between six hundred and thirteen hundred.

England's rivalry with France would grow even more intense in the next century, and colonists would draw upon their memories, real and imagined, of what they called Indian savagery. But the French were the true objects of their hatred, and a fierce anti-Catholicism, synonymous for many with anti-French sentiments, became the rallying cry until this old enemy became the colonists' new ally during the American Revolution.

CONCLUSION

By 1700, a clear ethnic and racial map of the mainland English colonies had emerged. To the north, New England remained the most homogeneous of the regions, populated primarily by English Calvinists in the countryside but with a growing urban population of Anglicans once Massachusetts became a royal colony in 1692. Few Indians remained in the area, for the wars against Pequot, Narragansett, and Wampanoag had ended the era of cooperation and coexistence between the races. The black population was small, concentrated in the slave-trading towns of Rhode Island and on the docks of Boston. The shortage of available land, already a problem by the end of the century, would discourage the waves of immigrants from Ireland and Germany that would fill the backcountries of the middle and southern colonies in the next century.

South of New England, Pennsylvania was just beginning to attract European settlers, drawn to the colony by its liberal land policies and religious tolerance. New York, and particularly New York City, remained the most cosmopolitan, heterogeneous spot on the English mainland, with the Dutch, German, and English in lively competition for cultural hegemony, and with Jews, French Huguenots, and Africans adding to the city's tradition of diversity.

The transition of the Chesapeake and the Lower South from a society with slaves to a slave society, defined by the presence of a social caste based on race, had begun by 1700. Despite the arrival of Scotch-Irish, Irish, and German immigrants in the next century, race rather than ethnicity would be the defining characteristic of this southern culture.

ANNOTATED BIBLIOGRAPHY

Acrelius, Israel. *A History of New Sweden, or The Settlements on the River Delaware*. New York: Arno Press, 1972.
    One of the few attempts to narrate the history of this small seventeenth-century colony of Swedes and Finns. The volume focuses on political origins of the settlement and the background of the immigrants themselves.

Axtell, James. *Natives and Newcomers: The Cultural Origins of North America*. New York: Oxford University Press, 2000.
    Axtell describes the major encounters between Indians and Europeans and analyzes how they ultimately shaped a unique American character. He explores both the short- and long-term consequences of these encounters on the two cultures.

Bailyn, Bernard *The Peopling of British North America: An Introduction*. New York: Vintage, 1988.
    In this introduction to Bailyn's multivolume work, *The Peopling of British North America*, one of the leading scholars in early American history identifies central themes relating to the transatlantic transfer of people from the Old World to the North American continent.

Bailyn, Bernard, and Philip D. Morgan. *Strangers within the Realm: The Cultural Margins of the First British Empire*. Chapel Hill: University of North Carolina Press, 1991.
    This collection of essays, dealing with British expansion in the seventeenth and eighteenth centuries, addresses the processes of Anglicization on the peripheries of the British Empire.

Calloway, Colin. *New Worlds for All: Indians, Europeans, and the Remaking of Early America*. Baltimore: Johns Hopkins University Press, 1997.
    This study, which encompasses continental America for a span of three hundred years, explores the various ways in which Indians and Europeans forged alliances in early America and sufficiently comingled to create a unique American identity and culture.

Games, Alison. *Migration and the Origins of the English Atlantic World*. Harvard Historical Studies. Cambridge: Harvard University Press, 1999.
    This in-depth analysis of the seventy-five hundred people who traveled from London to the New World in 1635 explores the attempt and ultimate failure of the travelers to re-create English society in their overseas outposts.

Goodfriend, Joyce D. *Before the Melting Pot: Society and Culture in Colonial New York City, 1664–1730*. Princeton: Princeton University Press, 1991.
    Exploring the vast ethnic diversity of New York City that was present from its

earliest days, Goodfriend seeks to discover the meaning of ethnicity in early America. Arguing against the prevailing notion of rapid Anglicization, she suggests that ethnicity proved to be a persistent force into the eighteenth century.

Jaffee, David. *People of the Wachusett: Greater New England in History and Memory, 1630–1860*. Ithaca: Cornell University Press, 1999.

Through the lens of one New England town, Jaffee paints a portrait of the cultural history of America's original frontier. Firsthand narratives of founding citizens are explored to provide a personal account of the founding of America, town by town.

Kupperman, Karen O. *Indians and English: Facing Off in Early America*. Ithaca: Cornell University Press, 2000.

Kupperman explores the complex interactions between colonists and Native Americans between 1580 and 1640. In examining the sources of precolonial stereotypes, she discovers the interconnectedness of the two cultures.

Lepore, Jill. *The Name of War: King Philip's War and the Origins of American Identity*. New York: Random House, 1999.

An exploration of King Philip's War, not only as a historical event but as a literary event. Lepore stresses the advantage the English enjoyed as a literate culture in controlling the accounts of this war, its motives, and the nature of its participants.

Merwick, Donna. *Possessing Albany, 1620–1710: The Dutch and English Experiences*. New York: Cambridge University Press, 1990.

This is a study of the role of the Dutch in shaping the political and cultural life of seventeenth-century New York. Merwick narrates early New York history from a Dutch rather than an Anglo perspective.

Morgan, Edmund. *American Slavery, American Freedom: The Ordeal of Colonial Virginia*. New York: Norton, 1975.

This award-winning examination of the roots of slavery in colonial Virginia traces its development to Bacon's Rebellion and the effort to ameliorate class tensions among English colonists by creating a caste system based on race.

Morgan, Philip. *Slave Counterpoint: Black Culture in the Eighteenth-Century Chesapeake and Lowcountry*. Chapel Hill: University of North Carolina Press, 1998.

This prize-winning book provides a richly textured comparison of African American life in eighteenth-century Chesapeake and Low-Country society, addressing such issues as work patterns, family organization, and black-white relationships in the two regions.

Rink, Oliver A. *Holland on the Hudson: An Economic and Social History of Dutch New York*. Ithaca: Cornell University Press, 1973

Instead of focusing on the failures of the Dutch West India Company, Rink explores the successes of private Amsterdam merchants in creating the Dutch colony on the Hudson. Rink paints a portrait of a thriving Dutch society, rather than a faltering one, on the eve of conquest by the British.

Shuffelton, Frank, ed. *A Mixed Race: Ethnicity in Early America*. New York: Oxford University Press, 1993.

This collection of essays suggests that American society was inescapably multicultural from its inception and that cultural differences fundamentally defined American culture. This topically and chronologically broad collection, which focuses on the eighteenth century, addresses issues such as the representation of cultural differences between European immigrants and Native Americans and the circumstances in which the first African American autobiographical narratives arose.

White, Richard. *The Middle Ground: Indians, Empires, and Republics in the Great Lakes Region, 1650–1815*. New York: Cambridge University Press, 1991. This compelling study of relations between Indians and Europeans in the Great Lakes concentrates on the necessity for the creation of a "middle ground" between two alien cultures. This middle ground allowed communication, alliances, and trade as well as the transference of cultural values and behaviors for almost three hundred years.

Wood, Betty. *The Origins of American Slavery: Freedom and Bondage in the English Colonies*. New York: Hill and Wang, 1997. Wood examines the role of the English in the development of slavery in this synthesis of the scholarly debate on the origins of slavery in America.

2

ETHNICITY IN EIGHTEENTH-CENTURY NORTH AMERICA, 1701–1788

Graham Russell Hodges

Ethnicity was a defining characteristic for early Americans. Among a plethora of New World societies where, except for Native Americans, few individuals could trace their residence back more than three generations, a person's language, personal habits, and customs often derived directly from roots in old-world cultures. Continuing waves of voluntary and coerced immigration from Europe and Africa between 1700 and 1788, along with religious revivals and celebration of secularized rituals, refreshed old-world cultures among colonial Americans. Two historical views have shaped discussion of ethnicity in early America. One side holds firmly that eighteenth-century Americans soon became acculturated or "Anglicized" into the dominant political English society. Opposing this view is one that contends that ethnicity and race proved strong enough for groups to resist Anglicization and maintain traditional customs and beliefs. A third view, adopted in this essay, is that Anglicization depended heavily upon English demographic dominance in particular regions. The English controlled the Atlantic seaboard but did not dominate demographically, except for New England.

In this essay I contend that although the English controlled the Atlantic Coast politically and militarily, the British Empire held no hegemony, which could have eliminated other cultures. A more nuanced term for the effects of English political and military control on ethnicity is Americanization. In this definition, members of an ethnic group necessarily accepted English rule, but within their culture sustained traditional traits. At the same time, they frequently interacted with other ethnic groups and melded particular cultural practices to their own.

Even though English political and religious authorities pined for immigrants from the British Isles, they often recruited enslaved and bonded peoples from other societies as laborers. At the outset of the eighteenth century, observers often commented on the heterogeneity of the Atlantic Coast colonies. New York City was the best example of this; in this port city lived English, Dutch, Scots, Irish, Germans, Walloons, Portuguese, Africans, and Jews. Such diversity held little appeal to English authorities. Yet their efforts to Anglicize African slaves and European servants often floundered under local pressures. Elsewhere, throughout the eighteenth century, drives to acculturate people to English ways had mixed results. Even in New England, which was dominated by English peoples, by midcentury, more than 30 percent of its inhabitants came from outside of England. As Jon Butler has observed, Africans, Scots, Scotch-Irish, and Irish were numerous enough to have a "critical mass" to support burgeoning group identities. Further south, African Americans presented a major alternative to English culture along with substantial influence from German arrivals. Westward from the Mississippi and Ohio River Valleys to the Pacific coast, Native American, French, and Spanish power held sway throughout most of the eighteenth century. In this essay, I treat the history of ethnicity in North America by emphasizing time and space. I have divided the essay geographically, and have attempted to cover all the regions that make up contemporary United States.

Although the English language generally served as a lingua franca, there was little commonality between the sections of the Atlantic Coast. These sections include New England, the Mid Atlantic, the Chesapeake or Upper South, and the Lower South. Further into the interior, English power dissipated rapidly. The Iroquois Confederacy controlled much of the land between the Onondaga region to present-day Illinois. The Midwest was a contested middle ground. In the Southeast, Native Americans maintained a precarious grip on traditional homelands, as European Americans with African slaves occupied ports along the Gulf of Mexico. In the Southwest, Spanish Tejanos exerted firm control over the remnants of Native American nations from New Mexico to California while warring against Apache and other guerilla Indians in the intermountain West.

ENCOUNTERING NATIVE AMERICANS

All nonindigenous settlers coming to North America in the eighteenth century had to interact with Native American societies. Although Native

America sustained control over most of the interior land of North America until after the American Revolution, genocidal war practices, forced removal, and disease directly decimated their numbers. It was during the eighteenth century that the balance of power tipped irretrievably away from Native Americans. Part of that loss was demographic. From an estimated population of 5 million persons in 1500, Native American nations dramatically declined to about six hundred thousand by 1800. Tributary groups of Native Americans around New England, New York, Pennsylvania, and down to Virginia were generally extirpated and survivors had to retreat behind a Proclamation Line established in 1676. By 1700, there were few Native Americans left close to the Atlantic Ocean. To stem this slaughter, Native Americans attempted to regroup by assembling new nations out of the remnants of older ones and practiced adoption into the tribe or band on a large scale. They were able to do this in the newer English colonies. The example of South Carolina is instructive. There refugees of the Saponis joined Tutelos or Occaneechees in a desperate effort to survive. They did not accept all comers, however, and rejected other tribal survivors because of language. For a short period, until the Tuscarora War of 1714, they were able to play off competing officials in Virginia and Carolina, but by 1717, the Saponis were restricted to a narrow reservation of six square miles. This method of contraction can be found elsewhere in the mission reserves of New France, praying towns of New England, settlement tribes of southwest New England, and small nations of Louisiana. Over the next few decades, their Native American traditions were swept away by the further impact of European trade. Worsening relations over local issues such as livestock, real estate, and personal conflicts often escalated into full-scale military confrontations, with Native Americans invariably ceding further rights in peace negotiations.

Native Americans experienced a brief respite from the downward cycle during the Long Peace following the imperial wars between European nations between 1689 and 1713. For about thirty years, there were small skirmishes, but most of the invasions of interior America were commercial. As Native Americans, especially the Iroquois, attempted to regroup, relations with Europeans centered on trade goods. Within Native American societies, distinct class lines emerged between those with access to consumer goods and those without. Pan-Indian revival movements led by Neolin in the 1760s and Handsome Lake at the end of the eighteenth century were attempts to exclude European American trade from Native American societies.

The situation was more complex in the interior of the continent. Native American survival techniques of adoption produced a plethora of multiethnic villages. The Iroquois federation was made up of a melting pot of peoples descended from evicted bands from the Northeast. West of Iroquoian lived Wyandots, Ottawas, Miamis, and others, occupying a territory known as the pays d'en haut, which Richard White has fittingly called a "middle ground" and a "world made of fragments." Similar configurations existed among the Cherokees, Muskogees, Chicasaws, and Choctaws of the Southeast. Of all ethnic groups of early America, Native Americans fit most closely the modern ideal of the melting pot.

Trade and warfare were not the only assimilating influences upon Native Americans. Religion was a key force. James Axtell has argued that the "Invasion Within" by Jesuit priests in the late seventeenth century, overcame the demographic superiority of the Iroquois over the French and helped to create New France. In the eighteenth century, as French power gradually dissipated from a long series of wars, English Protestantism grew in influence. Religious enthusiasms connected to the Great Awakening among European Americans in the 1740s were matched by contemporary revivals among Native Americans. The mid-eighteenth century saw continual diplomacy between Native Americans, the French, and the English. The last conflict emanating from this uneasy triangular relationship resulted in Native American alliances with the French, who lost the war and much of their territory. Although the English attempted to reinstate a boundary between white and Indian settlements, American settlers poured across the Appalachian Mountains and into the southeastern Indian homelands. One key theme of revolutionary discourse was Patriot discontent with English attempts to hedge settlements east of the Appalachians.

SPANISH TERRITORIES

Patriots also lusted for lands controlled by the Spanish since the late sixteenth century. In the southeast, English colonists established colonies in the Carolinas to raid and check Spanish settlements in Florida. The Spanish in turn welcomed runaway slaves from the English colonies; African American refugees were quickly adopted into Creek Indian villages, themselves a product of European rivalries. Around 1700, the Spanish governor estimated that around three hundred mixed-race refugees lived around St. Augustine. Successive wars drove more Creeks into the northern panhandle of Florida. By 1767, there were nearly two thousand Creeks and African Americans in Florida; together they became known as Seminoles, a corruption of the Spanish term *cimmaron*, or runaway. Native Americans and blacks quickly formed new communal systems for land, food distribution, and work. Although slavery was practiced, the slaves were more like prisoners of war than victims of the lifetime bondage evolving in the English colonies. Even after the Spanish ceded Florida to the British under the 1753 Treaty of Paris, the territory continued to be attractive to self-emancipated blacks from the Carolinas and Georgia.

Further west, Spanish influence was larger. New Spain extended from present-day Texas to far up the Pacific Coast. Its center was New Mexico. Demographic data for New Mexico is anecdotal before 1749, and even the census of that year was incomplete. At the close of the seventeenth century, about 3,000 nominally white Spanish people lived in the province, joined by about 9,000 Pueblo Indians. Fifty years later, the Spanish population had grown only slightly to 3,808; growth beyond 8,783 people virtually stalled among Pueblo Indians. Thereafter the Spanish population increased to 9,743 in 1776 and jumped to 16,358 by 1790. The Pueblo Indian population barely maintained itself through the second half of the eighteenth century and in 1790 was at 8,840.

Early in the eighteenth century, Native American ethnicity dominated California. Conjugal couples and their children and aged relatives formed basic units of small villages, which acknowledged a chief. Joined together these local organizations formed a tribe of up to one thousand people. Hierarchies of wealth, status, and power were hereditary. Throughout society, kinship constituted the fundamental social contract; communities were composed of extended residence groups that were linked by formal ties. Household economies were based upon hunting and gathering within a sexual division of labor. These highly traditional traits existed more purely in California than in eastern regions because of the lack of European contact. That changed in 1769, when Spanish settlers arrived. Many Spanish families shared such common traits with Native Americans as sexual hierarchy, dutiful alliances through marriage, and female control over the household economy. Intermarriage between Native Americans, Africans, and Spanish created a mestizo population. Although Roman Catholic missions worked steadily to eradicate Native American cultures, epidemic diseases were the strongest forces in the transition into Spanish rule.

THE ST. LAWRENCE VALLEY

The survival of the Iroquois Nations in the region from New France to the Midwest can be directly attributed to the weak population growth among the French. In the first two decades of the eighteenth century, after more than one hundred years of settlement, French immigration was concentrated in the cities of Montreal and Quebec City, with about fourteen thousand inhabitants in 1700. Further west, the French presence amounted to less than seventeen hundred people, of whom only 10 percent were females; many of those were celibate members of Catholic religious orders. Over the next twenty years, immigration crept up to only eighteen hundred souls, of whom women accounted for but seventy-five. The second largest group of immigrants came from prisoners. Despite these daunting numbers and the low social status of immigrants, the population grew because of high female fecundity, quick remarriage after spousal death, low general mortality, and large families of seven to eight children. With the sizable jump in immigration after 1740, the French demographic situation was very favorable at the time of the English conquest in 1763. By then the French population had reached seventy thousand along the St. Lawrence, allowing for retention of a staunch Franco-American peasantry well into the future.

NEW ENGLAND

From a total of 91,100 in 1700, the region's population grew steadily, passing 115,000 in the next ten years, to more than 360,000 by 1750, and then leaping to just less than 700,000 in 1790. Of all the North American colonial regions, New England was the best example of English ways. At the end of the colonial period, over 80 percent of the area's population was of English descent, with the rest largely of such related origins as Welsh, Scotch-Irish, and Scottish. While there were antagonisms among these groups, English language and culture was dominant.

The frontier proved no barrier to New England's growth in the eighteenth century. Population growth in New Hampshire after 1700 came from natural reproduction and from European immigration. The typical couple in New Hampshire produced at least four children who attained adulthood; few of these children left the colony for the West in the early decades of the century. This natural growth was interrupted in the mid-1730s by a "throat distemper," which combined diphtheria and scarlet fever. It killed over fifteen hundred inhabitants, many under sixteen years of age. Wars also hampered internal growth, but by 1750 the population of twenty-five thousand souls was large enough to absorb these losses. Any shortfall was also made up by immigration. English farmers, deserting sailors and soldiers, and arrivals from the British West Indies, who brought several hundred enslaved Africans with them, bolstered the colony's population. Other Englishmen came from southern New England in search of land. Major growth came from Ulster, from which enough Scottish Presbyterians arrived in New Hampshire to make up 10 percent of the colony's population by 1750.

The population of Massachusetts was overwhelmingly derived from England. The colony did not have its first census until 1764 and 1765, when its population stood at 245,698, making it one of the three largest English colonies in North America. It had been populous long before that; at the beginning of the eighteenth century, Boston was the dominant town in North America. The colony was 97.2 percent white, with the vast majority of English ancestry. Youth was a significant factor in eighteenth-century New England. In a number of urban counties, nearly half the population was under sixteen years of age. Connecticut also did not enumerate its citizens until late in the colonial period. In the first reasonable census of 1756, the colony's population stood at 130,612; it rose to 197,000 in 1774. As in Massachusetts and New Hampshire, whites made up over 96 percent of the population. Rhode Island displayed a bit more diversity, but primarily in the cities of Providence and Newport.

That was the case throughout New England. The continued involvement of New England merchants in the slave trade produced pockets of enslaved Africans in coastal towns. Though often sparsely distributed, there were more than four thousand blacks in Massachusetts in 1750 and three thousand in Connecticut. By 1770 that figure had jumped to more than fifty-seven hundred. Even New Hampshire was home to 550 African Americans. As many as 18.3 percent of Newport, Rhode Island was black in 1755. William Pierson has described how "Black Yankees" were often fully assimilated. Black New Englanders were spread broadly across the region; nearly every town in the region was home to a few African Americans. Even so, black Yankees were able to re-create African folk customs, such as the mock election of a governor, and sustained an African religious base throughout the colonial period. In addition, Africans intermarried with local Native Americans in rural New England.

Over the course of the seventeenth century, the living standards of whites and blacks in New England diverged sharply. African Americans in New England had significantly higher mortality rates than white servants by every measure. Boston's black infant mortality in the mid-eighteenth century was actually higher than experienced by their counterparts in Virginia. A smallpox epidemic in 1752 hastened the death of black adults in Boston. The living also showed disparities in health. White servants in Boston and in Philadelphia were generally taller and better fed than African Americans.

THE MID ATLANTIC

This region was the most ethnically diverse of the Atlantic colonies. Even at the end of the colonial period, after a strong wave of English migration just before the American Revolution, the proportion of the populace with English roots was only about 50 percent in New York and New Jersey and only 25 percent in Pennsylvania. In 1700, English military rule insured its political hegemony but could not stamp out ethnic traditions; English political and military power controlled New York, New Jersey, and Pennsylvania at the beginning of the eighteenth century and maintained suzerainty until the American Revolution. Nonetheless, in New York and New Jersey, English power uneasily held sway over a mixture of nations. The Dutch, who, one commentator claimed, would readily extinguish the English, incorporated French Huguenots into their churches and political organizations. Differences between city and countryside were sharp. In New York City, according to Randall Balmer, the Dutch elite gradually accepted English power by using the language of hegemony in church services. Joyce Goodfriend has cogently argued that among poorer urban Dutch, women retained their ancestral language at home and worship. Occupations continued to show ethnic retentions. The Dutch dominated the carting trade in New York City until after the American Revolution, even as they accepted English foremen. The urban Dutch presence was bolstered by internal migration from rural areas.

As persistent as Dutch culture was, arrivals from home slowed dramatically in the eighteenth century. More characteristic immigrants came from parts of the British Isles and the West Indies. From across the social strata came Londoners (the largest contributor to New York's population from abroad), Scotch-Irish, and Irish, adding complexity to the phrase

English New Yorker. Merchants and artisans came from London while farmers and their families came from rural England and provincial cities. As the conditions for white laborers worsened in the slave societies of the West Indies, Englishmen migrated up to New York in search of fortunes.

Scots differentiated themselves from the English by religion. Their Presbyterian faith was a strong dissent from the hegemonic Church of England. The controversy over King's College in the 1750s is illustrative. Anglican clerics, longing for a college that could train local priests and eventually establish a bishopric, proposed a new institution for those purposes. *The Independent Reflector*, edited by the Presbyterian Scotsman William Livingston, angrily attacked the plan and referred to the Anglican clergymen's "ghastly juggling, their Pride, and their insatiate Lust for Power." Anglicans were forced to open the tiny college without public support.

After 1730 the number of Irish soared in New York City. At first they remained undifferentiated from other members of the British Isles. Coming as indentured servants, as paying passengers, as soldiers in the British army, and as convicts, most Irishmen soon gained access to New York's occupations. Generally, they affiliated with Scot Presbyterians. During the eighteenth century, Catholicism was generally banned from most Atlantic colonies (except for Pennsylvania and parts of Maryland), but Catholic Irish came to New York as soldiers and sailors. Catholic priests occasionally traveled to private homes to conduct clandestine services. Discrimination against Catholicism in New York was so great that one unlucky priest was caught up in the repression of the 1741 Slave Conspiracy and condemned to death on flimsy evidence. In contrast to Catholicism, Jewish New Yorkers assimilated with the dominant culture. There were approximately 225 Jews in New York around 1730. Although local Jews opened a synagogue that year, other Jews, primarily Sephardic merchants, intermarried with Anglicans and joined the Church of England.

Recognized in importance only recently, the African presence in New York was critical to labor and social needs. Originally creolized captives taken from Spanish vessels, and later from the Angolan Coast, Africans in eighteenth century New York came increasingly from the West Indies and by direct importation from the West Coast of Africa. Between 1703 and 1775, the black population of New York City soared from 630 to over three thousand. Africans constituted about 15 percent of the city's population during the eighteenth century. Ethnic relations took on a variety of forms. For a privileged few, access to Anglican schools offered literacy and at least an illusion of potential freedom. Among Africans living among poorer Englishmen, the Dutch, and the Huguenots, who decided that their chattel had no souls, little acculturation was possible. Daily necessities demanded comprehension of European languages and some European mores, but African cultural survivals may be found in secularized rituals, among self-proclaimed religious leaders, and in the character of revolt reflected in the conspiracies of 1712 and 1741. In the planning of these two suppressed rebellions, conspirators swore oaths inside chalk circles, sucked blood from each other's self-inflicted wounds, and stated their allegiance to African nationality. A lively debate has recently arisen as to whether the conspirators used African military methods, as John K. Thornton has insisted, or drew from pan-Atlantic Christian forms of allegiance, as recently claimed by Marcus Rediker and Peter Linebaugh. In both cases authorities used brutal methods of torture and execution to quell the conspiracies. Ira Berlin has claimed that the effect of these revolts was to convince white slave traders to purchase human chattel directly from Africa rather than accept Creoles from the West Indies, who held dangerous views of freedom.

In rural New York and East Jersey, slavery was even more critical for the labor-starved farmers, millers, and coastal sea captains. Kings County in New York was more than one-third black in 1738, and about 20 percent of the inhabitants of Bergen County in East Jersey were enslaved Africans. Derived from the slave trade out of New York City, Philadelphia, and, to a small extent, Perth Amboy, New Jersey, Africans in East Jersey were an amalgam of Angolan, West African, and Creole. While high mortality was not a critical issue, the biggest problems for African reproduction in rural New York and Jersey were the gender imbalance of males over females and the small-farm character of slavery, which inhibited any family solidarity. As noted below, English religious hegemony failed outside of New York, and such ethnic groups as the French Huguenots, Dutch, and Lutherans made little attempt to acculturate Africans. The limited acculturation of enslaved Africans was mirrored among other groups and occupations. For mariners on the Hudson River, the Dutch language was the lingua franca among Dutch, English, African, and other sailors. Dutch, German, and French remained the tongues of worshipers in pietist rural congregations. Dutch farmers remote from New York City kept their cultures long into the nineteenth century. Earlier settlements of non-English Europeans were reinforced by migrations from the Palatine in the 1710s. German Lutherans, beckoned by colonial officials seeking settlement of northern New York, initially had a disastrous reception. Many quickly removed to Pennsylvania while the remnants maintained a precarious existence west of Albany, New York. The push into the frontier continued late in the colonial period with the arrival of several thousand immigrants from Britain through the port of New York en route to the northern counties above Albany.

Rural New Jersey proved a fertile ground for maintaining ethnicity. Considered the most diverse colony along the Atlantic coast, New Jersey lacked a dominant ethnic group. Religion was the dividing issue. Anglicans, whose theological authority lessened with each mile away from New York, vied for influence and power with Dutch Reformed in the north, Scotch-Irish Presbyterians in the north-central counties, and Quakers in the middle and southern regions. Monmouth, the largest county, was home to all, although sharp divisions by religion showed in the formation of agricultural townships. Generally, enslaved Africans served as farm laborers and domestics throughout Jersey. Arrivals from the West Coast of Africa and seasoned slaves from the West Indies gradually supplanted earlier forced immigrants from Angola and Congo.

In Pennsylvania, the Society of Friends, a dissident sect with significant ties to the English Crown settled Philadelphia and its immediate hinterland. In order to develop what became known as the "poor man's best country," the Quakers invited other denominations to settle outside of Philadelphia. From the beginning of settlement in the 1680s and into the eighteenth century, there was segregation of national groups. English Quakers controlled the city of Philadelphia and the eastern rural regions.

German Dunkards, Schwenkfelders, and Moravians occupied the north. The German immigration in the second quarter of the eighteenth century was one of the largest mass arrivals of the era. Between 1710 and 1775, more than eighty thousand Germans arrived in America through the port of Philadelphia; the vast majority came before 1756. Many came as redemptioners or as indentured servants. Sharon Salinger has pointed out that the presence of Germans in these key immigrant groups transformed these methods of immigration from paternalist to capitalist ventures. The eighty thousand arrivals accounted for over 72 percent of all Germans coming to America in the colonial period. Germans, Jon Butler has argued, retained much of their cultural solidarity because of their rural isolation, density of population, and reaction to English prejudice. For example, German women married outside of their culture only occasionally. German insularity, language differences, and communal economics placed them apart from Anglo-Americans. Germans became the first European immigrant group viewed with suspicion and prejudice. Such differences had political consequences. The dominant Society of Friends in Philadelphia refused to allot colonial tax revenues for a militia, which angered Germans living in close proximity to Native Americans who were anxious about white imposition upon their homelands. By the 1760s, acrimony between Friends and Germans became so sharp that rural dwellers nearly marched into Philadelphia to enforce their demands. In following years, Friends largely withdrew from politics.

The Scotch-Irish, who were largely Presbyterian, lived in the west with some overlap in the east. All of these immigrants were European Protestants who shared common agricultural methods and dietary preferences and had common beliefs in bourgeois liberal individualism (which quickly overcame earlier communalism). Despite national differences, these sects shared perfectionist beliefs. Exclusive and self-righteous, and occasionally otherworldly, Pennsylvania's theological communities attained a fairly equal economic status. Tensions arose over the rising power of non-English groups over the course of the eighteenth century. Distinct minorities early in the century, Germans and Scotch-Irish accounted for well over half by 1790. Much of this population was on the frontier, where frequent conflicts with Iroquois nations resulted in demands for stronger defenses, expenditures the pacifist Quakers would not fund. Even so, David Fischer has argued, the Society of Friends was able to construct a polity within which various ethnic groups coexisted. In Delaware, Irish Protestants arrived in a small but steady flow of a few hundred immigrants annually.

THE UPPER SOUTH

Though often regarded as strongly Anglicized, Maryland, Virginia, and North Carolina were actually quite pluralistic. Sixty percent of Virginia's stock was English, but North Carolina and Maryland were only about 50 percent English. Scotch-Irish settlers accounted for almost sixteen percent of North Carolinians. North Carolina was the goal of several hundred German Lutherans around 1728.

The counterpart to English mores in the Upper South was its African presence. As the tobacco colonies moved from indentured to chattel bondage in the late seventeenth century, farmers large and small became steady customers of the Atlantic slave trade. After a slow start at the beginning of the eighteenth century, the arrival of Africans soared. Between 1720 and 1750, the numbers of enslaved African people in Maryland jumped from 12,500 to more than 43,000. In Virginia, the increase was even more dramatic. From about 26,000 slaves in 1730, the Old Dominion became home to more than 100,000 black people just twenty years later. By 1790, Virginia slave masters owned more than 287,000 enslaved Africans. North Carolina slave owners, who also started slowly, accelerated their purchases so that a populace of 1,000 enslaved people became 100,000 by 1790. These colonies merited the definition of slave societies in which servitude was the principal mode of labor relations. Not all of the ethnic contact in Virginia was conflicted. Mechal Sobel has demonstrated how Africans and European Americans derived culture from each other. Sobel has shown how premodern whites and blacks shared similar perceptions of time, key events, space and the natural world, and death and the afterlife. They also created new people. As recent collections by Martha Hodes and Catherine Clinton have demonstrated, rural areas were the locales for interracial sex among Native Americans and European Americans. Whatever cultural interaction did occur, the general experience of African Americans was servitude. Edmund Morgan's exploration of Virginia's tilt toward human bondage for blacks and freehold promises for whites continues to shape the discussion of race relations. Alan Kulikoff has shown how white migrants to the frontier tried to take enslaved peoples with them. Kathleen Brown has demonstrated how over the course of the eighteenth century, the experiences of white and black women differed. White females, as the plantation economy boomed, became less tied to farm work, owned more consumer items, and became generally wealthier. In contrast, as the slave trade brought increased numbers of Africans to Virginia, the childbearing potential of black women became devalued. As a result, black females were more likely to be field hands in 1790 than at the beginning of the century. The experiences of Virginia were magnified in the lower colonies.

THE LOWER SOUTH

South Carolina and Georgia were more pluralistic than were the tobacco colonies to the north. Less than 50 percent of South Carolina's population hailed from England; nearly 20 percent were Scotch-Irish and 10 percent were from Scotland. French Huguenots accounted for a sizable number of new arrivals. Whatever ethnic controversies existed between low- and up-county residents in South Carolina, the racial imbalance of the colony congealed ethnicity into whiteness. South Carolina landowners adopted rice as a staple crop late in the seventeenth century and chose West Africans as their principal laborers. In this slave society, the number of Africans rose from about 3,000 in 1700 to 39,000 in 1750 and 107,000 in 1790. It then doubled again by the close of the century. Georgia initially resisted slavery. Only six hundred enslaved Africans lived there in 1750. The colony soon overcame its hesitancy. Masters purchased more than 15,000 enslaved Africans by 1770, a figure dwarfed by the black population of 105,000 at the start of the nineteenth century.

LOUISIANA

Sparsely settled at the time of its first census in 1726, French Louisiana was home to 1663 whites, 1,385 Africans and Indians, and 570 soldiers in a total population of 3,618. It comprised tiny settlements along the Mississippi River below Red River, a handful of interior clusters in Arkansas and near Natchez, and Gulf Coast settlements. New Orleans was the largest community, with 630 people. Generally, males outnumbered females; in some instances, such as the African population below German Village on the West Bank of the Mississippi, where 210 males lived with four females, family life was impossible. African slaves were far more consolidated than French, German, or Spanish. Over three-quarters of enslaved Africans lived along the lower Mississippi River. Slaves were often channeled into skilled occupations, which caused resentment among some European workers. The answer was for white artisans to purchase skilled slaves, a process that further implanted servitude in this frontier society.

Growth was slow in Louisiana over the course of the century. Shortly after the American Revolution, the total population of the territory had grown only to 30,471. Of these 13,076 were white, 16,248 were black (Louisiana was rapidly becoming a slave society), and 1,147 were Creole or free people of color. The impact of direct importation of enslaved peoples directly from Africa amplified the racial identification of people of color. Although free people of color were becoming the norm in the northern states and had sizable numbers in the Upper South, their presence in Louisiana owed less to abolitionism than to their unique status as people of mixed blood. Creoles in Louisiana, survivors of the intermingling of peoples common in the early seventeenth-century colonies, were virtu-ally stamped out by hardening racial lines along the Atlantic Coast. Soon after this, the introduction of the cotton culture into the region and the arrival of ambitious German farmers would herald the further decline of the Creoles and the triumph of a slave society.

ETHNICITY AND THE AMERICAN REVOLUTION

The American Revolution was as much a war to determine who should rule at home as it was a war to see who would rule. That dictum, used by Carl Becker early in the twentieth century to describe the class nature of the War for Independence, might also be used to enable us to comprehend the importance of ethnicity at the start of American nationhood. The war was a civil war in many regions, disrupting political economies and folding local animosities into an imperial conflict. So it was that recently arrived Englishmen in upper New York and North Carolina remained loyal to the Crown. So too did the Dutch in New Jersey side with the English against their Patriot enemies. Lord Dunmore, the English gover-nor of Virginia, and several generals made appeals to slaves and inden-tured servants and offered freedom in exchange for military service. This time-honored method of undercutting a foe by riling up its servants proved highly successful in the revolution as tens of thousands of slaves left their masters in search of freedom behind the British lines. The English specialized so heavily in ethnic appeals that Bishop Henry Muhlenberg condemned the Crown practice of raising regiments of German, Irish, Indians, and blacks to repress the rebellion. The American Revolution churned the black population as enslaved and free people joined marauding armies, sending Afro-Virginians up to New York and New Yorkers to the South Carolina front. Florida remained highly attrac-tive to African American refugees from slavery.

Eventually, more than ten thousand African Americans left with the British from the ports of New York and Savannah. As important as were these hegiras to freedom, the major impact of the American Revolution was the close of the slave trade. Cutting off the supply of new Africans to America and bringing together a congregation of Black Loyalists within the British army should have created a separate African American society. Of such persuasion is the claim of Jon Butler, who contends that African Americans had to accept European theologies because of the holocaust of African beliefs. Yet it is striking that after just a few frustrating years in Nova Scotia, Black Loyalists successfully petitioned for assistance to move their society to Sierra Leone and founded a new nation there. Within a few years, these Black Loyalists formed a leadership cadre yet also resuscitated African cultural traits. For the white population, as much as things changed, they remained the same. The first federal census of the United States, taken in 1790, provided information about ethnicity among white Americans. Overall, 60 percent of Americans were of English descent, ranging from a high of 82.5 percent in Massachusetts to 35 percent in Pennsylvania and 47 percent in New Jersey. The Mid Atlantic proved to be the most pluralistic region. New York and New Jersey (with 17.5 and 16.6 percent) were the only states with sizable Dutch populations. Pennsylvania was one-third German; only Kentucky, Tennessee, and Maryland also had more than 10 percent (14 and 11.7 percent). Scots lived primarily in the upper and lower southern regions. Eighteen percent of Georgia's residents were Irish. What these figures indicate is that, although the ethnic breakdown of the Atlantic coast states remained much as before the American Revolution, the newer western regions experienced greater diversity. Further west, American claims on Northwest and Spanish territories would include regions in which English residents were a distinct minority. In Louisiana, for example, 65 percent of white residents were French-speaking and only 11.2 percent were English. Nearly as many residents of Louisiana were German. The egalitarian promises of the Declaration of Independence did not apply equally. The egalitarian promises of the Declaration of Independence did not apply equally across ethnic and racial lines. Native American populations continued their tumble into near oblivion anywhere whites encroached upon their territories. Scholars generally agree that the American Revolution was a major setback for Native Americans. The claims of the new nation to lands west of the Appalachian Mountains into the Ohio Valley meant constant white migration and seizure of Indian homelands. In the South, white farmers moved into Cherokee and Choctaw homelands in Georgia. In upstate New York, Native Americans were quickly pushed far to the north and west. Within twenty years, virtually no Indian nation held land east of the Appalachians. The Euro-American drive across the continent seemed inexorable.

Easily the biggest change in American society was the renewed importance of African Americans. In New England, blacks remained a tiny percentage of the population; nearly all were free by 1790. In the

Mid Atlantic, where the institution of slavery survived into the nineteenth century, free blacks formed a new force. In the South and Southwest, after a brief period of self-examination and religious soul-searching over slavery, English, Scots, Germans, and French quickly transformed their states into slave societies. Louisiana had the most striking change, but South Carolina, Georgia, and the newer territories of Kentucky and Tennessee all tightened their embrace with slavery.

The post-Revolutionary movement of white yeoman farmers, going west in search of new lands, created a sense of "whiteness" among settlers. Whether Anglo-Americans from New England, Dutch from the Mid Atlantic, or Scotch-Irish from the Carolinas, postwar settlers—many of them veterans paid by the federal government with promises of western lands—wanted a society free of slavery and of African Americans. Although the northern states passed gradual emancipation laws in the first two decades of the nation's history, African Americans remained significant portions of these societies well into the nineteenth century. In the Old Northwest (the Ohio Valley), that was not the case. New settlements tended to be entirely white. The Continental Congress had passed a bill in 1707 that promised to end the slave trade twenty years later. The effect differed by region. In the North, state laws gradually eroded the legality of any slave sales. As immigration from Europe resumed, the percentage of African Americans in the populations sharply declined. At the same time, white prejudice toward African Americans increased. Encouraged by the philosophical musings of Thomas Jefferson on race, white Americans viewed blacks as different and biologically inferior. State after state passed legislation insuring that even free blacks would have little or no say politically and that permitted economic isolation and discrimination. In the next century, the chief Euro-American reaction to the growing numbers of free blacks in the north and to the national debate over slavery was to encourage, however fantastic, the mass migration of blacks to Africa, a choice very few African Americans were willing to make. As the stock of Euro-Americans gradually congealed into a white race, African Americans and Native Americans came to be regarded as separate and unequal.

BIBLIOGRAPHIC ESSAY

The demographic history of the colonial period can be found in John J. McCusker and Russell R. Menard, *The Economy of British America, 1607–1789* (Chapel Hill:

University of North Carolina Press for the Institute of Early American History and Culture, 1985) and Michael R. Haines and Richard H. Steckel, eds., *A Population History of North America* (New York: Cambridge University Press, 2000), 99–143. See also Thomas L. Purvis, "The European Ancestry of the United States Population, 1790," *William and Mary Quarterly*, 3rd ser. 41 (1984) and Robert Wells, *The Population of the British Colonies in America Before 1776* (Princeton: Princeton University Press, 1975), 85, 95–103; *Historical Statistics of the United States, Colonial Times to 1970* (Washington, DC: U.S. Government Printing Office for the Department of Commerce, 1976), 2 vols.

A general study on the colonial period that emphasizes English influence is David Hackett Fischer, *Albion's Seed: Four British Folkways in America* (New York: Oxford University Press, 1989). Three books by Jon C. Butler, which combined Anglicization and cultural diversity, are *The Huguenots in America: A Refugee People in New World Society* (Cambridge: Harvard University Press, 1983); *Awash in a Sea of Faith: Christianizing the American People* (Cambridge: Harvard University Press, 1994); and *Becoming America: The Revolution Before 1776* (Cambridge: Harvard University Press, 2000).

The most emphatic study of the continued impact of ethnicity on a colonial society is Joyce Goodfriend, *Before the Melting Pot: Society and Culture in Colonial New York City, 1664–1730* (Princeton: Princeton University Press, 1992). Books that argue for continued African influences are Michael Gomez, *Exchanging Our Country Marks: The Transformation of African Identities in the Colonial and Antebellum South* (Chapel Hill: University of North Carolina Press, 1998) and Margaret Washington Creel, *A Peculiar People: Slave Community Culture among the Gullahs* (New York: New York University Press, 1988).

For studies of the demography of Native Americans, see Henry F. Dobyns, *Their Number Become Thinned: North American Population Dynamics in Eastern North America* (Knoxville: University of Tennessee Press, 1983). Influential studies of Native American regrouping include James H. Merrill, *The Indians' New World: Catawbas and Their Neighbors from European Contact Through the Era of Removal* (Chapel Hill: University of North Carolina Press for the Institute of Early American History and Culture, 1989) and Daniel K. Richter, "Native American History: Perspectives on the Eighteenth Century," in Michael V. Kennedy and William G. Shade, eds., *The World Turned Upside Down: The State of Eighteenth-Century Studies at the Beginning of the Twenty-first Century*, 268–89 (Bethlehem, Penn.: Lehigh University Press, 2001). The most important study about the intersections of Native Americans, French, English and Americans is Richard White, *The Middle Ground: Indians, Empires, and Republics in the Great Lakes Region, 1650–1815* (Cambridge: Cambridge University Press, 1991). See also Daniel H. Usner, Jr., *Indians, Settlers, and Slaves in a Frontier Exchange Economy: The Lower Mississippi Valley Settlers, and Slaves in a Frontier Exchange Economy: The Lower Mississippi Valley Before 1783* (Chapel Hill: University of North Carolina Press for the Institute of Early American History and Culture, 1992), Gregory Evans Dowd, *A Spirited Resistance: The North American Indian Struggle for Unity, 1745–1815* (Baltimore: Johns Hopkins University Press, 1992); Martha Hodes, ed., *Sex, Love, Race: Crossing Boundaries in North American History* (New York: New York University Press, 1999); and Catherine Clinton and Michele Gillespie, eds., *The Devil's Lane: Sex and Race in the Early South* (New York: Oxford University Press, 1997). For a study that emphasizes ideological influence, see James Axtell, *The Invasion Within: The Contest of Cultures in Colonial North America* (New York: Oxford University Press, 1985). The fullest studies of changes in southwestern Indian cultures are Ramon Guttierrez, *When Jesus Came, the Corn Mothers Went Away: Marriage, Sexuality, and Power in New Mexico, 1500–1846* (Stanford: Stanford University Press, 1991) and Albert Hurtado, *Indian Survival on the California Frontier* (New Haven: Yale University Press, 1988). For studies of Native Americans and African Americans together, see Kenneth W. Porter, *The Black Seminoles: History of a Freedom-Seeking People*, Revised Edition (Lexington: University of Kentucky Press, 1996); Kevin Mulroy, *Freedom on the Borders: The Seminole Maroons in Florida, the Indian Territory, Coahuila, and Texas* (College Station: Texas Tech University Press, 1993); Jane Landers, *Black Society in Spanish Florida* (Urbana: University of Illinois Press, 1999).

On black Americans in New England, see William D. Piersen, *Black Yankees: The Development of an Afro-American Subculture in Eighteenth-Century New England* (Amherst: University of Massachusetts Press, 1988) and Ira Berlin, *Many Thousands Gone: The First Two Centuries of Slavery in North America* (Cambridge: Harvard University Press, 1998), 366.

For a good study of the Mid Atlantic, with emphasis on the intersection of politics and diversity, see Gary B. Nash, *The Urban Crucible: Social Change, Political Consciousness, and the Origins of the American Revolution* (Cambridge: Harvard University Press, 1979). Carl L. Becker, *The History of Political Practice in the Province of New York, 1760–1776* (Madison: University of Wisconsin Press, 1909). For studies of ethnicity in the Mid Atlantic, see Joyce D. Goodfriend, *Before the Melting Pot* (Princeton: Princeton University Press, 1992) *and Goodfriend,* "The Irish in Colonial New York City," in Ronald H. Bayor and Timothy J. Meagher, eds., *The New York Irish*, 35–48 (Baltimore: Johns Hopkins University Press, 1996).

On blacks in the Mid Atlantic, see Graham Russell Hodges, *Root & Branch: African Americans in New York and East Jersey, 1613–1863* (Chapel Hill: University of North Carolina Press, 1999.) and Hodges, *Slavery and Freedom in the Rural North: African Americans in Monmouth County, New Jersey, 1660–1865* (Madison, Wisc.: Madison House Publishers, 1997). For a discussion of the role of blacks in the military see John K. Thornton, *Warfare in Atlantic Africa, 1500–1800* (London: UCL Press, 2000). On the Pan-Atlantic influences see Peter Linebaugh and Marcus Rediker, *The Many Headed Hydra: Sailor, Slave, Commoners and the Hidden History of the Revolutionary Atlantic* (Boston: Beacon Press, 2000). On the Dutch, see Randall Balmer, *A Perfect Babel of Confusion: Dutch Religion and English Culture in the Middle Colonies* (New York: Oxford University Press, 1989) and David Steven Cohen, *The Dutch-American Farm* (New York: New York University Press, 1992). On Germans, see A. G. Roeber, *Palatines, Liberty, and Property: German Lutherans in Colonial British America* (Baltimore: Johns Hopkins University Press, 1993) and Marianne S. Wokeck, *Trade in Strangers: The Beginnings of Mass Migration to North America* (University Park: The Pennsylvania State University Press, 1999). On later English migration, see Bernard Bailyn, *Voyagers to the West: A Passage in the Peopling of America on the Eve of the Revolution* (New York: Knopf, 1986), 573–80. on ethnicity generally in New Jersey, see Peter Wacker, *Land & People: A Cultural Geography of Preindustrial New Jersey: Origins and Settlement Patterns* (New Brunswick: Rutgers University Press, 1975). On the Scotch-Irish, see Ned C. Landsman, *Scotland and Its First American Colony, 1683–1765* (Princeton: Princeton University Press, 1985). For the story of changing ethnicity in labor relations see Sharon V. Salinger, *"To Serve Well and Faithfully": Labor and Indentured Servants in Pennsylvania, 1682–1800* (New York: Cambridge University Press, 1987).

For the complicated story of African and Euro-Americans in the tobacco colonies, see Mechal Sobel, *The World They Made Together: Black and White Values in Eighteenth-Century Virginia* (Princeton: Princeton University Press, 1987); Woody Holton, *Forced Founders: Indians, Debtors, Slaves, and the Making of the American Revolution in Virginia* (Chapel Hill: University of North Carolina Press for the Institute of Early American History and Culture, 1999); Edmund S. Morgan, *American Slavery, American Freedom: The Ordeal of Colonial Virginia* (New York: Norton, 1975); Allan Kulikoff, *Tobacco and Slaves: The Development of Southern Cultures in the Chesapeake, 1680–1800* (Chapel Hill: University of North Carolina Press, 1986), and Kathleen M. Brown, *Good Wives, Nasty Wenches, and Anxious Patriarchs: Gender, Race, and Power in Colonial Virginia* (Chapel Hill: University of North Carolina Press for the Institute of Early American History and Culture, 1996). On the Southeast, see Gwendolyn Midlo Hall, *Africans in Colonial Louisiana: The Development of Afro-Creole Culture in the Eighteenth Century* (Baton Rouge: Louisiana State University Press, 1992).

3

THE LIMITS OF EQUALITY

Racial and Ethnic Tensions in the New Republic, 1789–1836

Marion R. Casey

There is no place in the world where a man meets so rich a reward for good conduct and industry as in America.
— John Dunlap, Philadelphia, 12 May 1789

In the wake of the ratification of the Constitution, the United States ventured forth into a democratic experience without any road map and with a wary eye on the French version evolving across the Atlantic. By the time Andrew Jackson's presidency was coming to a close, the republican ideal of equality for all had been put to the test on several fronts. Four overlapping spheres—broadly labeled citizenship, religion, language, and segregation—dominated political and social intercourse during this half-century. An increasingly multiethnic, multiracial population pushed at their interstices, forcing Anglo-Americans to attempt reconciliation between policy and practice.

The Constitution called for uniform rules of naturalization and of representation based on the population of the United States. It allowed for the regulation of commerce with Indian tribes, permitted the migration or importation of "such persons as any of the states now existing shall think proper to admit" until 1808, provided for equal legal jurisdiction in all the states over persons "held to service or labour," and banned religious tests as the basis for holding public office. This appressed form of articulation is, in fact, the document's only commentary on issues related to race and ethnicity. There appears to have been no need to make explicit in the actual Constitution that which its intended audience already understood: in practice there were limits to equality.

Despite its basis in the philosophy of natural rights, the Constitution did not create a polycracy. During the ratification process between November 1789 and December 1791, ten amendments emerged to address personal liberties in more specific language. Even so, the Bill of Rights did not anticipate areas of civil interaction that would require delicate negotiation in a diverse population, save for the proscription on an established religion in the first amendment. In practice, the socially vulnerable and the politically disfranchised—immigrants, indentured servants, redemptioners, Indians, and slaves—often remained marginalized or ineligible for the privileges of natural rights and their political corollary, equality, throughout the New Republic.

Between 1789 and 1836 the profile of the United States changed in fundamental ways. There was a fourfold increase in the total population, from 3.9 to 17 million. The number of square miles within its territorial jurisdiction—stretching from the Atlantic to the Rockies—doubled to 1.8 million, up from 889,000 at the end of the Revolution. This was accompanied by an administrative expansion as a dozen new states were admitted to the Union, encompassing Maine to Louisiana. Even as the majority of the American people were concentrated in rural areas, there was a dramatic increase in the residents of cities. The number of urban places with more than twenty-five hundred people jumped from twenty-four in 1790 to ninety in 1830. New York City's population multiplied by six—easily taking the lead as the country's largest—but Baltimore, Boston, Philadelphia, Charleston, and New Orleans also grew during that period, though in less spectacular demographic proportions. Significantly, much of this was the result of in-migration rather than natural growth.

A federal law mandating an enumeration of the population was passed in 1790, and the census count began on August 1. Once the tally of all fifteen states was in, the population of the United States stood about evenly divided between the North, with 1,968,040, and the South, with 1,961,174. Because of a political compromise, enslaved blacks counted for only three-fifths of a white when determining proportional representation in Congress. The categories developed for the census to calculate this "three-fifths compromise" embodied a classification system in which everyone was measured against "white"— the designation into which 80.7 percent of the 1790 population fell.

While the dominant race of the United States may have been "white," by no means was this homogeneous. The word encompassed much ethnic and linguistic variety—Irish, Scots, Welsh, Germans,

Dutch, Swiss, French, Swedes, and Spanish as well as English. The composition of this foreign-stock population was determined by three surname analyses of the 1790 census completed in the twentieth century. Although not without error and controversy, the surname method is a rudimentary measure (in the absence of any better) that serves to document the diversity of the country's Northern European roots. The very broadest generalizations point to the predominance of peoples from the British Isles (including Ireland) and Germany, with settlement patterns that were increasingly non-English the further south and west of New York City one went in the early national period. The regional dispersion of this population was focused on the Middle Atlantic states, partly a reflection of the preeminence of Baltimore, Philadelphia, and New York as ports of arrival. The most ethnic states in 1790 were Pennsylvania, with its large German element, and New York and New Jersey, where colonial Dutch settlement had been concentrated.

By contrast, the most "racial" states were Virginia, Maryland, and the Carolinas. The black population was ten times greater in the South than in the North in 1790. The North-South racial disparity is best illustrated by Massachusetts, which (with a population of 378,787) was almost as dense as North Carolina (with a population of 393,751), although the former had no slaves and the latter had more than one hundred thousand. The census established that 18 percent of the American population was enslaved and 42 percent of all slaves lived in Virginia. In addition, it counted 59,557 free blacks, or 12.7 percent of a total black population of 757,181.

Native Americans, on the other hand, were not considered citizens and therefore were neither taxed nor counted in the 1790 census. Under the Constitution, tribes were classified as foreign nations, and their relationship to the United States was diplomatic. It was 1820 before enumerators broke out figures for the 4,631 Native Americans who paid taxes within the borders of the United States and, by including a question on citizenship, counted some fifty-three thousand resident aliens.

The naturalization of foreign-born whites became one of the key issues to emerge during the era of partisan politics that began in the 1790s. The first Congress required only two years residency for citizenship. This entitled a propertied man to the vote but, in the wake of the French Revolution, it also gave many Americans pause. The European who had simply been a "colonist" before Independence was, in the period of the New Republic, reconceptualized as an "immigrant," a word with increasingly pejorative connotations. It came to symbolize all that was the opposite of the Anglo-American ideal, a convenient scapegoat for any national ill. Restrictionist attitudes appeared, such as that expressed by Federalist Congressman Harrison Gray Otis (1765–1848): "If some means are not adopted to prevent the indiscriminate admission of wild Irishmen and others to the right of suffrage, there will soon be an end to liberty and property."

At the end of February 1794 Albert Gallatin's Swiss birth was used to prevent him from taking his elected seat as a Senator from Pennsylvania on a residency technicality. With bipartisan support, the residency requirement was raised to five years in 1795 during a spate of Gallophobia. By the spring of 1797 attitudes had hardened further. The Federalists proposed a $20 tax on naturalization certificates, arguing that the United States needed to discourage immigration. Harrison Gray Otis declared that America could no longer afford to invite the "turbulent and disorderly of all parts of the world, to come here with a view to disturb our tranquility, after having succeeded in the overthrow of their own Governments." The tax was not passed; nevertheless, the following year Congress enacted four laws to suppress domestic dissent that had implications for those of foreign birth. Thereafter, ethnicity was a factor to a certain extent in determining political alignments: Anglo-Americans were typically Federalist, whereas Irish, Scots, and Germans were Democratic-Republicans.

The most severe of the alien laws was a Naturalization Act that again lengthened the residency requirement for citizenship from five to fourteen years and mandated the registration of all foreigners living in the United States. Combined with the Sedition Act, it effectively blocked those with European sympathies from influencing American elections. The first victim of the speech provisions of the Sedition Act was Irish-born Matthew Lyon, a naturalized citizen serving as a Republican congressman from Vermont. He was fined $1,000 and sentenced to four months' imprisonment for criticizing President John Adams in print. He served his term in the Vergennes jail, which he described in a letter to the *Independent Chronicle* in November 1798 as the "common receptacle for horse-thieves, money-makers, runaway-negroes, or any kind of felons." Indeed there was an element of racism in the selective way in which the sedition law was put into effect. The Federalists called Lyons an "animal who apes a monkey," who "talks and writes a gibberish between Wild Irish and vulgar American."

Likewise, when Dr. James Reynolds of Philadelphia protested the Alien and Sedition Acts, he was actually prosecuted for "seditious riot." Reynolds was a United Irish political refugee. Following a short but bloody uprising in Ireland in 1798 that had had French support, the British government banned these rebels from its territories. Hundreds, like Reynolds, sailed immediately from Belfast for New York or Philadelphia. But the American ambassador in London, the Federalist Rufus King, vigorously protested further banishment to the United States, and the leaders of the United Irishmen were imprisoned in Scotland instead. As he wrote to the American secretary of state, "I cannot persuade myself that the Malcontents of any character or country will ever become useful Citizens of ours." King lived to rue these words. Once Thomas Jefferson took office, draconian anti-immigrant legislation was allowed to expire, restoring the five-year naturalization period and clearing the way for the emigration of the Irish political prisoners. Among them were the able lawyers Thomas Addis Emmet (1764–1827) and William Sampson (1764–1836), who encouraged Irish support for the pro-immigrant party of Jefferson.

Naturalization again surfaced as an issue during the Napoleonic Wars, but this time the United States was forced to defend its foreign-born. The Royal Navy boldly stopped American trading vessels and forcibly impressed former British subjects into service to replenish its ranks under the principle "once an Englishman, always an Englishman." An estimated six to eight thousand citizens were impressed between 1803 and 1812 despite American efforts to protect them through trade sanctions and military force. Thirteen American ships sailing from Ireland were intercepted in 1812, including four still in Irish waters. At the same time, federal restrictions limited the freedom of English immigrants on the mainland who had maritime activities. New York City merchants of English birth, for example, were interned upstate at Fishkill, and a similar relocation occurred in Charleston, South Carolina, to prevent potentially subversive acts.

Suspicion of foreign-born loyalties was perennial. In 1835, in response to a suggestion by the *New York Evening Post* editor that immigrants be naturalized after twelve months in a state and six months in a town or ward, New York University professor Samuel F. B. Morse (1791–1872) wrote:

> he would put the Foreigner, the moment of his landing, on the same footing with native American citizens no matter from what country

he may come, no matter what his early habits, his character or condition, whether Hottentot or Turk, or Russian serf, or New-Zealand cannibal; the moment he sets foot on our shores, and simply signifies a wish to become a citizen, he is to be a citizen. He would in fact give foreigners of all kinds, not merely the protection, and instruction, and other advantages of citizenship, but the privilege also of electing our rulers; yes, and of being themselves preferred and elected over native Americans.

Immigrant entitlement during this period hinged not only on citizenship. While the federal Constitution guaranteed religious expression, some states continued to distinguish it from civil rights. In New York all naturalized citizens seeking political office were required to take an oath of loyalty. Other states, like New Jersey, Delaware, and North Carolina, restricted elective office to Protestants, a policy that excluded Jews as well as Catholics. Catholicism, in particular, presented a challenge to republican ideals. Early Catholic leaders were sensitive to their position as a barely tolerated minority, acutely aware of American Protestant suspicions about any foreign jurisdiction. Their immediate priority following the Revolution was to change the status of the American church from "mission" to "national" in order to remove any dependency on the Propaganda office in Rome. The connection with the Vatican was to be spiritual rather than temporal, given current political prejudices.

At the end of the eighteenth century association with the Pope—a "foreign prince"—was compounded by a rise in the number of foreign-born Catholics. In addition to French speakers who had been inherited from the Diocese of Quebec in the recently acquired territory between the Appalachians and the Mississippi, Irish immigrants had already begun to dilute what had hitherto been an English- and German-stock Catholic population on the eastern seaboard. This caused significant administrative problems because, although the understaffed church needed priests, many itinerant European clergymen refused to take direction from American church leaders. Irish priests in New York, French priests in Boston, and German priests in Philadelphia all caused internal dissent that reflected poorly on Catholicism in general at the very moment that Catholics were struggling to gain civil rights in various states as well as independent jurisdiction from Rome.

A new era of ecclesiastical structure or authority for the Catholic Church in the United States began with the selection of John Carroll

(1736–1815) as its first Bishop in 1789. Based in Baltimore, Carroll took charge of an estimated thirty-five thousand Catholics, nearly two-thirds of whom were in Maryland (including approximately three thousand African slaves). The timing of Carroll's appointment coincided not only with these image problems but with political upheaval on the Continent. The American Catholic Church was thus in a unique position to offer refuge to European religious orders, like the Sulpicians, who were threatened by the French Revolution. In the continued absence of a native-born clergy, the public face of Catholicism at the parish level during this period therefore continued to be foreign. Carroll insisted that European priests serving under him in America learn English as well as American laws and customs. With Carroll's encouragement, a vernacular edition of the Catholic Bible was published by Mathew Carey in 1790. Nevertheless, by 1820 the consequences of a foreign-born clergy were being felt through a more traditional and conservative strand of practice appearing in the American church.

A critical turning point in the acquisition of civil rights for Catholics was the refusal of Fr. Anthony Kohlmann, a Jesuit from Alsace, to divulge the identity of a thief because he had received the information while hearing confession. This 1813 test case became the first free-exercise-of-religion litigation in American constitutional history and, in the words of legal historian Walter J. Walsh, the "jurisgenerative origin of the priest-penitent evidentiary privilege." Arguing in New York's Court of General Sessions, William Sampson, a Protestant lawyer from Ireland, darkly contrasted England's history of Catholic discrimination with the protections promised by the American constitution. He concluded that providence had decreed this land to be "the grave of persecution, and the cradle of tolerance," declaring, "every citizen here is in his own country. To the protestant it is a protestant country; to the catholic, a catholic country; and the jew, if he pleases, may establish in it his New Jerusalem."

Sampson published the trial as *The Catholic Question in America* (1813), but minds and hearts were slower to change than the law. The problem with religious toleration was that by the second decade of the nineteenth century, Catholics from Ireland vastly outnumbered those of any other ethnicity. Their immigration became particularly significant to the rapid expansion of the Catholic Church in America after 1820. "Its growth here appears to me almost impossible," Frances Kemble (1809–1893) noted, for if ever there were two things more opposite in their nature than all other things, they are the spirit of the Roman Catholic religion, and the spirit of the American people. It's true, that of the thousands who take refuge from poverty upon this plenteous land, the greater number bring with them that creed, but the very air they inhale here presently gives them a political faith, so utterly incompatible with the spirit of subjection, that I shall think the Catholic priesthood here workers of miracles, to retain anything like the influence over their minds which they possessed in those countries, where all creeds, political and polemical, have but one watch-word—faith and submission.

The United States was still culturally Anglo-Saxon, and soon, inherited racial attitudes toward the Irish surfaced that, combined with anti-Catholicism, resulted in the rise of virulent nativism. In 1827 the Society for the Defence of the Roman Catholic Religion from Calumny and Abuse, in response to what it felt was a libelous attack by the Gideonite Society in Philadelphia, published a fourth edition of Mathew Carey's pamphlet *Letters on Religious Persecution* for free distribution. The parliamentary campaign for Catholic emancipation in Ireland in 1829 no doubt exacerbated nativist conditions in the United States, particularly in cities like New Orleans, where moral and financial support for Daniel O'Connell was very public among Irish immigrants. The backlash included anti-Irish employment ads such as those in New York protested by *The Truth Teller*, a Catholic weekly:

Wanted.—A woman well-qualified to take charge of the cooking and washing of a family—any one but a Catholic who can come well recommended may call at 57 John Street.
(*Journal of Commerce*, 8 July 1830)

Wanted.—A Cook or a Chambermaid. They must be American, Scotch, Swiss, or African—no Irish.
(*Evening Post*, 4 September 1830)

Passions were further aroused by the mob burning of St. Mary's in New York City the following year and an Ursuline convent and school in Charlestown, Massachusetts, in 1834, as well as by the publication of sensational tracts like Samuel F. B. Morse's *Imminent Dangers to the Free Institutions of the United States Through Foreign Immigration* (1835) and Maria Monk's *Awful Disclosures of the Hotel Dieu Nunnery of Montreal* (1836).

Not only was Catholicism perceived as "immigrant" in the 1820s and 1830s, it was also seen as urban. The confluence of cities, race, and ethnicity had ramifications when cholera struck the United States in 1832. Lack of understanding about its scientific causes led to an assumption of moral depravity, seemingly confirmed through accepted stereotypes of the urban poor—often African Americans or Irish living in crowded and unsanitary conditions—who were its principal victims. "Whether he was free or slave, Americans believed, the Negro's innate character invited cholera," wrote medical historian Charles Rosenberg in 1962. "He was, with few exceptions, filthy and careless in his personal habits, lazy and ignorant by temperament. A natural fatalist, moreover, he took no steps to protect himself from disease." A similar profile was drawn of Irish immigrants, with the additional onus of supposedly having aided cholera in breaching the Atlantic divide. In September 1832, New Yorker Philip Hone confided to his diary,

> they have brought the cholera this year and they will always bring wretchedness and want. The boast that our country is an asylum for the oppressed in other parts of the world is very philanthropic and sentimental, but I fear that we shall before long derive little comfort from being made the almshouse and refuge for the poor of other countries.

Underpinning relations with (not between) African Americans and Irish lay a widely accepted hierarchy of race that degraded the humanity of both groups. Nevertheless "whiteness" mattered—in the decennial census as we have seen—and in other legislation such as New York State's suffrage extension in 1821 and again in 1826, which removed property qualifications and voting restrictions for all men except for blacks. This gave the Irish a ballot but little else; from this point until the Emancipation Proclamation in 1863, the relationship of the two groups to northern Protestant Americans diverged considerably in the political arena. The abolitionist movement elevated the African American to a cause célèbre at the same time that Irish were denigrated by Whig elites. During the election of 1834, the *New England Review* called the Irish "the most corrupt, the most debased, and the most brutally ignorant portion of the population of our large cities" while the *Journal of Commerce* wrote that "Colored Persons" were "attached to our institutions, and are intelligent, and in many respects far better qualified to participate in our elections." Nevertheless, compared to the average American, blacks and the Irish were on a par socially and economically. And, like the Irish, African Americans had developed religious congregations and institutions that set them apart from white Protestants, such as the A.M.E. Zion Church, established in 1796, and the African Methodist Episcopal Church, founded in 1816.

While the moral tensions inherent in perpetuating bondage in a democratic society were part of the new federal political discourse, it was pure economics that kept slavery alive in the United States after 1790. The invention of the cotton gin in 1792 resolved the impending crisis in the southern plantation system by facilitating a shift away from tobacco, rice, and indigo toward a more lucrative cash crop. Growing cotton was labor-intensive and, as it dominated the southern economy, the number of slaves nearly tripled—from more than seven-hundred thousand in 1790 to 2.3 million in 1830. Slavery was increasingly a southern institution, especially after New York (1799) and New Jersey (1804) joined the other northern states that had already outlawed it.

Fear in the aftermath of the 1791 uprising in Haiti led to the passage of legislation regulating slave imports, especially in southern states like the Carolinas, Virginia, and Maryland. Fear was also the genesis of the Fugitive Slave Act of 1793, which gave wide latitude to masters in retrieving their human "property." Under this law, African Americans could be convicted on oral testimony only and were not privy to trial by jury, rights which white ethnics enjoyed under the Bill of Rights. About ninety thousand slaves arrived in the United States between the end of the Revolution and January 1, 1808, the date after which Congress—under abolitionist pressures from Great Britain and New England—expressly banned the overseas slave trade. However, lax enforcement and the domestic sale of slaves to plantations in the new Louisiana Territory—as well as their intentional breeding for sale—allowed the slave trade to flourish during the early national period. As late as 1836, twelve thousand slaves from Virginia were sold further south when prices for prime field hands were nearing $1,200 to $1,300 in Kentucky, Georgia, Alabama, and Louisiana. A profitable adjunct to slave trading was slave hiring, which placed blacks in service and laboring work in cities and factory towns and on railroad and canal projects.

At the same time the number of free blacks in the United States increased, from 108,000 in 1800 to 386,000 in 1840. There was a concomitant drop in the number of white indentured servants in response to British restrictions on the emigration of skilled labor to the United States. Combined with relaxed—even fashionable—attitudes toward manumissions, this facilitated black entry into the northern economy, at least until Nat Turner's slave revolt in 1831 when there was considerable retrenchment:

> The calm, deliberate composure with which he spoke of his late deeds and intentions, the expression of his fiend-like face when excited by enthusiasm, still bearing the stains of the blood of help-less innocence about him; clothed with rags and covered with chains; yet daring to raise his manacled hands to heaven, with a spirit soaring above the attributes of man; I looked on him and my blood curdled in my veins.

This 1832 excerpt from Thomas R. Gray's widely circulated version of Turner's confession increased white fears and the imposition of legal restrictions became inevitable. Fanny Kemble, an English actress turned wife of plantation owner Pierce Butler, was horrified to learn about southern restrictions on basic rights. In December 1832 she recorded in her diary, "To teach a slave to read or write is to incur a penalty of fine or imprisonment. They form the larger proportion of the population, by far; and so great is the dread of insurrection on the part of the white inhabitants, that they are kept in the most brutish igno-rance, and too often treated with the most brutal barbarity, in order to insure their subjection."

The enforcement of these "black codes" encouraged freed slaves to move to the north, bringing them into direct competition for jobs with Irish immigrants, especially in the mid-Atlantic cities. There were race riots between the two groups in Philadelphia in 1832 and again in 1842. In addition, both peoples faced employment and housing discrimina-tion; relegated to the lowest service-sector positions—such as cooks, servants, waiters, and day laborers—and to the cheapest-rent districts, Irish and African Americans were the victims of pernicious stereotyp-ing. "I never hear an Irishman called Paddy, a colored person called nigger, or the contemptuous epithet 'old beggar man,' without a pang in my heart for I know that such epithets, inadvertently used, are doing more to form the moral sentiments of the nation, than all the teachings of the schools," wrote Lydia Maria Child in 1841.

Verbal portraits of racial and ethnic groups in antebellum literature published before 1840 commonly focused on their inferior intelligence and moral capabilities rather than on extrinsic characteristics like appearance that would gain popularity at midcentury (the epitome being the simian depictions of Thomas Nast). The relationship of language to perceptions of the ethnic Other was critical, especially as Americans were defining themselves nationally in the first four decades of the nineteenth century. As the new nation rebuilt a commercial base in its port cities, colonial trading links were renewed. The demand for foreign luxury goods increased their quantity and visibility in American households. One of the consequences was a direct cognitive relationship between product and country of origin.

In other words, a product's identification with specific ethnicity or race entered Anglo-American cultural discourse. Gallophobia, for example, did not preclude a taste for French style in dress or dance fashions. The recruitment of skilled workers from England for certain industries in the United States was independent of political Anglophobia. Immigrants from Staffordshire—with an established reputation for ceramic tableware—were the backbone of the emerging American pottery manufactories at Trenton, New Jersey, from 1832. The highly desired textile printing and metal-working techniques of Lancashire and Sheffield were transferred to Massachusetts and Connecticut factories through British immigrants, enabling American-made products to compete favorably with their English counterparts in the marketplace.

But by far the greatest commercial influence on perceptions of ethnicity was the post-war trade with China. The New York firm of William Constable and Company reaped enormous profits from the 1790–1791 voyage of the *Washington*, heralding a new era in American business. Not only did China become the basis of several mercantile fortunes but chinoiserie became pervasive in social circles with disposable income. Chinese silk, tea, porcelain, and opium contributed to Orientalism, especially among the upper classes. Tea became a necessity rather than a luxury, while the practical value of other items—such as china tea sets—was surpassed only by their value as curios. Although the Chinese presence in America was negligible at the turn of the nineteenth century, Chinese goods were already well established when the Siamese twins Chang and Eng first made appearances in Boston and New York in 1829. For the thousands of Americans who paid to see the brothers over the next decade, it was their first contact with Chinese people. The physical attachment of Chang and Eng, while startling, was nevertheless in keeping with exotic perceptions of China and the Chinese that were current in the early national period. Their duplication literally made flesh a much-admired Oriental art, as the following excerpt from the diary of Anne Gorham Everett in 1835 illustrates:

> I read . . . a very curious account of the exactness of the Chinese. A lady wishing to match some beautiful china, which her husband had received from the East India Company, sent a plate to China to have some more made like it. In due time the plates arrived, and were unpacked; but every one looked as if it had a crack in it, and on examining the pattern it was found that there was a crack in the middle of it.

On the other hand, whereas by the late eighteenth century the word "Irish" in the marketplace was descriptive of good-quality, inexpensive linen, as well as salted herring and mackerel, by the early nineteenth century it had become a synonym for "barbarity." Likewise, Fanny Kemble commented on how the blackness of slaves had been transformed into an even darker concept. Americans, she wrote, had "learned to turn the very name of their race into an insult and a reproach." In 1833 Thomas Hamilton, a Scottish traveler in the United States, remarked, "It has often happened to me, since my arrival in this country, to hear it gravely maintained by men of education and intelligence, that the Negroes were an inferior race, a link as it were between man and the brutes." This went beyond skin tone, as the New York Irish schoolmaster Patrick S. Casserly grimly observed in 1832: "If a swindler, thief, robber, or murderer, no matter what his color or country commit any nefarious or abominable act, throughout the Union, he is instantly set down as a native of Ireland." Descriptions of the Irish as lazy, unreliable, improvident, childlike, and foolish mirrored descriptions of blacks, creating a popular idiom that was deficient in the very virtues deemed necessary to good republicanism. These were familiarly summed up by the rubric "Paddy" or "Sambo," "Bridget" or "Mammy"—the serving class of white America. In New York's Sixth Ward successive mob violence by native-born whites in 1834 and 1835 targeted blacks and Irish equally, sparked by general trepidation over amalgamation (miscegenation) and foreigners.

Indians, on the other hand, were "noble savages" until at least the late 1820s. Rather than an inherently inferior people, Native Americans were perceived as victims of social, political, and economic circumstances who could be civilized. Why? Indian tribes had been defined as sovereign nations in the earliest treaties made by the United States and, unlike blacks and Irish, were not viewed as an exploitable or cheap source of labor. There were federal and religious attempts to transform tribes into yeoman stock by encouraging the adoption of cash agriculture, Anglo-American education, and political institutions. In 1790 Congress appropriated $20,000 for farming supplies for the Cherokees and in 1819 began annually endowing an Indian Civilization Fund with $10,000. The Cherokees, Chickasaws, Choctaws, and Creeks were the first to respond well but their motives were practical: the need to avoid dispossession of their lands and "black" classification in an increasingly biracial southern society. One of the hallmarks of their successful acculturation was the acquisition of the English language. The *Cherokee Phoenix*, a bilingual newspaper founded in 1828, as well as eighteen Cherokee schools, clearly demonstrated this by the mid-1820s.

All foreign languages suffered in the rising sense of American nationality after 1790. The supremacy of English as the dominant tongue of the United States was settled by 1815. Giovanni Antonio Grassi, an Italian Jesuit serving as president of Georgetown University at that time, observed, "English is the language universally spoken, and it is not corrupted here as in England by a variety of dialects." In fact, the appearance of books emphasizing accent elimination, such as John Walker's *A Critical Pronouncing Dictionary and Expositor of the English Language* (1818), hastened the adoption of an "American" English standard. Yet, by the early national period, English as spoken in the United States had already absorbed many ethnic words and inflections, particularly from the intermingling of German and Irish immigrants in the backcountry. This was most pronounced in Appalachia, where the one distinct variation of American English was already evident by 1800. Words like "chaw," "ingine," and "picter" were typical of the region's so-called broad speech.

Unlike immigrants from the British Isles—among whom even these linguistic variations were still recognizable as English—communities who spoke a foreign language were marked off as different. There was natural attrition as immigration failed to replenish the supply of native speakers among the Welsh, French, and Swedes. But for others, abandoning their mother tongues was more difficult because its use was reinforced not only in the home and in the marketplace but also in church.

In the Middle Atlantic states commercial interaction with a rapidly expanding economy eroded the language faster, of necessity, so that the pulpit became the bastion of preservation, especially among the Germans of Pennsylvania and the Dutch of New York. As early as 1794 the Dutch Reformed Church of America began to adopt English, making religious services in Dutch obsolete by the late 1830s. In 1800 Lutheran Church authorities in New York favored English as the language of its official business just as fellow Germans on the western and southern frontiers began to adopt it too. Generally, urban congregations were more successful than rural ones in obtaining dispensations regarding language preference. Clergy trained abroad contributed to resistance to change, but compromises were inevitable as American-born generations pressed for religious services, Bibles, hymn books, and catechisms in English. Translation and dissemination were among the principal activities of the American Bible Society, formed in New York City in 1816. The acceptance of English by German and Dutch Protestants directly diluted a sense of ethnic identity and enhanced an American one.

On the other hand, minority religions retained foreign language services—particularly when multiple ethnicities made a common language more critical. Jews had Spanish, Portuguese, and German roots that made Hebrew integral to worship just as Latin took precedence over mother tongues in Catholic rituals. But Jews and Catholics were not immune to the influence of English. In 1824 the Sephardic congregation in Charleston, South Carolina, petitioned for bilingual services, "so as to enable every member of the congregation fully to understand every part of the service." The issue was so volatile that the petition's refusal led to a splinter Reform congregation that lasted for eight years.

Bishop John Carroll mused on the drawbacks of Mass in Latin: "It is an unknown Tongue, and in this Country, still more than in yours [England] either for want of Books or desirability to read, the greatest part of our Congregation must be entirely ignorant of the meaning and Sense of the publick Offices of the church." For German and French Catholics—minorities within a minority religion—the vernacular assumed a great importance as a marker of identity as well as a source of interethnic friction with the increasingly more numerous Irish. National parishes, such as New York's St. Nicholas founded by Germans in 1833, were one solution. Such linguistic independence had its limits as far as the church hierarchy was concerned, and Germans repeatedly had to capitulate on broader administrative matters.

There are always historical exceptions. Father Felix Varela (1788–1853), a Catholic priest and Cuban political exile, ministered in English to his New York Irish parishioners as well as publishing *El Haberno*—in the 1820s one of the first Spanish-language newspapers in America—to advocate for minority rights, religious toleration, and bilingual cooperation. Scholars continue to debate whether African Americans spoke a form of English learned from contact with white immigrants in the United States or a creole version brought from Africa and the Caribbean, such as the distinctive Gullah of coastal South Carolina and Georgia spoken since the mid-eighteenth century. And, in a rare example of the use of an indigenous language to acculturate to white norms, the Rev. Thomas Roberts of North Carolina oversaw a Cherokee translation of the *American Sunday School Spelling Book* (*Sunalei akvlvgi no 'gwisi alikalvvsga zvlvgi Gesvi*), that was published in 1824 "for the benefit of those who cannot acquire the English language."

Native American interaction with white settlers increased due to eastern population pressures after the American Revolution. Several treaties attempted to stabilize tribal boundaries, particularly with the Iroquois at Fort Stanwix on the New York–Canadian border (1784), with the Choctaw, Chickasaw, and Cherokee nations at Hopewell, South Carolina (1785–86), and with the Creeks in Georgia (1790). The result was a nearly tenfold increase in the number of Americans west of the Appalachian Mountains and south of the Ohio River during the 1780s. In the old Northwest (Ohio, Indiana, Illinois, and Michigan) there were more than a dozen agreements made with tribes between 1795 and 1809. However, the provisions of Indian treaties were weakly enforced by the federal government and routinely violated by ambitious settlers. Governor William Henry Harrison (1773–1841) reported that many trespassing frontiersmen in Indiana Territory considered "the murdering of the Indians in the highest degree meritorious."

Treaties with France (Louisiana Purchase 1803), Great Britain (1818), and Spain (Adams-Onis 1819) opened up further migratory possibilities to the west of the Appalachian Mountains and reopened the issue of Native American relations along a wide swath of territory from the Canadian border to Florida and Mexico. The migrants included not only New Englanders and southern planters but black slaves and foreign-born laborers, making the frontier the crucible of racial and ethnic interaction in the early nineteenth century. There is considerable anthropologic, folklore, and cultural geographic evidence that frontier settlers learned from each other and creatively adapted to a challenging natural environment. The Irish borrowed the log cabin from the Germans and, by the time they reached Indiana, had altered its design to suit domestic customs from Ulster. Both groups used Indian methods of hunting and forest pharmacology to survive in the wilderness. African Americans were frequently trappers and interpreters, negotiating the middle ground between white immigrants and Indian tribes. Yet once again, outside perceptions of the frontier inhabitants were colored. In 1801 William Strickland, an English farmer, declared, "none emigrate to the frontiers beyond the mountains, except culprits, or savage back-woodsmen . . . the outcasts of the world, and the disgrace of it."

Like the opposition of "immigrant" to Anglo-American, "frontier" served to highlight the civility of life in the East. Well into the 1830s some Americans remained uncomfortable over the presence of the foreign-born in their midst. After remarking in his diary on the arrival of 15,825 passengers at the port of New York in May 1836, Philip Hone complained, "All Europe is coming across the ocean; all that part at least who cannot make a living at home; and what shall we do with them? They increase our taxes, eat our bread, and encumber our streets, and not one in twenty is competent to keep himself." Throughout the early national period one of the solutions frequently proposed was the creation of colonies, particularly in the West. The impetus for this kind of segregation sometimes came from within an ethnic or racial group, and sometimes it was imposed from without.

One of the earliest colonization efforts was Gallipolis, founded on the LaBelle River in Ohio by French-Catholic immigrants in 1790. Several were in Pennsylvania: an Irish settlement begun in 1795 at Buffalo Creek and Slippery Rock in Butler County was flourishing fifty years later under the name Sugarcreek; in Cambria County, a mixture of Germans, Swiss, and Irish Catholics gravitated to Loretto after 1799; and at Silver Lake in Susquehanna County, Fr. Jeremiah F. O'Flynn erected a church in 1827 that shortly drew Catholics from rural public works projects to live in its vicinity. In northwestern New York, French, German, and Irish Catholics farmed several of the Black River Settlements. Bishop Fenwick started a Catholic colony at Benedicta in Maine in 1834, toward which he directed many of his Boston Irish parishioners.

Ethnic colonies were not exclusively Catholic. English political radicals founded Jacobin and Quaker communities in Pennsylvania in the 1790s. Wanborough and Albion, prairie colonies established in Illinois in 1818 by immigrants from Surrey and Hertford, were heavily promoted back home in England. In 1824 Mordecai Manuel Noah, the former American consul at Tunis, purchased fifty square miles on Grand Island in the Niagara River from the New York State Legislature. There he proposed a haven for Jews to be called Ararat, until such time as they could return to the Holy Land. Despite an elaborate ceremony in nearby Buffalo in September 1825, this Jewish colony never materialized.

The Irish leaders in New York, Baltimore, and Philadelphia petitioned Congress in 1818 to set aside lands in the Illinois Territory on easy credit for newly arrived immigrants from Ireland. Their argument was essentially a desire to protect the vulnerable and to guide the innocent:

> They have fled from want and oppression—they touch the soil of freedom and abundance; but the manna of the wilderness melts in their sight. Before they can taste the fruits of happy industry, the tempter too often presents to their lips the cup that turns man to brute, and the very energies which would have made the fields to blossom make the cities groan. Individual benevolence cannot reach this evil. Individuals may indeed solicit, but it belongs to the chosen guardians of the public weal to administer the cure.

This appeal by the Irish Emigrant Association was rejected. In contrast, an attempt by the African Colonization Society to repatriate blacks to the west coast of Africa was modestly successful. Between 1817 and 1830, approximately 1,420 were resettled in Liberia. Although the movement was fraught with ideological conflicts—it was all too easy to see it either as deportation or as a method of Christianizing Africa—a total of twelve thousand eventually migrated from the United States under the auspices of the Society. Abolitionists in particular objected to colonization on the grounds that, by siphoning off the free black population, it strengthened the position of American slaveholding interests.

A far less idealistic colonization scheme was the United States government's Indian reservation policy. Prior to 1815, Native Americans were pressured to yield their eastern lands either through sale or in exchange for land in the West, at the same time that private acculturation programs—typically run by Christian missionaries—were underwritten by Congress. Success had been qualified, as Rachel Lazarus reported to novelist Maria Edgeworth in 1824:

> I lately saw another very sensible and well written letter from an Indian, in reply to one that made some enquiries relative to the situation of his tribe. He says they are fast advancing in civilisation, that exclusive of Missionary schools, they have established several for the education of their youth; that many of them have embraced the Christian Religion, and that there are among them several men of property, who cultivate flourishing farms which exhibit every appearance of neatness and comfort. He nevertheless deprecates the idea which appears to have been suggested of a free intercourse with the whites. He says, "do not force nature; we are improving, but we are not prepared to live among you, or to receive you among us; time has done a great deal, and may do a great deal more for us, if we are left to ourselves."

Thereafter "removal" was added to the strategies used by Washington, D.C., to deal with Native Americans. "He is unwilling to submit to the laws of the States and mingle with their population," President Andrew Jackson argued in 1830 on behalf of the Removal Act, "To save him from this alternative, or perhaps utter annihilation, the General Government kindly offers him a new home, and proposes to pay the whole expense of his removal and settlement." Once formally implemented by Congress, Indians were to be moved west of the Mississippi—either bought out or forcibly relocated—ostensibly to keep them out of harm's way through isolation. John C. Calhoun (1782–1850) reckoned removal would permit a generation of Indians to become civilized enough for reintegration into white society. In reality, the policy was meant to appease the insatiable demands of white frontiersmen for Mississippi Valley land, which had been building ever since the signing of the Pickney Treaty with Spain in 1795.

The Indian Removal Act affected about seventy-three thousand Native Americans during the 1830s. The Cherokees resisted by suing the state of Georgia in two landmark cases that went to the U.S. Supreme Court. In *Cherokee Nation v. Georgia* (1831) and *Worcester v. Georgia* (1832), Justice John Marshall decided in favor of the Indians, describing them as "domestic dependent nations." President Jackson chose to ignore the Court, enforcing a dubious treaty that gave 7 million acres to the United States and removed fifteen thousand Cherokees under duress to Oklahoma in the winter of 1838–1839. Nearly four thousand did not survive the "Trail of Tears." Likewise, Jackson took aggressive action against the Sac, Fox, and Seminoles when they proved uncooperative about removal. The Black Hawk War (1832) in Illinois and the Second Seminole War in Florida, fought between 1835 and 1842 under the leadership of Osceola, ultimately saw the triumph of federal policy.

In some ways Andrew Jackson (1767–1845) is the classic fulfillment of John Dunlap's prediction in the epitaph that opens this essay. On the other hand, he was born and raised in the Southern backcountry, on the border of North and South Carolina, in an area whose native Waxhaw tribe was eradicated by smallpox and wars, then resettled in the 1740s by an influx of Germans and Irish. Its frontier days were waning even though it was still quite isolated from "civilization." Jackson was also the son of immigrant parents from the north of Ireland, who spoke with a foreign accent and espoused Presbyterianism, a nonconforming brand of Protestantism. By the standards of the New Republic, was he truly an ideal American?

As defined by the Constitution of 1789, he was a native-born white citizen with the right to vote and freedom of conscience. But by then he was living in Nashville, beyond the western edge of the United States and outside its jurisdiction. When Tennessee was admitted to statehood in 1796, it drafted a liberal constitution that even extended suffrage to free blacks. Jackson, in his subsequent professional career, manifested the attitudes of (and accommodations commonly made on) the frontier. As a military officer, he fought alongside free African Americans in the battles of Horseshoe Bend and New Orleans, but never lifted a finger to abolish slavery. During the War of 1812, he also fought against the British with companies of Cherokees and Choctaws, the same tribes he would later dispossess while seventh President of the United States. Their clearance permitted a new generation of Irish and German immigrants to grow up on the settled frontier, just as Jackson had more than half a century earlier. Although Jackson was hailed by "the sons of his father's land" at the St. Patrick's Day 1828 banquet of the Friendly Sons of St. Patrick in New York City, his presidency nevertheless marks the emergence of a bitter Scotch-Irish versus Irish rivalry in American ethnic history, mirroring the rural/urban and Protestant/Catholic tensions already rife in the country. Jackson was a kind of new American for the nineteenth century, the complicated and anomalous result of the interplay of citizenship, religion, language, and segregation during the early national period.

BIBLIOGRAPHIC ESSAY

For general overviews of race and ethnicity in the Early National period, see Leonard Dinnerstein and David M. Reimers, *Ethnic Americans: A History of Immigration*, 3rd ed. (New York: HarperCollins, 1988); Leonard Dinnerstein, Roger L. Nichols, and David M. Reimers, *Natives and Strangers: A Multicultural History of Americans* (New York: Oxford University Press, 1996); and Marcus Lee Hansen, *The Atlantic Migration, 1607–1860* (Cambridge: Harvard University Press, 1951).

On the 1790 census and early republican demographics, see *The Statistical History of the United States from Colonial Times to the Present* (Stamford, Conn.: Fairfield Publishers, Inc., 1947); Peter D. McClelland and Richard J. Zeckhauser, *Demographic Dimensions of the New Republic: American Interregional Migration, Vital Statistics, and Manumissions, 1800–1860* (New York: Cambridge University Press, 1982); and Margo J. Anderson, ed., *Encyclopedia of the US Census* (Washington, D.C.: CQ Press, 2000). For the twentieth-century surname analyses of the 1790 census, see U.S. Bureau of the Census, *A Century of Population Growth* (Washington, D.C.: Government Printing Office, 1909); American Council of Learned Societies, "Report of Committee on Linguistic and National Stocks in the Population of the United States," American Historical Association, *Annual Report for the Year 1931* (Washington, D.C., 1932); and "The Population of the United States, 1790: A Symposium," *William and Mary Quarterly* 41 (January 1984): 85–135, which includes revised estimates of the ACLS figures by Thomas L. Purvis; see especially Table II, p. 98, although these figures are disputed by Donald Akenson, pp. 102–119. Students should note that despite this lively debate, the U.S. Historical Census Data Browser for 1790 on the Web at http://fisher.lib.virginia.edu/cgi-local/censusbin/census/cen.pl?year=790 is based solely on the controversial *A Century of Population Growth* (1909).

For a good summary of the effects of early restrictionist legislation, see James Morton Smith, *Freedom's Fetters: The Alien and Sedition Laws and American Civil Liberties* (Ithaca: Cornell University Press, 1956).

On the issues of image and language, see Dale T. Knobel, *Paddy and the Republic: Ethnicity and Nationality in Antebellum America* (Middletown, Conn.: Wesleyan University Press, 1986); John Kuo Wei Tchen, *New York Before Chinatown: Orientalism and the Shaping of American Culture, 1776–1882* (Baltimore: Johns Hopkins University Press, 1999); Robert McCrum, William Cran, and Robert MacNeil, *The Story of English* (New York: Viking Penguin, 1986); and John R. Rickford, "The Creole Origins of African American Vernacular English: Evidence from Copula Absence," in Salikoko S. Mufwene, John R. Rickford, Guy Bailey, and John Baugh, eds., *African American English,* (London: Routledge, 1998).

For the history of ethnic and racial Catholics during this period, see John Tracy Ellis, *Catholics in Colonial America* (Baltimore: Helicon Press, 1965); Jay P. Dolan, *The American Catholic Experience: A History from Colonial Times to the Present* (Notre Dame: University of Notre Dame Press, 1992); and Dolan, *The Immigrant Church: New York's Irish and German Catholics, 1815–1865* (Notre Dame: University of Notre Dame Press, 1983; Baltimore: The Johns Hopkins University Press, 1975); and Sister Mary Gilbert Kelly, "Irish Catholic Colonies and Colonization Projects in the United States, 1795–1860," *Studies* (Dublin), Vol. 29 (1940), pp. 95–109.

On turn-of-the-nineteenth-century black history, see John Hope Franklin and Alfred A. Moss, Jr., *From Slavery to Freedom: A History of African Americans*, 7th ed. (New York: McGraw-Hill, 1994). There is an electronic version of *The Confessions of Nat Turner, the Leader of the Late Insurrection in Southampton, VA as fully and voluntarily made to Thomas R. Gray* (Richmond: Thomas R Gray, 1832) on the Web at http://odur.let.rug.nl/_usa/D/1826-1850/slavery/confeso1.htm.

Essays by Theda Perdue and R. David Edmunds in *Indians in American History: An Introduction*, Frederick E. Hoxie, ed. (Arlington Heights, Ill.: Harlan Davidson, 1988) are helpful. See also Angie Debo, *A History of the Indians of the United States* (Norman: University of Oklahoma Press, 1970). Andrew Jackson's Case for the Removal Act, First Annual Message to Congress, 8 December 1830, is reproduced in *A Compilation of the Messages and Papers of the Presidents, 1789–1908*, Volume II, by James D. Richardson, published by the Bureau of National Literature and Art, 1908. The full text of the landmark Supreme Court decisions *Cherokee Nation v. Georgia* (1831) and *Worcester v. Georgia* (1832) are on the Web at http://www.pbs.org/weta/thewest/ resources/archives/two/cherokee.htm

For the Irish, see *Essays in Scotch-Irish History*, E. R. R. Green, ed. (London: Routledge & Kegan Paul Ltd, 1969; reprint Ulster Historical Foundation, 1992), especially essays by Maldwyn A. Jones, E. R. R. Green, and E. Estyn Evans; Earl F. Niehaus, *The Irish in New Orleans, 1800–1860* (Baton Rouge: Louisiana State University Press, 1965); Dennis Clark, *The Irish in Philadelphia: Ten Generations of Urban Experience* (Philadelphia: Temple University Press, 1973); and essays by Walter J. Walsh and Graham Hodges in Ronald H. Bayor and Timothy J. Meagher, eds., *The New York Irish* (Baltimore: The Johns Hopkins University Press, 1996). *The Harvard Encyclopedia of American Ethnic Groups*, Stephan Thernstrom, ed. (Cambridge: Belknap Press of Harvard University, 1980) remains an excellent starting place for the early history of the English, Germans, Swedes, Jews, French, and Spanish in the United States.

Quotes from primary documents used in this essay are from the following: "Encouragement to Irish Emigrants," U.S. Senate Doc. No. 449, 15th Congress, 1st Session. 1818; Giovanni Antonio Grassi, *Notizie varie sullo stato presente della repubblica degli Stati Uniti dell'America* ("Observations on the United States"), originally published in 1819, reproduced in *The Annals of America*, Vol. 4, *1797–1820, Domestic Expansion and Foreign Entanglements* (Chicago and London: Encyclopedia Britannica, 1968); Thomas Hamilton, *Men and Manners in America* (Edinburgh: W. Blackwood, 1833), quoted in Walter Allen ed., *Transatlantic Crossing* (London: William Heinemann Ltd., 1971); Samuel F. B. Morse, *Imminent Dangers to the Free Institutions of the United States Through Foreign Immigration, and the Present State of the Naturalization Laws* (New York: E. B. Clayton, 1835); Bayard Tuckerman, ed., *The Diary of Philip Hone, 1828–1851* (New York: Dodd, Mead, 1889), as well as Allan Nevins, ed., *The Diary of Philip Hone, 1828–1851* (New York: Dodd, Mead, 1936); *Journal of Frances Anne Butler*, vol. 2 (Philadelphia: Carey, Lea and Blanchard, 1835); and Philippa C. Bush, *Memoir of Anne Gorham Everett, with Extracts from Her Correspondence and Journal* (Boston: privately printed, 1857). There are electronic versions of these last two on the Web at http://www.alexanderstreet2.com/NWLDlive/

4

RACIAL AND ETHNIC IDENTITY IN THE UNITED STATES, 1837–1877

Michael Miller Topp

In recent years the specter of identity politics—of people identifying themselves and organizing themselves around their ethnicity or race, for example—has created enormous concerns in American society. Critics, from Michael Kazin and Todd Gitlin on the Left to Arthur Schlesinger, Jr., and Lynne Cheney on the Right, have raised alarms across the political spectrum about the dangers of splintering American reform efforts or American society as a whole. In an age when accusations of reverse discrimination, ethnic and racial separatism, and even Balkanization and tribalism are ubiquitous, we would do well to remember that identity politics—that racial and ethnic identity—have always mattered in the United States.

The period between 1837 and 1877, during which economic and geographic growth thoroughly changed the face of the nation, offers an excellent window on how these aspects of identity defined a person's place in or outside of American society. In these years immigrants began to flood into the United States in unprecedented numbers: the Irish, the Germans, and, on the West Coast, the Chinese foremost among them. American expansionism and industrialization affected each of these populations directly and often dramatically. These forces also touched other populations—Indians, Mexicans, and African Americans—already living in the United States, or in what became the United States, profoundly altering their relationship to American society.

In 1837, American expansionism had tremendous momentum. Texas had just declared its independence from Mexico and was pushing for entry into the United States. Georgians, working with Andrew Jackson's full cooperation, were just completing their successful effort to expand their access to tillable soil by forcing the Five Civilized Tribes westward. The federal government sponsored expeditions into the West throughout this period, scouting out accessible transportation routes and valuable resources; in these years, overland trails were replaced by the transcontinental railroad. Through the Mexican American War, fought between 1846 and 1848, and the Gadsden Purchase in 1853, the United States added California and parts of present-day Arizona, Utah, Nevada, and New Mexico. In the course of these few years, the United States increased in size by more than 70 percent. By 1877, thirteen new states entered the Union, and the rest of what became the continental United States was organized into territories.

Industrialization and economic growth went hand in hand with territorial expansion. The new lands provided raw materials for burgeoning American industries and provided access to new markets for goods. Slave owners in the South migrated west as the nation expanded, leaving tired soil behind them. As cotton production shifted west, it increased its importance to the American textile industry and to the export economy of the country. The new lands spurred the transportation revolution, which produced a transcontinental railroad and the first American corporations by 1869. One clear marker of economic growth was the increase in American production. The goods produced in the United States increased several fold in these decades. The nation produced $483 million in manufactured goods in 1840. In 1870 the gross national product had grown to $7.4 billion, and by 1880 it had climbed to $11.2 billion.

All of this growth and development offered seemingly endless opportunities to people living within the nation's borders. But these opportunities were starkly defined in racial terms. The notion of Manifest Destiny—that American expansion was inevitable because it was the will of God—had obvious racial implications. It indeed offered boundless possibility for those who laid claim to God's blessings, but it had dire consequences for those who stood in the way. Likewise, industrial and geographic expansion opened up new jobs and new acres to farm by the tens of thousands. But as this essay will argue, access to jobs and farms were by and large determined racially as well. Simply stated, those defined as white could opt for inclusion and participation in American society—and access to economic opportunities—while those defined as nonwhite by and large could not. This was, however, no simple binary of exclusion and inclusion. The reconstitution of the American population during these decades provoked a reassertion—and in many ways a complex reworking—of racial identity and racial hierarchy in the United States.

The Irish were the first white population in the United States to face significant challenges to their racial identity, and to their presence in the country in general. Irish immigrants began to arrive in the United States in the 1820s, and by 1840 they constituted nearly half of all immigrants entering the country. Over the next forty years, more than 2.5 million more Irish immigrated into the United States. So many of them settled in urban areas in the Northeast that immigrant historian Marcus Hansen referred to them as the "second colonization of New England." Though they arrived at an opportune moment in American economic history, they faced serious opposition to their presence in the United States. Not only their racial identity, but also the dire circumstances of their arrival and their Catholicism made them targets of people concerned about their potential impact on the country. These challenges, and their ability to overcome them, determined the extent of Irish access to American society.

Those who came in the 1840s left a country in dire straits. A blight struck potato crops, on which most Irish depended for survival, and between 1845 and 1849 the population of Ireland fell by more than a million. Many left the country, considering themselves involuntary exiles, and many more starved to death. But as Hasia Diner has argued, the famine did not so much create the enormous problems Ireland faced as exacerbate them. English colonialism had created the context for the deadly famine long before it struck, and the downward spiral in population continued well after the blight ended. From 1841 to 1891, Ireland lost almost 50 percent of its population. Marriage rates plummeted as economic conditions grew worse. Family ties nonetheless remained vital to many immigrants; one historian has argued that the Irish were the first to practice chain migration. As often as not, though, it was siblings who traveled together rather than husbands, wives, and children.

The Irish who made their way to the United States were predominantly impoverished and poorly educated, and thus often confined to manual labor. The Irish entered at the bottom of the social and economic scale and took jobs that few others would. Nonetheless, the labor that they provided was vital. Irish men began to arrive just as the United States turned seriously to developing its infrastructure. Irish labor helped build canals in the Northeast, the National Road, and eventually the transcontinental railroad. In general, they eschewed rural life, settling almost exclusively in urban areas. In many northeastern towns and cities, Irish men dominated day labor by the middle of the 1840s.

Unlike any other immigrant group, the majority of the Irish who came to the United States were women. They were not only forced from Ireland by conditions there, but also drawn to this country because of an economic niche open to them—domestic service. This job was always available to Irish immigrant women. By the 1850s they were 80 percent of the domestic servants in New York City. Even decades later their association with this work remained strong. Irish women moved fairly quickly into the textiles industry and into needlework as well. But as late as 1900 over 60 percent of all Irish-born women in the United States still worked as domestics.

Despite the hard labor that Irish immigrants provided, they were routinely maligned by native-born Americans and by those who had immigrated earlier. While there had been Catholics in the United States from its first days, the Irish Catholic population grew enormously in the mid-nineteenth century, reaching 2 million by 1842. This religious difference, and increasing Irish demands for the right to open their own schools, caused alarm among certain Americans. The Irish also gained a reputation for criminality, for pauperism, and for alcohol abuse that increased opposition to their presence.

Opposition to the Irish coalesced into a nativist movement as early as the 1830s. In 1837 New York City elected a nativist mayor and city council. Nativists, who drew on the secretive nature of their organization in calling themselves "Know-Nothings," gained power through the 1840s. Though broadly antiforeign, they focused the majority of their attention on the Irish. By the 1850s, nativists had formed the American Party, which for a time vied with the new Republican Party to replace the defunct Whigs. In 1856, the American Party scored its greatest successes. It elected 7 governors, 8 United States senators, and a staggering 104 members of the United States House of Representatives. Though the North, consumed by the issue of slavery, soon turned to the Republicans, nativist impulses—and racialized threats to Irish presence—still ran deep and strong in American society. In facing challenges to their racial identity as white, the Irish presented one of the most complex reworkings of racial identity and hierarchy in this era. Irish immigrants were often associated—and often associated themselves—with African Americans. Free blacks and Irish often lived

in the same neighborhoods and socialized together. They often competed for the same unskilled labor because these were the only jobs
open to either; Irish women vied with black women (and with the few
Chinese women in the West who had immigrated) for domestic service
jobs. Slave owners even occasionally hired Irish day laborers to perform
jobs deemed too dangerous for their slaves.

But historians of the construction of whiteness have recognized that
as challenged as certain white European immigrant groups might have
been, they nonetheless enjoyed access to rights that nonwhites did not.
Thomas Guglielmo's analysis of Italian immigrants applies equally to
Irish immigrants. He argues that the "whiteness" of these populations
was rarely called into serious question; rather the *quality* of their whiteness was. Thus, for example, unlike immigrants like the Chinese, who
were defined as nonwhite, the Irish could naturalize as citizens under the
1790 Naturalization Act, which allowed only whites this access. As
Matthew Jacobson has argued, they were "the first to immigrate in huge
numbers at once well within the literal language but well outside the
deliberate intent of the 'free white persons' clause of 1790." The act's
authors may not have intended to include them, but these immigrants
were included nonetheless.

Irish immigrants had other ways to separate themselves from their
nonwhite counterparts, and they used them to full advantage. Their
concentration in urban areas made them the target of scorn and even
violence. (The Irish notoriously established the first American "ghettoes," and anti-Catholic riots erupted in Philadelphia and in other cities
in the 1840s.) But it also eventually helped them, especially because
they arrived just at the outset of American urban development. This not
only helped them dominate construction and domestic service jobs in
their early years, it also made them critical components of the power
base the Democratic Party was trying to build in northeastern cities. As
David Roediger has argued, the Irish found in the Democratic Party not
only a route to political power, but also a way to assert their whiteness.
As the Democrats became outspokenly antiblack (and at times proslavery), Roediger asserts, in northeastern cities, "In areas with virtually no
black voters, the Democrats created a 'white vote.'" The Irish were also
able to use their ties to political party machines to move into municipal
jobs. Irish immigrants used their labor in other ways to gain access to
American society. Many Irish women working as domestics had long
thought of their jobs as inroads into the American middle class. If they

could not join the middle class through their labors, they could at least observe it firsthand. Many Irish men and women also became prominent members of the labor movement that was growing rapidly, if unevenly, in the United States between the 1830s and the 1870s. According to Hasia Diner, "Irish women provided much of the female trade union leadership in the last half of the nineteenth century." Irish men and women became instrumental members of many labor unions in these years, including the newly formed Knights of Labor. Their municipal jobs, their union membership, and the spiritual and institutional strength that the Catholic Church provided them elevated the status of the Irish in American society.

Many, though not all, also used their realization that, as Kerby Miller noted, blacks could be "despised with impunity" to their advantage. Irish attacks on blacks became so common in New York City that bricks were known as "Irish confetti." In 1863 tension in that city over the draft turned violent as many Irish, who saw the war as a battle over slavery, took their frustration at conscription out on the black residents. But if some Irish used attacks on blacks in an attempt to cement their relationship to American society, others used more noble means. General Thomas Meagher's Irish Brigade, for example, suffered losses of two-thirds of its men at Fredericksburg. All told, thousands of Irish Catholics fought for the Union during the Civil War.

Despite these numerous inroads into American society, the status of the Irish in the United States by 1877 in many ways remained insecure. Irish behavior during the 1863 draft riot had horrified many observers; some of them described the Irish, in terms usually reserved for Indian foes, as "savages," "savage mobs," and "demons." At the same time as the riots were taking place, the enigmatic Molly Maguires launched a series of mortal attacks against employers and other officials they deemed unjust in the anthracite region of Pennsylvania. As Kevin Kenny's work makes clear, the Molly Maguires were hardly representative of all Irish immigrants. He notes that ethnic identity is "historical, contingent and contested rather than essential [and] fixed," and many Irish immigrants worked arduously to counter the Molly Maguires' version of Irish ethnic identity. Kenny argued that "in the anthracite region at least, a specific Catholic definition of Irishness emerged victorious in the 1870s." It may have been victorious, but it was not the only one. In June 1877, ten Molly Maguires were hung in a single day, and once more, despite the enormous progress Irish immigrants had made, comparisons with "savage Indians" filled indignant editorials. The Irish by 1877 had taken full advantage of their whiteness; their status in the United States, however, was still being contested.

Germans were, with the Irish, the largest group of white ethnic immigrants to the United States in this period. Unlike the Irish, German immigrants were largely able to avoid vilification and faced far fewer impediments in their efforts to take advantage of American expansionism and industrialization. Highly skilled, well educated, predominantly Protestant, and largely rural (and thus more often able to avoid harmful attention), they were able to make the adjustment to life in the United States with little of the duress experienced by Irish immigrants, much less by those identified as nonwhite. Even the sizable German Jewish population (there were fifty thousand German Jews in New York City by 1860 and as many as ten thousand in smaller cities like Cincinnati in the same year) achieved considerable success in retail industries and in banking. It is little wonder that the metaphor of the United States as a "melting pot" was coined by German immigrant Christian Essellen in 1857, about fifty years before it gained currency in English.

Between 1840 and 1880, almost 3 million Germans arrived in this country; in these decades they were never less than one-fourth of incoming immigrants. Most historians agree that Germans came predominantly for economic reasons—not because of poverty or economic duress, but because changing economic conditions at home made the move across the ocean seem more advantageous. There were, however, some Germans who migrated for religious reasons. For example, some Lutherans made their way here because of the discrimination they faced in their homeland. Still others came for overtly political reasons, like the small but extremely vocal and articulate number of refugees from the failed revolution in 1848.

German immigrants stood out in this period as an unusually skilled and educated population. This was at least true of the men, who were quickly able to exploit their skills in the labor market. By 1850, for example, almost half of the German immigrants living in Chicago were employed as artisans or skilled workers; almost another 9 percent were small businessmen. German women by and large found work in the service sector, employed in jobs ranging from domestic servant to baker to hotelkeeper to nurse.

German immigrants also distinguished themselves from the Irish by settling predominantly away from northeastern urban areas. Taking full advantage of the United States' push west, and of the benefits it held out to white settlers, a considerable number of these migrants took up farming to earn their livelihood. They settled so broadly in rural areas away from the Atlantic coast that what came to be known as a "German Belt" stretched across eighteen states from the Northeast to the Midwest. As late as 1870, one in four German immigrants was still involved in agricultural pursuits.

Though German immigrants did not endure anything approaching the challenges the Irish faced, German presence in the United States did not go uncontested. Some of their social habits—their unwillingness to give up drinking on Sundays, and certain Germans' willingness to socialize with blacks—created consternation. Many working-class Germans engaged enthusiastically in union activity and in radical politics. They helped establish the Socialist Labor Party, the first socialist party in the United States, in 1877. By that time German anarchists were also organizing Lehr-und-Wehr-Vereins, "Instruction and Protection Societies," which focused on education and military training. The first one, founded in Chicago in 1875, was soon one of the largest workers' militias in the United States. These radical activities caused concern almost immediately. And while German Jews faced little overt discrimination in these decades, Carey McWilliams and John Higham have both argued that religiously and economically based anti-Semitism began to take hold in the United States by 1877.

German immigrants also faced occasional racial challenges. European racial theorist Joseph Arthur Comte de Gobineau, in his 1855 *The Inequality of Human Races*, a book widely read by American scholars, condemned not only Italians and Irish, but also Germans as "the human flotsam of all ages." Germans in the United States—and especially the Catholics among them—were included as well in the objections that nativists raised about immigration.

But these challenges did little to damage Germans' sense of security in their adopted home. They were able to point to a number of lofty cultural achievements and to draw on an organizational life that one historian has described as unrivaled by other immigrant groups. The German press in the United States dated back to the colonial era; German theater productions and music recitals appeared regularly in midwestern and northeastern cities. German immigrants established fraternal organizations, mutual aid societies, and labor associations on neighborhood, urban, and regional levels.

They were able to make inroads into American society in other ways as well. Like Irish women, German women who worked as domestics could use their proximity to American middle-class women as models for their own patterns of behavior and consumption. Unlike the Irish, whose enthusiasm for the Union during the Civil War was hardly unanimous, Germans established a solid reputation for supporting the Union. German Free-Soilers and members of the German immigrant community in Chicago, for example, were staunch opponents of slavery by the outbreak of the war. During the war, ten German immigrant regiments were raised in New York City alone.

These immigrants withstood challenges to their presence in the United States because of their remarkable level of cultural and racial confidence. Applying many of the same racial theories used to malign other immigrants and races, they were able to argue the equality—at the very least—of Anglo-Saxons and Teutons. During the Mexican American war, when the notion of Manifest Destiny was evoked to justify the conquest of supposedly "inferior" races, one German immigrant was able to assert, "We too, even though we are not Anglo-Saxons, believe in 'manifest destiny' and—we add for the benefit of the nativists—'manifest destiny' also believes in us." In a nation in the process of reformulating its notions of racial hierarchy, German immigrants boldly placed themselves at the top of that hierarchy.

Nevertheless, German immigrants would remain a challenged population in the United States. Their involvement in radical politics and unionizing would make them targets of a Red Scare in 1886. Their insistence on language maintenance—through building their own schools or pushing their local schools to teach German—would make them a highly visible target again in 1917. But before 1877 most problems they faced were internal to their community. There were so many divisions—geographic, religious, and ideological—that historian Kathleen Conzen has questioned whether German immigrants could even be called an ethnic group. Nonetheless, the skills and levels of education many Germans brought with them, their organizational prowess, and especially the confidence that their standing as "superior" whites gave them placed them in a position unrivaled by other immigrant groups in this or any era.

Chinese immigrants did not arrive in nearly the same numbers as German or Irish immigrants, but their concentration on the west coast—itself a product of and a spur to American expansionism and industrialization—and their identity as nonwhites meant that their presence in the United States would be both significant and severely embattled. The first Chinese began to arrive soon after gold was discovered in California in 1848; 325 Chinese were among the first fortune seekers. By 1852, Chinese immigrants numbered more than twenty thousand, most of them still in California. In ensuing decades the Chinese immigrant population continued to climb; the census showed sixty-three thousand Chinese in the United States in 1870, and more than 105,000 in 1880. Almost all of these immigrants were men; for reasons often rooted in cultural traditions, women tended not to travel abroad. They were also discouraged from immigrating by the 1875 Page Law, which in practice treated all Chinese women as potential prostitutes. As late as 1880, Chinese men in the United States still outnumbered women by more than twenty to one. They were drawn not only by the allure of potential riches, but because of the enormous turmoil in China. The first Opium War, fought between the English and the Chinese beginning in 1839, created great unrest and despair in China. Western intervention in the country and internal tensions produced a series of revolts. The Taiping Rebellion, for example, begun in 1850 by a man who claimed he was Jesus' younger brother, would claim 10 million lives across south and central China.

The work that the Chinese did, and the ways in which their work experiences and opportunities evolved, were inseparable from their reception in the United States. For a time they were well received; the Governor of California in 1852 referred to them as "one of the most worthy classes of our newly adopted citizens." In these early years, two-thirds of the Chinese immigrants worked in the gold mines, most of them panning for gold in small placer claims. By 1870 only about one in four were still mining, by then often as company employees, and spread across six states. Two things had happened that caused the numbers of Chinese immigrant miners to drop. First, the most easily accessible gold had been found; companies with capital to purchase extractive equipment now dominated the mines. But even before this development, white miners had pushed the California state legislature to remove the Chinese from the mines. The 1852 Foreign Miners tax targeted Chinese miners because they were ineligible for citizenship, requiring them to pay $3 a month until the law was overturned in 1870. In 1859, the state legislature passed another law expressly "to protect

Free White Labor against competition with Chinese Coolie Labor, and to Discourage the Immigration of the Chinese into the State of California." The law, which misidentified Chinese immigrants as coolies, imposed an additional monthly tax on them (with few exceptions) simply for living in the state.

Chinese immigrants soon found another source of employment helping to build the transcontinental railroad. Once again, racial identity was the definitive issue. The Central Pacific Railroad hired one hundred Chinese workers in 1865, and white workers quickly insisted that they be fired. Leland Stanford, the head of the railroad, weary of labor troubles with white workers, made the decision to hire Chinese workers exclusively for the remainder of the project. By 1869, when the railroad was completed, twelve thousand Chinese were working for the railroad—90 percent of its workforce. They were hired not only to send a warning to unruly white workers, but also because their employers regarded them as an easily exploitable workforce. During the infamous winter of 1866, railroad officials forced their Chinese employees to work despite sixty-foot snowdrifts. They worked in tunnels dug through the snow. A number of Chinese workers were buried when the tunnels gave way; some were not found until the spring thaw. When they struck the next summer, to protest their abusive treatment and the fact that they were paid far less than white workers, their employees cut off their food and starved them into submission.

After the railroad work was completed, Chinese immigrants went in two different directions for employment. Many turned to agriculture, finding jobs as farm laborers throughout California. By the end of the 1870s, they constituted most of the farm labor in four California counties and nearly half of the farm labor force in two others. Many more Chinese moved into urban areas, especially San Francisco. At first they were able to find employment in a variety of burgeoning enterprises— forming almost half of the work force in boot and shoe manufacture, woolen goods, cigars, and sewing. Before long, however, protests from whites drove them almost entirely into self-employment. By the 1860s and 1870s, Chinese restaurants and especially Chinese laundries were ubiquitous. Although self-employment offered certain benefits, external forces confined the Chinese to these economic niches. Their dominance of the laundry business, for example, was entirely a product of immigration. There was no tradition of male launderers in China; laundering was simply one of the only occupations open to them.

Chinese immigrants had faced enormous resistance, and even violence, in California from the first. In 1849, just after they arrived, sixty
Chinese miners were chased off their jobs by angry white miners. As
Sucheng Chan points out, in 1862 the California State legislature
received a list of eighty-eight Chinese miners who had been killed by
whites—including eleven killed by collectors of the Foreign Miners tax.
Job competition was particularly fierce in San Francisco; by one estimate, in 1870 there were two white workers and one Chinese worker for
every job in the city. Especially after the economic depression of 1873
began, anticoolie club members attacked Chinese in the streets, and
several were suspected of starting suspicious fires at factories that still
hired Chinese workers. In 1877, the local press reported the establishment of the Order of Caucasians, which dedicated itself to driving the
Chinese out of the city entirely.

Chinese immigrants sustained themselves in the face of this opposition through a rich organizational life. They quickly formed *huiguan*,
associations of immigrants from the same districts in China, which provided mutual aid and an arena for socializing. By 1862 the leaders of six
large *huiguan* in California organized the Chinese Six Companies,
which fought effectively for Chinese immigrants' rights in the United
States. Chinese immigrants often formed rotating credit associations,
which enabled each member in turn to use the collective resources of
the group to found a business or embark on some other economic enter-
prise. Less wealthy immigrants were often drawn to Tongs, secret
societies with revolutionary roots in China, which functioned as "alternative, antiestablishment" institutions in the new land.

But this organizational life, and the contributions that their labor
wrought in agriculture, mining, and railroad construction, were not
enough to prevent attacks against the Chinese. Even those who recognized the rich and complex history of China dismissed these immigrants
as the product of a decaying culture. Opposition to the Chinese had
always been strong in California, among both political and working-
class leaders. When they were drawn to other regions of the country as
prods to uncooperative workers, concern about Chinese immigrants
became national.

The first national legislation barring the entry of the Chinese targeted women. The proportion of women among Chinese immigrants
had remained very small, and a substantial number of them—as many as
60 percent by 1870—worked as prostitutes. The Page Law, passed in

1875, ostensibly banned Chinese prostitutes from entering the country. But the examinations into their personal lives that Chinese women faced as potential immigrants discouraged most of them from even trying to enter the United States.

By 1877, the Chinese were about to become the first national population to be excluded from entering the United States. This exclusion was rooted solely in their racial identity. President Rutherford B. Hayes asserted that the Chinese "invasion" was "pernicious and should be discouraged." Putting Chinese immigration in the context of "our experience in dealing with the weaker races—the Negroes and the Indians," he argued, "I would consider with favor any suitable means to discourage the Chinese from coming to our shores." The effort to end Chinese immigration almost entirely would succeed a few short years later.

They had made substantial contributions to the American, and especially the Californian, economy, but they found little opportunity to make inroads in this country. Even the 1870 Civil Rights Act, which provided certain protections for Chinese immigrants, gave little solace. Senator Charles Sumner's amendment to strike the word "white" from congressional acts related to naturalization met with widespread opposition. One senator protested, "Mongolians will never lose their identity as a peculiar and separate people." In the ensuing years of the nineteenth century, Chinese immigrants in the United States would become an increasingly secluded—and exoticized—population.

Mexicans—although they are now so commonly associated with immigration, especially by its critics—were not immigrants in this era. They lived on land that became part of the United States through expansionism—through colonial conquest and usurpation justified on racial grounds. Some of the first incursions into Mexican territory came in Texas. Initially invited to settle, Anglos continued to move into the province after the Mexican government banned their migration. A revolt against the Mexican government at first involved both Anglo immigrants and Tejanos (Texas-born Mexicans), some of whose families had lived in Texas for generations. But as Arnoldo de Leon has argued, Texans never experienced enormous hardship under the Mexican government, which was thousands of miles away and wracked by internal dissension. The rebellion quickly became, in the words of historian Reginald Horsman, "a racial clash, not simply a revolt against an unjust government or tyranny."

Relations between Tejanos and Anglos in Texas after the revolt set the tone for the Mexican American War, and for Anglo-Mexican relations after the war. A "peace structure" devised between Anglo immigrants and the Tejano ranch-owning elite, especially in predominantly Mexican areas of south Texas, prevailed for a short time. According to David Montejano, ambitious Anglo men married into Tejano families, often in these early years adopting aspects of Mexican cultural identity as their own. But competition over resources doomed the peace structure. Juan Seguin, a Captain in the Texas army, had fought against Mexico at San Jacinto and would have been at the Alamo, as thirteen Tejanos were, had he not been sent out for reinforcements. In 1840 he was elected mayor of San Antonio. But Sequin's valiant defense of Tejanos against abuses by land-hungry Anglos spelled his ruin. In 1842, he was forced to flee to Mexico, the country against which he had just fought, to protect himself and his family. At least two hundred Tejano families left San Antonio for similar reasons.

The Mexican American War, the United States' first foreign war, was again waged as an explicitly racial conflict. Popular travel journals written by Americans like Richard Henry Dana created lasting stereotypes of sexually accessible Mexican women and slothful, inept Mexican men. Mexicans in general were derided as bestial; one Tennessee soldier described them as "more degraded than the African race among us." Certain Americans compared them unfavorably to Indian populations and predicted that the Mexican "race" would soon become "extinct." Americans fighting against the Mexicans dehumanized them, and acts of brutality against Mexican soldiers and citizens were widespread. In Monterey, for example, Texas Rangers made a sport of shooting Mexicans off rooftops.

The racial ideology that underscored the war did more than justify repeated acts of cruelty. It was at the heart of Americans' sense of self-definition. "Manifest Destiny" was part of a broader assertion of racial superiority by Anglo-Saxons—who, for the first time in this country, defined themselves as a distinct racial group—and of other white ethnics who sought in its guise an explicit acceptance of their ownership of American identity. In this sense, it is not surprising that the phrase was coined by Irish immigrant John O'Sullivan. Those seeking acceptance into American society defined themselves in contrast to those outside its boundaries. For the latter, any manner of treatment was justified. As Horsman described it, "In effect, by mid-century, America's racial theorists were explaining the enslavement of blacks, the disappearance of Indians, and the defeat of Mexicans in a manner that reflected no discredit on the people of the United States."

Once the United States won the war, the 1848 Treaty of Guadalupe Hidalgo brought not only California and much of what is now the American Southwest, but also thousands of Mexicans into the country— by treaty, and as a "defeated race." Nonetheless, Mexicans entered the political framework of this country in the legal sense in complex and not altogether unfavorable ways. On paper, the treaty promised rights that seemed surprising, given the ways that Mexicans had been positioned racially during the war. Described in disparaging terms as a mixed-race population, they were nonetheless granted citizenship rights in the treaty—rights to this point granted to people entering American civic society only if they were white. Acting on these rights, however, and especially on the right to vote, would prove difficult and often impossible.

Moreover, the treaty did little to protect Mexican claims to land ownership. The United States Senate struck a clause from the treaty that would have guaranteed protection of Mexicans' rights to their lands. This had profound implications for the class system that had characterized the preconquest northern Mexican provinces. Tejano and Californio elites had controlled huge tracts of land in Texas and in California. Californios had relied on Indian peonage, establishing a seigneurial system to sustain the comfortable existence that Anglo travelers like Dana (whose uncle had married into a Californio family) had held in such contempt. Tejano ranchers had established a similarly paternalistic attitude toward the mestizo and Indian *peones* under them. Tied only marginally into the market economy, especially compared to more commercially minded Anglos, they were land rich and cash poor. Over several decades after the war, most of these rancheros lost their lands through a variety of means. Land claims were difficult and very expensive to establish in American courts, especially without treaty protection. Taxation under the new government forced many rancheros to sell off more and more of their land. Outright theft by unscrupulous Anglos was common.

Less wealthy Mexicans were often deprived of the means to provide for their livelihood. They were also frequent victims of violence. One particularly ironic example was the fate of the Californios who attempted to join the gold rush in California just months after the war. They were obligated, along with Chinese immigrants, to pay the Foreign Miners Tax—in a land in which many of their families had lived for generations. Along with the Chinese, they were also routinely assaulted, and sometimes killed, by Anglo miners who identified them as nonwhite competitors. The combination of the tax and the assaults drove them from the mines. The first Mexican woman known to have been lynched in the United States, a prostitute named Juanita, also met her fate in California in 1851.

Mexicans, in the decades after the war, resisted Anglo incursions and theft, at times informally, at times in more organized fashions. Historian Deena Gonzalez has analyzed how Mexican women in the territory of New Mexico defiantly maintained their cultural practice of unfettered public behavior and their work habits. They also strived through the courts to maintain property and inheritance rights they had enjoyed before the war. Other forms of protest were more violent. In 1859, for example, Juan Cortina, the son of a wealthy Tejano rancher, killed a Brownsville, Texas, sheriff he saw beating one of his father's employees. That incident sparked the "Cortina War." Cortina, who had initially fled, returned to Brownsville with sixty men, freed every Mexican prisoner he found, and executed four Anglos who had killed Mexicans and gone unpunished. Texas Rangers, unable to find him or his followers, retaliated against Mexicans throughout the region. Cortina's brand of informal justice, which some historians have labeled "social banditry," was reproduced throughout the 1860s and 1870s. Mexicans in the 1870s who removed cattle from Anglo ranches, for example, did not consider themselves thieves—they called it reclaiming "Nana's cattle." Anglo ranchers and especially Texas Rangers, whose enmity for Mexicans had only increased after the war, in turn considered killing Mexicans like "killing an enemy in the independence war."

Battles between Mexicans and Anglos continued throughout these years. Mexicans in Texas continued to incur the wrath of ranch owner Richard King, whose ambition at one point had been to own the entire territory between the Nueces and the Rio Grande once disputed by Mexico and the United States. King routinely drew on the Texas Rangers, known by some as the "King Ranch Rangers," to go after Mexican "cattle rustlers." By the end of 1877, battles between them had left more than a dozen Anglos and more than one hundred Mexicans dead. That same year, Anglo officials in El Paso attempted to assume control of salt beds west of the city that had traditionally been used communally by Mexican residents. Judge Charles Howard tried to claim the beds for commercial purposes. When he killed Luis Cardis, who led

Mexican opposition to the move, the "El Paso Salt War" began. Angry Mexican residents of El Paso killed Howard and two other Anglos, and defeated a troop of Texas Rangers before being quelled.

By the end of this period Mexicans in the United States were in many ways a subject population. Many Tejano and Californio rancheros had lost their holdings or were in dire financial straits, or both. The process of the proletarianization of this population—its reduction largely to manual, unskilled labor—was well under way. Even vaqueros, Mexican cowboys who had had such enormous pride in their skills and who had taught many incoming Anglos, now had difficulty finding suitable work. The racial hierarchy under which Mexicans lived was clearest on the King Ranch—Mexicans worked as ranch hands, overseen by Anglos, many of whom were former Texas Rangers. Before long, as Arnoldo de Leon has pointed out, Jim Crow signs in south Texas would read "for Mexicans" instead of "for Negroes."

The transition that African Americans made in this era was easily one of the most dramatic. They began the era as an enslaved population (only a fraction of the antebellum population was free). In 1860, the slave population in the South had reached an estimated 4 million. Slave labor sustained all major southern crop production—rice, sugar, tobacco, and especially cotton. Though perhaps in less immediately obvious ways than the other populations discussed in this essay, African Americans too were profoundly affected by the major developments occurring in American society. Expansionism and industrialization in the North and West combined to put the North and South on a collision course that led to civil war. By the end of this era African Americans had been freed, though with the end of Reconstruction the racial challenges they faced remained daunting at best.

The nature of slave labor varied enormously according to where slaves worked. Enslaved African Americans worked not only on various crops throughout the South, but also in both urban and rural settings, on small farms and enormous plantations, in masters' houses and in surrounding fields. Under slavery, everyone worked—men, women, and, as soon as they were able, children. Field hands labored from sunrise to sunset, and even longer during harvest time. House slaves performed a wide range of tasks, including cooking, cleaning, serving as butlers and valets, and providing care for young children. This work was often less physically taxing than field work, and provided access to more and better food. Work in the proximity of whites meant access to valuable information—especially as the war approached. But house servants also were expected to be on twenty-four-hour call, and compelled to live away from family and friends, and from the sustenance of slave culture. The small number of slaves who worked as artisans, or who lived in urban areas, often had increased opportunities. Masters who "hired out" their slaves sometimes let them keep some of their wages. There were even instances in which masters let them buy their freedom. Urban areas and work with free men and women also provided tremendous access to information—and even chances to escape.

But despite these slim windows of opportunity, slavery as a system was based on coercion and cruelty. Slave owners relied on violence, or the threat of it, to maintain control over the human beings they owned. Whippings were commonplace, and dismemberment of particularly recalcitrant slaves was not unheard of. Enslaved women could face not only these punishments but routine sexual abuse as well. Escaped slave Harriet Jacobs wrote of the horror of having lost her virginity when she was raped by the man who owned her. Rebellious slaves could also be punished through sale away from their loved ones, or by having their spouses or children sold. An estimated one in five slave marriages were broken up by sale; one in three children were sold away from their families.

Nor was sale or forced migration necessarily administered as punishment—it was often a product of American expansionism. Crop production, especially in cotton, shifted westward in the decades before the Civil War. Whereas in 1810, 80 percent of slaves had lived in Virginia, Maryland, and the Carolinas, by 1860 one in three slaves lived in the fabled "black belt" spanning Georgia, Alabama, Mississippi, Louisiana, and further west. An estimated 1.5 million slaves had been forced to migrate west during that half century.

In the face of unrelenting hardship, enslaved African Americans strived to establish space for their own humanity. They relied first and foremost on their families. Slave men and women routinely fought for control over their choices of marriage partner and over the process of childbirth—midwives were valued members of their communities. Slave women formed informal networks—quilting and sewing circles, systems of shared labor away from the fields—that sustained them socially and spiritually. Slave culture was also organized centrally around the church and religious ritual. By 1860, most enslaved African Americans professed some sort of Christianity.

Their relationship to Christianity, however, was a complex one. As scholar Sterling Stuckey has argued, under slavery they created a synthetic religious faith that merged African burial ceremonies, circle rituals, and ring shouts with Christian practices. In Stuckey's words, "Christianity provided a protective exterior beneath which more complex, less familiar [to outsiders] religious principles and practices were operative." These aspects of African religions facilitated the synthesis of diverse African ethnicities into a singular culture—circle rituals, for example, were central to a number of African populations in one form or another. They also enabled people to retain ties to their homeland or, eventually, to the homes of their ancestors, up to and beyond the last days of slavery. When Frederick Law Olmstead traveled through the South in the 1850s, for example, he declared that three-fourths of the slaves on Louisiana and Mississippi plantations were profoundly influenced by African survivals.

The establishment of an African American culture, and the insistence on preserving aspects of African culture, were both survival strategies and implicit forms of resistance. They were by no means the only ones. Although there were few slave rebellions after Nat Turner's 1831 revolt, one important exception was the Seminole Wars in Florida. The Seminole Indian community had been a haven for runaway slaves since the colonial era, and by the 1830s it was in open resistance to the American government. Most resistance occurred on a much more personal level. Occasionally slaves violently attacked their masters, but retribution for these acts was so fierce that resistance was usually much more subtle. Feigning illness, breaking tools, mistreating livestock, destroying crops—all of these were acts of resistance that occurred daily during slavery.

There were also 225,000 free blacks in the North on the eve of the Civil War, and a smaller and shrinking number in the South, whose very existence was an indictment of the implicit assumption that African Americans could not survive, much less prosper, outside of slavery. But they lived very difficult lives, enduring increasing discrimination and segregation in the North, and ever more urgent efforts to expel them or return them to slavery in the South. They had few employment options available to them, and even these began to disappear when European, and especially Irish, immigrants entered the country. As Frederick Douglass noted, "Every hour sees us elbowed out of some employment to make room perhaps for some newly arrived immigrants, whose hunger and color are thought to give them a title to special favor." There were nonetheless instances of resistance to their conditions, and to the conditions endured by African American slaves. Martin Delany, who was able to trace his family roots back to African royalty, called for an early version of African nationalism, and even briefly attempted to organize a collective return to Africa. Free blacks in the North, moreover, were among the first and most enthusiastic participants in the abolitionist movement.

They contributed enormously to growing tensions between anti- and proslavery forces in the decades leading up to the Civil War. In the 1830s and 1840s, the abolitionist movement both grew and diversified, as more and more whites and blacks organized to voice their opposition to slavery. By 1840, political, religious, and radical factions had emerged as abolitionists split over the means to attack slavery. These abolitionist forces were countered by increasingly vehement defenses of slavery emerging out of the South. In the decades immediately following the Revolutionary war, many southern slave owners had rationalized slavery as a "necessary evil"—difficult to justify, but absolutely essential to the southern, and the American, economy. By the 1830s, in the face of slave rebellions, economic downturns, and especially the flood of abolitionist literature making its way into the South, southern slave owners began to argue that slavery was, in the words of John Calhoun, a "positive good." Southern politicians and academicians worked in the ensuing decades to defend slavery and to compare it favorably to capitalist labor relations in the North. They viewed the emergence of the Republican Party in the 1850s with considerable alarm. The new party was staunchly antislavery, though its members were hardly of one mind on racial equality. Some Republicans were abolitionists and upholders of the principle of racial equality. But even more were former Free-Soilers, many of whom wanted neither slavery nor blacks moving into new territories in the West. Disagreement over slavery finally erupted into war in 1861.

The ultimate act of African American rebellion against slavery was their participation in the Civil War. Free blacks from the North and South threw themselves into the war effort. Slaves ran away by the tens of thousands, attaching themselves to Union armies, enduring dismal conditions in "contraband" camps, and offering their services in whatever way possible. Although their assistance was refused early in the war, and they were often relegated to menial labor behind the scenes, blacks organized their first regiment in 1862; the following year, they were fighting on the front lines. By 1865, 186,000 blacks had participated in the war effort.

Postwar Reconstruction represented a seemingly extraordinary opportunity for blacks. Eric Foner described the period as "a massive experiment
in interracial democracy." The era held out the promise—though in many
ways, only the promise—of freedom. Again in Foner's words, "'freedom'
itself became a terrain of conflict." Every aspect of freedom African
Americans sought—personal, institutional, political, and economic—was
contested by former slave owners and other southern whites.

Nonetheless, blacks after the war were able to act autonomously in
unprecedented ways. They reasserted the centrality of family life;
literally thousands left their homes in an effort to find spouses, children,
and other loved ones who had been sold away under slavery. They
reestablished gender roles within their families; the opportunity for
black women not to have to work in the fields was extremely important.
African Americans were now free to establish their own churches. By
1877, almost all southern blacks had left white-dominated churches
for autonomous institutions like the African Methodist Episcopal
Church. They sought not only education but the opportunity to educate
themselves; by 1869, black teachers outnumbered white ones in the
South. Blacks took advantage of the Fifteenth Amendment not just by
voting; they won office in the Reconstruction South in remarkable
numbers. All told, African Americans won six hundred legislative seats;
between 1868 and 1876, fourteen blacks served as U.S. congressional
representatives; two were elected as U.S. Senators; and six served as
lieutenant governors.

But the central issue in the minds of many newly freed American
citizens was economic. Many blacks fully anticipated that the federal
government would provide them the fabled "forty acres and a mule" in
return for generations of uncompensated labor. The hope was by no
means unfounded. In January 1865, Union General William T.
Sherman set aside lands to be distributed to blacks in allotments of forty
acres; he later added a proviso enabling the army to loan mules to blacks
on these lands. Congress took up a broader land distribution program
after the war. But no such program was ever instituted; in fact, lands that
had been awarded to blacks to farm and improve were in many instances
confiscated. Freed blacks soon found themselves under enormous pressure—often from the Freedman's Bureau, which had been established to
oversee their transition to freedom—to sign labor contracts. Their work
producing cotton and other crops vital to the southern economy, in
some cases on the same plantations they had worked as slaves, soon

devolved into a binding system of sharecropping. Working "on shares" offered blacks some semblance of autonomy. But in the cash-poor South, sharecroppers quickly became indebted to exploitive credit merchants. Most ended up in a form of debt peonage, in which the produce women grew became absolutely essential to survival, and from which the only escape was death.

Just as the prospect of economic freedom seemed increasingly remote by the end of Reconstruction, so too did many other freedoms. Most states and localities had passed Black Codes right after the war— oppressive laws that punished blacks severely for a wide range of offenses. After these laws were overturned, whites still sought to control and intimidate blacks at every turn. Even under Reconstruction governments, even having organized themselves into Union League militias, blacks could never be sure of their personal safety. They were killed for petty offenses—for refusal to work, for "insolence," even for being seen as too ambitious. One estimate was that more than two thousand blacks were killed in 1865 alone around Shreveport, Louisiana; another one thousand were reported murdered in Texas between 1865 and 1868. The atmosphere of terror that many southern whites sought to create among newly freed blacks had sexual overtones as well. During Reconstruction, many white southerners still considered black women to be sexually accessible. They acted without fear of punishment. As Deborah Gray White points out, from the end of the Civil War through two-thirds of the twentieth century, no southern white man was convicted of raping a black woman.

Blacks who sought to buy their own land, or who ran for office, became targets of the Ku Klux Klan. Formed in 1869, the KKK served as the armed militia of the Democratic Party in the South, attacking white—but especially black—members of the Republican Party and the Union Leagues. By the time the Ku Klux Klan Acts of 1870 and 1871 were passed, giving the federal government sweeping powers to combat the Klan, it had driven blacks and sympathetic whites from politics in the South.

The Republicans did make one last attempt to assist the efforts of blacks to combat discrimination in the South. The Civil Rights Act of 1875 outlawed discrimination against blacks in public places. But the law ultimately accomplished little in the eight years before the Supreme Court declared it unconstitutional. A critical clause mandating integrated schools in the South did not pass. The enforcement procedure, moreover, compelled blacks to take their cases to federal court, which was a preventively expensive and cumbersome process. The following year, the Republicans' secretive bargain with the Democrats to resolve disagreement over the election of 1876 signaled the end of the era.

The removal of federal troops in 1877, not from the South entirely, as legend has it, but from the statehouses they had been defending in Louisiana and South Carolina, did not mark the abrupt end of Reconstruction. But it spelled its inevitable demise. The era of promise for blacks ended slowly and unevenly; the South did not begin to pass formal segregation legislation until the early 1880s. But the implications were already clear. Blacks were, in Foner's words, "enmeshed in a seamless web of oppression, whose interwoven economic, political, and social strands all reinforced one another."

American expansionism had dramatic effects on every person living in the United States. But its most profound, and devastating, effect was on American Indians, people who in these years were defined as outside the boundaries of American society. European colonizers, then land-hungry Americans, had been moving into Indian territory and pushing Indians off their lands, either by force or through negotiations, from the first days of contact. Between 1837 and 1877 this process continued with a vengeance, until the fates of Indian populations were all but sealed.

As the era began, one of the most important moments in the history of Indian displacement was just being concluded. In 1837, Cherokees were on the "Trail of Tears," their forced march during which thousands died en route to a newly constructed Indian territory in what became Oklahoma. They had made concerted efforts to assimilate themselves into American society. By the time of the coerced removal they had their own newspaper and a constitution modeled on the American document; some Cherokees even owned African American slaves. But the federal government and anxious American farmers and settlers made it clear that Indians, that "ill-fated race" in the words of Andrew Jackson, had no place in American society. This was the deeper meaning of this removal. As Richard White put it, "Removal made it clear that there was no room for a common world that included independent Indians living with whites." The Jeffersonian notion that assimilated Indians could live among Americans was no longer deemed a possibility.

Their removal was a harbinger of things to come for American Indians. Indian communities already in the Southwest and West faced increasing encroachment on their land, both from other Indians forced into their territories and from Americans seeking land and wealth. Through the middle of the 1840s, federal officials were nonetheless still able to make promises to Indian populations like the Cherokees that they would be undisturbed in their new homes. They constructed an Indian territory on the assumption that American movement west would not prohibit the possibility of a "permanent Indian frontier." This frontier would define the outer boundary of the United States, beyond which Indians could live freely. If the possibility of inclusion of Indian populations within the country no longer existed, at least they could live in relative safety on their own. This possibility too disappeared after the Mexican American War. American victory in the war, and the prospect of settlement on the vast territory it brought into the United States, meant there would be no safe haven for Indian populations between the Atlantic and Pacific Oceans.

The threat to Indian ways of life as Americans engulfed them was already evident in the fates of those who had resisted Jackson's policy of removal. The Choctaw, who had managed to remain in the Southeast rather than moving to the Indian territory that became Oklahoma, fought to keep their cultural traditions alive. They held on to their language, unlike those who had made the move, and they had remained a matrilineal culture. But under increasing pressure from the United States government, their efforts to preserve their culture and traditions faltered. Men who married into the Choctaw community found it impossible to substantiate their wives' land claims in American courts. By the end of the 1850s, the matrilineality of the Choctaws in Mississippi was under serious challenge, and male descent lines were being privileged.

The effort to break down Indian cultural identity became systematic with the formal implementation of the reservation system. There had been reservations east of the Mississippi, but with the end of the prospect of the permanent Indian frontier, reservations became national policy. In theory, their purposes were clear-cut: to remove Indians from travel routes and from areas being settled by Euro-Americans and to attempt, in the words of one federal official, "the great work of regenerating the Indian race." Reservations were supposed to protect Indians by separating them from Euro-American settlers and to facilitate their assimilation—to detribalize and individualize them. In reality, the reservation system was put into place unevenly and even haphazardly. As Richard White has suggested, it "was an improvisation the way survivors of a shipwreck might fashion a raft from the debris of the sunken vessel." Any high-minded ideas about protecting Indians were quickly subsumed under the more pressing effort—in terms of the imperatives of American expansion—to enclose and imprison them. It was an effort that would be successful only after a series of fierce wars fought on the Plains and further west, and one that would leave most Indians either dead or bereft of the cultural and material resources to live their lives on their own terms.

There was only one area of Indian settlement that remained relatively peaceful in the two decades after the Mexican American War—Indian territory in present-day Oklahoma, where many Cherokees and others among the Five Civilized Tribes (the Choctaws, Chickasaws, Creeks, and Seminoles) had been forced to relocate. They spent much of the first decade simply trying to reestablish a sense of unity within the tribes themselves, who had been divided by bitter disagreements over the issue of removal. But within a very short time, they were able to recreate much of their society—still based significantly on the American model—in their new homes. As Robert Utley notes, by the 1850s their public school systems were better than those in Arkansas or Missouri.

But this peace did not prevail elsewhere. Despite the efforts of those like the Five Civilized Tribes who tried to adopt American ways, Indians continued to be seen as savages standing in the way of civilization. In fact, as scholars like Matthew Jacobson and David Roediger have argued in other contexts, the definition of Indians (and various other non-whites) as savages was an essential foundation of the definition of civilization itself. As Roediger pointed out, "'Civilization' continued to define itself as a negation of 'savagery'—indeed, to invent savagery in order to define itself."

During the 1850s and the 1860s, in every corner of the country west of the Mississippi, Indian populations resisted the reservation system, trying to maintain their autonomy and independence, and Americans sought to contain them through negotiation, betrayal, and, ultimately, violence. The United States' effort to turn reservations into national policy was rarely very successful. The reservation system was brutally implemented in Oregon and Washington. It failed terribly in Texas and in California, where Indians were murdered by the thousands by gold rushers. Navajo resistance in New Mexico led to another, if less famous, forced removal. In 1864 the Navajos endured a "Long Walk" to Bosque

Redondo, a reservation across the New Mexico territory from their established homeland. Conditions on the reservation were so severe that
General William Sherman compared it to Andersonville, the infamous
Confederate prisoner of war camp. They would not be permitted to return
to a reservation on a reduced section of their homeland until 1868.

Meanwhile, some of the fiercest Indian resistance occurred on the
Plains, especially after 1865, when the United States turned its attention from the Civil War back to the West. Warfare between American
forces and Plains Indians like the Cheyenne, the Arapahoes, the
Lakotas, the Comanches, and the Kiowas became incredibly brutal.
Despite the lines between civilization and savagery that they wished to
draw so neatly between themselves and Indian populations, white com-
batants and their supporters often behaved in utterly shocking ways. In
one attack on a group of Cheyenne encamped in Sand Creek, Colorado,
in 1864—there because their leader, Black Kettle, was attempting to
negotiate a peace settlement—Colorado soldiers killed two hundred
people, most of them women and children. They scalped and mutilated
their bodies and paraded their remains through the streets of Denver. At
a local theater, according to one historian, "Theater patrons applauded
a display of Cheyenne scalps, some of them of women's pubic hair,
strung across the stage at intermission." Though these soldiers were
forced out of the service, they remained heroes to many in Colorado.
Despite having legitimized any and all methods of warfare by thoroughly
dehumanizing their foes, American soldiers remained unable to secure
Indians on reservations through the 1860s.

There were brief moments when the American government
attempted to negotiate some sort of peace with resistant Indian populations. A Peace Commission was established after the Civil War, and
Ulysses Grant tried to implement a Peace Policy during the first term of
his Presidency. Certain Indian leaders were willing to negotiate—Black
Kettle had been attempting to do so in Colorado; Oglala Lakota leader
Red Cloud visited Washington, D.C., in 1870 on a similar mission. But
the end goal of the American government—settlement of all of the land
from ocean to ocean—and the perspective most Americans shared of
Indians—that they were a race of savages who could not exist within
the boundaries of American civilization—made the outcome of these
efforts predictable.

By 1877, Indian populations were almost completely enclosed on
reservations. Neither battle nor flight proved effective. In June 1876, a

collection of Indian tribes killed an overconfident General Custer and all of his men at the Little Bighorn in Montana. Despite the exhilaration the battle evoked, retribution against the victors was swift and fierce. A year later, Chief Joseph and what remained of the Nez Perce raced American troops to Canada. In October 1877 they were caught, just forty miles shy of the border. Sitting Bull and a few Sioux would not surrender until 1881; Geronimo and a handful of Apaches would hold out until 1886.

Most historians agree that Indians' ultimate confinement on reservations was not the result of a military defeat. In the words of historian Elliott West, they "were not muscled on to reservations because soldiers defeated and sometimes butchered them. They ended up there because they lost command of the resources they needed to live as they wished." What they fought, in other words, were battles not only over territory, but also over the right to maintain control over their identity and their culture. These are battles that in many ways continue to the present day.

This essay has argued the central importance of racial identity in determining the experience of the various racial and ethnic groups who, through various means, came to be included in—or excluded from—American society between 1837 and 1877. American expansionism and industrialization left no population within the United States untouched; distinct experiences of those developments, however, were defined by racial identity and by the racial hierarchy that was reformulated in this era.

It has also sought to provide an overview of Irish, German, Chinese, Mexican, African American, and American Indian experiences in the United States between 1837 and 1877; this is a far more hazardous task than generating a framework within which to understand their particular relations to this country. Inevitably, in a brief summary of the historical experiences of any population, generalizations can hide as much as they reveal. In the hope of suggesting the underlying complexity of each population's history, this essay will sketch out one more issue before closing—how regional distinctions might complicate perceptions of each of these populations.

The experiences of each population varied widely, though to considerably differing degrees, across the regions of the United States. As Matthew Jacobson has argued, Irish immigrants' relationship to whiteness was not the same on the East Coast as it was in California. In New York, when these immigrants rioted against the draft in 1863, they were compared to savage Indians. In California, they merged with and often led other whites united to fight against labor competition from the Chinese. There are other possible complications as well. In Texas, several Anglo ranchers—including the King family, with its enormous holdings—were Irish immigrants or of Irish descent. They ruled over the Mexican population who worked under them with increasingly autocratic power. In New Mexico, on the other hand, many Irish men married Nuevomexicanas and adopted their culture as their own. In Texas and New Mexico, in other words, there were still other possible variations of Irish immigrants' relation to whiteness.

For German immigrants, regional variations were as compelling, if less racially charged. In urban areas in the Northeast and Midwest, the involvement in unions and the radical politics of certain German workers and intellectuals concerned wary Americans. Away from the cities, German immigrants could more easily look like defenders of the American heartland. In western Pennsylvania, for example, German immigrants were prominent on the juries that sat in judgment of the Molly Maguires.

For Chinese immigrants, increasingly maligned nationally as threats to the racial sanctity of the nation, regional variations mattered less but were nonetheless evident. In the late 1860s, after the transcontinental railroad was completed and when Chinese immigrants were increasingly confined to racial economic niches, they were still recruited by employers in the South and the Northeast. Their recruitment was cynical; they were used as strikebreakers in Massachusetts and as prods to ex-slaves in the South. But the fact remains that at this point, away from California, there were certain employers who remained willing to see Chinese immigrants as something other than a threat.

For Mexicans who became Mexican Americans after the war, regional differences reflected profound cultural differences. Californios, Tejanos, and Nuevomexicanos had much in common, but there were also significant differences in their cultural practices. In California, for example, a distinctive Californio culture had emerged by the time of the conquest, centered around ample leisure time and flamboyant ceremonies and celebrations. And although the wealthy among each population suffered the loss of land and prestige, there are historians who argue that Nuevomexicanos were able to hold on to more of their power and influence than the others. Not only was New Mexico less rich in resources and thus less attractive to incoming Anglos, but some wealthy Mexicans in New Mexico, though by no means all, claimed pure Spanish lineage—claimed, in other words, that they were white descendants of Europeans and had no Indian ancestors. Elite Tejanos and Californios made similar claims, and eventually they all found themselves surrounded by Anglos who rejected these assertions of racial purity. Nonetheless, many Nuevomexicanos continue to make these racial claims in the present day.

Likewise for American Indian populations, regional differences underscored significant cultural differences. Most Indian populations had certain things in common—subsistence economies, the worship of nature, and some sense of collective ownership of property. But Sioux living on the grassy plains, Pueblos living in the arid Southwest, and Yakima living on the plush West Coast, for example, constructed their lives, their cultures, and their traditions very differently. These differences were based on numerous factors, including what their natural environments did or did not provide, and the number, or lack, of foes or allies surrounding them. As with the Mexican population, the region in which various Indians lived also determined the nature of their interaction with Euro-Americans. Although few if any Indians avoided the onus of conquest, the severity of their experience varied considerably. In California, gold rushers engaged in a murderous campaign against the Indian population, whose numbers fell from 150,000 in 1845 to 35,000 in 1860. In the nearby southwest, by stark contrast, certain Indian populations were left relatively free to remain true to their culture and traditions. In the 1860s, for example, the United States government largely ignored Kiowa and Comanche raids against Anglos and Mexicans in Texas. As Utley describes it, the Indian raiders "had always regarded Texans, like Mexicans, as a people distinct from Americans— a view reinforced by the . . . Civil War."

For African Americans, the contrast between regions for much of this period could not have been more stark—the South meant slavery, and the North, freedom. Their hope that change of location—that regional variation—would bring better things remained strong in the face of the disappointments that came with the end of Reconstruction. In 1877, African American "exodusters" founded Nicodemus, Kansas, one of their first communities in the West, hopeful that they had left the angry white South and an increasingly cynical North behind.

ANNOTATED BIBLIOGRAPHY

Blassingame, John. *The Slave Community*. New York: Oxford University Press, 1972 [rev. 1979].
When first published in 1972, Blassingame's book was one of the first to examine slave culture and slave life systematically. He takes up issues of African heritage, culture and family, plantation life, resistance, and slave personality types.

Chan, Sucheng. *Asian Americans: An Interpretive History*. Boston: Twayne Publishers, 1991.
Chan provides a synthesis of Asian American history with an overt interpretive edge, focusing particularly on placing Asian Americans in a global perspective.

Chen, Jack. *The Chinese of America*. San Francisco: Harper and Row, 1980.
Chen's book is a thorough examination of Chinese American culture, from earliest arrivals through exclusion to the post–World War II era.

Conzen, Kathleen Neils. *Immigrant Milwaukee, 1836–1860: Accommodation and Community in a Frontier City*. Cambridge: Harvard University Press, 1976.
This community study traces the German American presence and involvement in Milwaukee from its earliest days, placing issues of the construction of ethnic identity and eventual accommodation in the context of other immigrant groups and the city's public culture.

De Leon, Arnoldo. *They Called Them Greasers: Anglo Attitudes Toward Mexicans in Texas, 1821–1900*. Austin: University of Texas Press, 1983.
This pointed analysis traces the emergence of Anglo Texans' anti-Mexican attitudes through the Texas revolt and the antebellum and postbellum eras.

Diner, Hasia. *Erin's Daughters in America: Irish Immigrant Women in the Nineteenth Century*. Baltimore: Johns Hopkins University Press, 1983.
Diner analyzes the culture of Irish immigrant women and their relations with American society and culture through their familial connections, work experiences, and associational life.

Foner, Eric. *Reconstruction: America's Unfinished Revolution, 1863–1877*. New York: Harper and Row, 1988.
This masterful book is now the standard work on Reconstruction. He draws together existing scholarship on the era and creates a new frame for this comprehensive study by emphasizing the experiences, actions, and goals of the newly freed African American population.

Genovese, Eugene. *Roll, Jordan, Roll: The World the Slaves Made*. New York: Pantheon, 1974.
Genovese's classic study examines slave culture in the context of slave-owner paternalism. He explores the possibilities of acquiescence and resistance to slavery, finding in the culture of enslaved African Americans a form of "protonationalism."

Gonzalez, Deena. *Refusing the Favor: The Spanish-Mexican Women of Santa Fe, 1820–1880*. New York: Oxford University Press, 1999.
Gonzalez's work makes effective use of archival sources like wills and trial transcripts to reveal how Spanish-Mexican women faced, and responded to, and resisted Anglo colonizing efforts in New Mexico.

Griswold del Castillo, Richard. *The Treaty of Guadalupe Hidalgo: A Legacy of Conflict*. Norman: University of Oklahoma Press, 1990.
Griswold del Castillo offers a detailed study of the treaty that ended the Mexican American war, focusing on its impact on the new Mexican American population.

Gutman, Herbert. *The Black Family in Slavery and Freedom, 1750–1925*. New York: Random House, 1977.
Gutman asserts the autonomy of the African American family both during and after slavery. He argues that slave families were constituted not only within, but despite slave owners' paternalism. He also counters arguments by sociologists Daniel Moynihan and Nathan Glazer, who argued the dysfunctionality of the African American family.

Horsman, Reginald. *Race and Manifest Destiny: The Origins of American Racial Anglo-Saxonism*. Cambridge: Harvard University Press, 1981.
Reginald Horsman links the development of American racial ideology, and particularly Anglo-Saxons' explicit identification as a distinctive racial group, to American expansionism in the 1840s and 1850s.

Jacobson, Matthew. *Whiteness of a Different Color: European Immigrants and the Alchemy of Race*. Cambridge: Harvard University Press, 1998.
Jacobson's complex and rich work explores a wide variety of historical documents and cultural products in analyzing the construction of whiteness—and the challenges many European immigrants faced in asserting their whiteness—throughout American history.

Johannsen, Robert W. *To the Halls of the Montezumas: The Mexican War in the American Imagination*. New York: Oxford University Press, 1985.
Johannsen argues that the United States' first foreign war produced both assertions of American identity and the demonization and degradation of Mexicans.

Kenny, Kevin. *Making Sense of the Molly Maguires*. New York: Oxford University Press, 1998.
Kenny uses impressive empirical evidence and postmodern methodologies to explore the enigmatic Molly Maguires, and to place them in the broader context of Irish ethnic identity formation.

Limerick, Patricia Nelson. *The Legacy of Conquest: The Unbroken Past of the American West*. New York: Norton, 1987.
One of the first synthetic works to substantially revise American Western history, Limerick's book presents the region in all of its racial complexity.

Miller, Kerby A. *Emigrants and Exiles: Ireland and the Irish Exodus to North America*. New York: Oxford University Press, 1985.
This standard work in Irish immigrant history focuses especially on the exile mentality of the Irish.

Montejano, David. *Anglos and Mexicans in the Making of Texas, 1836–1986*. Austin: University of Texas Press, 1987.
Montejano's work analyzes relations between Mexicans and Anglos from the Texas revolt to the very recent past, from the short-lived "peace structure" through land confiscation and anti-Mexican Jim Crow laws to a new period of relative inclusion and equality.

Pitt, Leonard. *The Decline of the Californios: A Social History of the Spanish-Speaking Californians, 1846–1890*. Berkeley: University of California Press, 1966. Pitt's path-breaking work analyzes the distinctive Californio culture and its demise at the hands of encroaching Anglo Americans.

Roediger, David. *The Wages of Whiteness*. New York: Verso Press, 1991. Roediger analyzes the implications of whiteness for the construction of working class identity in the decades before and just after the Civil War. He focuses centrally, especially in his last section, on the efforts of Irish immigrants to establish, and to benefit from, their identity as white.

Saxton, Alexander. *The Indispensable Enemy: Labor and the Anti-Chinese Movement in California*. Berkeley: University of California Press, 1971. Saxton explores the complex reasons for the emergence of anti-Chinese sentiment in California, especially among white workers. He argues that Chinese immigrants were "indispensable," not only for the inexpensive labor they provided but because their presence served to galvanize the white working class as few other issues did.

Stuckey, Sterling. *Slave Culture: Nationalist Theory and the Foundation of Black America*. New York: Oxford University Press, 1987. Stuckey offers a compelling argument for African survivals in African American slave culture and beyond. He reads emergent black nationalist and liberation thought into the 1940s through this Africanist lens.

Takaki, Ronald. *Strangers from a Different Shore: A History of Asian Americans*. New York: Penguin Books, 1989. Takaki offers a comprehensive synthetic examination of the history of Asians in the United States.

Trommler, Frank, and Joseph McVeigh, eds. *America and the Germans: An Assessment of a Three-Hundred-Year History*. Philadelphia: University of Pennsylvania Press, 1985. This collection provides a number of useful essays on German American immigration, ethnicity and politics, language, and literature.

Utley, Robert. *The Indian Frontier of the American West, 1846–1890*. Albuquerque: University of New Mexico Press, 1984. Utley explores the last fifty years of open conflict between Indian populations and the expansionist United States, from the 1840s through the "passing of the frontier" in 1890.

West, Elliott. *The Contested Plains: Indians, Goldseekers, and the Rush to Colorado*. Lawrence, Kansas: University of Kansas Press, 1998. In this provocative book, West argues that the battle between Indians and whites over the Great Plains, specifically Colorado, was a contest over resources that both, in their own ways, were ill-prepared to fight.

White, Deborah Gray. *Ar'n't I a Woman?: Female Slaves in the Plantation South*. New York: Norton, 1985. In this highly readable study, Deborah Gray White explores the distinctive world of the enslaved African American woman. She examines stereotypical images of women slaves, family and work life, women's networks under slavery, and the particular dangers that enslaved women faced. She closes with a chapter on African American women after slavery.

White, Richard. *"It's Your Misfortune and None of My Own": A History of the American West.* Norman: University of Oklahoma Press, 1991.
This broad revisionist survey of American Western history focuses centrally on the frequently combative and destructive interactions between racial groups in the region.

5

RACE, NATION, AND CITIZENSHIP IN LATE NINETEENTH-CENTURY AMERICA, 1878–1900

Mae M. Ngai

In the summer of 1893 the World's Columbian Exposition was held in Chicago, celebrating the four hundredth anniversary of Columbus's arrival in the New World. It was a huge exposition, with gleaming neoclassical buildings that housed triumphant displays of American science, industry, and commerce as well as exhibits from other nations of the world. More than 27.5 million Americans visited the fair. Dubbed the "White City," it was projected as a utopian dream that marked America's progress since 1492 and called the nation to its future.

Myriad symbols and practices of racial exclusion and hierarchy pervaded the ideas of nation and world embodied by the Columbian Exposition, themes that captured and unified the trends of race and nationalism in the late nineteenth century. The fair's governing boards excluded African Americans, prompting black leaders to protest and boycott the event. Of the few African American exhibits, the most popular was the living advertisement of Aunt Jemima, performed by a former slave, for the RT Davis Milling Company's pancake mix. The fair's Department of Anthropology displayed living American Indians from various reservations making and selling handicrafts. The popularity of that exhibit seemed to indicate white Americans' desire to situate Indians in the past as an exotic, backward race.

These representations of African Americans and American Indians underscored their exclusion from the mainstream of American society and from the fair's notions of national progress and achievement. Indeed, the dream of the White City could be understood only as it stood in relation to the exposition's other major feature, the Midway Plaisance, a mile-long row that combined honky-tonk entertainments with an encyclopedic exhibition of the world's races. Living "ethnological villages" set out a racial order from barbarism to civilization—starting at the far end with American Indians, Africans and Dahomeyans, the latter considered by white fair goers as the most savage and threatening, then proceeding to East Asia, West Asia, and the Islamic world (with exotic Orientalist themes) and then, finally, nearest to the gates of the White City, German and Irish villages, representing the Teutonic and Celtic races. Because China boycotted the exposition in protest of the Chinese exclusion laws, the presentation of Chinese civilization was reduced to a Midway display described by the *Chicago Tribune* as "Freaks of Chinese Fancy at the Fair."

The White City and the Midway were designed as an object lesson for the masses in the evolutionary path of humankind, which marked the racial identity and "place" of the world's peoples. The obsession with anthropology and ethnology at the Columbian Exposition reflected the emergence and influence of scientific racism in the last quarter of the nineteenth century. The "scientific" ordering of civilization according to race not only explained cultural difference and Anglo-Saxon superiority, it justified both the extreme economic exploitation and the second-class political status of peoples who had been marked as colored races. Racial segregation in the South, the conquest of American Indian and Mexican lands in the West, Chinese exclusion, and the colonial possession of Hawai'i, the Philippines, and Puerto Rico—these policies were integral to American national development during the last quarter of the nineteenth century. In many ways these policies may be understood as a continuation of old practices. The Old South, of course, haunted the new; and the conquest of the West and the acquisition of new colonies bore a family resemblance to European colonialism in the New World in the seventeenth and eighteenth centuries. But race and colonialism were not simply reproduced; they were constructed anew out of the demands of changing economic and political conditions, out of dynamic processes of national territorial consolidation, rapid industrial development and economic growth, and projections of United States power abroad.

The Columbian Exposition narrated those processes as an inevitable march of scientific and cultural progress, in which material abundance held the key to democracy. Indeed if the Civil War and the expansion of the railroads had established the national market, technological and business innovations in the decades following the war—electrical power, telegraph and telephone, hard steel, precision machine and tool making, and modern corporate management—propelled a vast expansion of the nation's productive capacity. By 1880 American manufacturing output exceeded that of Germany and France combined.

Yet while American economic growth was phenomenal, it was neither linear nor smooth. Between 1873 and 1896 nearly all industrial nations in the world, including the United States, experienced a prolonged economic depression plagued by chronic overproduction and falling prices. In the United States recurrent cycles of boom and bust characterized the economy; the rise to power of the great "robber baron" industrialists like Carnegie, Frick, and Rockefeller took place along with business failures, tightening credit, and the impoverishment of small farmers and workers. The tensions of industrial life were expressed most forcefully in the growing number of labor strikes, involving hundreds of thousands of workers in the peak years of 1877, 1886, and 1892–1893.

The expanding economy had a voracious appetite for labor, especially of the unskilled variety. Immigrants from capitalism's rural peripheries, from Southern and Eastern Europe, Asia, and Mexico, supplied the needed muscle and dramatically diversified the nation's population." Not every foreigner is a workingman," observed a Chicago clergyman in 1887, "but every workingman is a foreigner." The new immigrants confronted both the disdain of elite Anglo-Americans, who welcomed their brawn but questioned their racial fitness for citizenship, and native-born white workers, who often blamed immigrants and blacks for depressing wages or for strikebreaking. The great antimonopolist agrarian movement of the 1880s and 1890s, led by the People's Party (Populists) and militant labor organizations like the Knights of Labor, which fought for the eight-hour day, were inconsistent at multiracial solidarity. They sometimes organized blacks in segregated units and at worst practiced racial exclusion of nonwhites. Thus in this period of national consolidation, economic growth and class conflict, race and ethnicity complicated and cut across the meanings of citizenship and national identity. To understand the patterns of race and racism that emerged in the last quarter of the nineteenth century, we must first turn to the South.

JIM CROW AND THE NEW SOUTH

The Civil War and the passage of the Thirteenth, Fourteenth, and Fifteenth Amendments to the U.S. Constitution abolished slavery, established national citizenship, and extended the principle of democracy to all Americans. In the South, Reconstruction (1867–1877) brought about profound changes and hopes for African Americans. The former slaves established the autonomy of their personhood and of their families and built churches, schools, and other community institutions. They resisted working on the old plantations as waged gang labor, preferring the semiautonomous work of sharecropping and tenant farming. And with the vote, they won office—sixteen seats in Congress and more than six hundred in state legislatures.

Reconstruction was not, however, a period of steady advance, but rather one of constant and often bloody conflict. By 1876 most state governments in the South had been "redeemed" by white southern Democrats. Only four states—North Carolina, South Carolina, Louisiana, and Florida—remained under the control of Republicans. Just as important, by the mid-1870s, federal commitment to black equality had foundered. Northern opinion wearied of it, especially after the economic depression of 1873, and Republicans in Congress became increasingly divided over the efficacy of continued federal intervention in the South.

The elections of 1876 assured the reversal of Reconstruction and completed Redemption. As a black southerner sadly stated, "The whole South—every state in the South—had got into the hands of the very men that held us as slaves." Under "home rule," white supremacy retook the South. The Redeemers included both traditional planters and new commercial and industrial interests that championed a "New South." But while politically and socially diverse, Redeemers agreed on a new southern order of racial subordination based on fiscal retrenchment, labor control, and reduced black political power.

In the name of efficiency, Redeemers dismantled the Reconstruction state, slashing state budgets and property taxes. The Mississippi state budget was cut in half between 1875 and 1885. Across the South, public hospitals, asylums, and penitentiaries were closed. Texas imposed fees for schooling and Alabama abolished state-wide school taxes. The crippling of public education—for both black and poor white southerners—was perhaps the most enduring consequence of fiscal retrenchment. New laws asserted firmer control over black labor. Vagrancy and antienticement laws limited black people's mobility. Laws prohibiting the sale of unginned cotton and other farm products after dark cut directly into black farmers' ability to make a living. Most important were the crop lien laws, which, by giving the landowner first rights to the sharecropper's crop, shifted the entire burden of risk to the latter. Black farmers fell into permanent debt and impoverishment as sharecropping turned into debt peonage, which some called a new form of slavery.

Perhaps the cruelest form of coerced labor was convict leasing. During the 1880s southern prisons were filled with young black men, who were incarcerated as a result of new laws that punished blacks severely for crimes against white property. (On the other hand, states repealed Reconstruction laws that had been passed to restrict Klan violence.) Mississippi's notorious "pig law," for example, made theft of any farm animal or any other property valued at ten dollars or more a felony punishable by five years in jail. Convict laborers hired out to private contractors laid three thousand miles of new railroad track across the South; they worked on cotton plantations in Mississippi, on turpentine farms in Florida, and in iron foundries and coal mines in Alabama. Working in shackles and beneath the whip, in water and muck and under the blazing sun, convict laborers were sometimes literally worked to death. During the 1880s not a single leased convict in Mississippi lived long enough to serve out a sentence of ten years.

In Louisiana and South Carolina, where sugar and rice plantations employed waged workers, labor militancy continued from the Reconstruction period, in some areas into the late 1880s. The former slaves in the bayou parishes in Louisiana had a history of worker organization, strikes, and armed defense of the right to vote. In 1886 sugar workers in Terrebonne Parish joined the Knights of Labor, forming an integrated local. Their efforts suggest the possibilities that existed for cross-racial alliances. But a region-wide strike in 1887 was brutally crushed by the planters' use of mass evictions, armed force, and the mobilization of white racism.

Changes in social relations and politics were relatively slower than in the economic sphere. Segregation, which began almost immediately after the Civil War in public schools, proceeded unevenly throughout Reconstruction and into the 1880s and 1890s. During the 1880s blacks and whites increasingly withdrew from each other, but segregation was not absolute and southern race relations were still somewhat flexible. Black people still entered theaters, bars, and some hotels and could get equal seating on streetcars and railway cars.

The process of narrowing black political rights was also uneven and contested. During the 1880s Democratic state governments gerrymandered districts to dilute black voting strength and committed wholesale ballot fraud in counties with black majorities. Yet in other states, where whites had large majorities, such as Arkansas and Texas, black voting continued during Redemption. A few blacks continued to serve in state legislatures and pockets of black political power endured in some plantation counties. It was not until the 1890s that complete racial segregation and legal disfranchisement took place.

Historian C. Van Woodward has argued that while extreme racism had always existed in the South, it had been checked by the conservative paternalism of the old planter class, northern liberal opinion, and southern white radicalism. But in the latter decades of the century, the influence of these elements waned. Northern liberalism had retreated in the 1870s, and the U.S. Supreme Court's ruling in 1883 overturning the Reconstruction civil rights acts sealed federal abandonment of black rights. The Populists' support for a class-based alliance of black and white farmers against monopoly proved to be short-lived. Under pressure of the agricultural depression and bitter political battles with white conservative Democrats, white Populists turned against their black allies in the 1890s.

The policy of strict racial segregation—nicknamed "Jim Crow" after a minstrelsy character—took hold and consolidated during the 1890s as a concession to poor white people, a bid to rebuild a "solid South" unified across class lines by white racism. The Jim Crow laws reached into every nook and cranny of southern life. Their relentless logic created not only separate railroad cars, building entrances, and drinking fountains, but also separate Bibles for swearing witnesses in the courtroom, separate streets for prostitutes, even separate gallows for hanging condemned men.

The chief aim of white supremacy was not so much racial separation, although that was its form, but racial subordination. Jim Crow was a system of countless daily humiliations intended to remind black people of their inferior position. Middle-class blacks were special targets of white resentment, indicating both the progress that black people had made since slavery and the precariousness of lower-class whites' racial confidence. These white southerners resented "uppity," independent-minded Negroes in general and economically successful blacks in particular, described by one white southerner as "that insolent class who desired to force themselves into first-class coaches."

In fact, streetcars and trains were contested public spaces because they were among the very few places in the South where blacks and whites came together on equal footing. An observer explained, "In their homes and in ordinary employment, [whites and blacks] meet as master and servant; but in the street cars they touch as free citizens, each paying for the right to ride; the white not in a place of command, the Negro without an obligation of servitude. Streetcar relationships are, therefore, symbolic of the new conditions."

During the 1880s and 1890s many blacks refused to observe the new rules segregating streetcars and railroad coaches. The transportation companies were also not always keen on assuming the additional expense and responsibility for policing the color line. In 1887 a black newspaper in Georgia encouraged black passengers who purchased first-class tickets to stand their ground. "When a conductor orders a colored passenger from the first-class car it's a bluff, and if the passenger goes to the forward or smoking car, that ends it; should he refuse, it ends it also, for the trainman will reflect seriously before he lays on violent hands."

While some blacks successfully called the trainman's bluff, others were not as fortunate, including a young Ida B. Wells who, while traveling from Memphis in 1884 was dragged from her seat in the first-class ladies car after she refused to move. Wells got off the train at the first stop rather then sit in the smoking car, and then successfully sued the railroad. A few others won similar judgments. But in 1896 Homer Plessy, a light-skinned Negro from Louisiana who sued over his ejection from the first-class car, lost his case before the U.S. Supreme Court. In *Plessy v. Ferguson* the court legitimized racial segregation with the "separate but equal" doctrine. The court ruled that the Fourteenth Amendment protected the rights of black people only in narrow terms of formal political equality. "If one race be inferior to the other socially," it said, "the Constitution of the United States cannot put them upon the same plane."

Many black people made individual decisions to walk rather than ride on segregated cars. Efforts were made at collective action as well, although these were difficult to sustain. Between 1890 and World War I, black people staged boycotts of streetcars in twenty-five cities in every southern state. "Do not trample on our pride by being 'jim crowed'- WALK!" exhorted the Savannah *Tribune*.

The street, too, could be contested terrain. Historian Glenda Gilmore found evidence of street altercations between black and white women in the late 1890s in North Carolina towns where black power had not yet been completely displaced. In Wilmington, where blacks held local office until 1898, a black woman refused to yield the sidewalk to a group of white women. When one of the white women tried to push her aside, the black woman retaliated with her umbrella. "That's right, damn it, give it to her," a black male observer reportedly shouted. Incidents such as these suggest that the generation born in freedom did not easily acquiesce to the reassertion of white supremacy.

But, while it is important to acknowledge resistance to Jim Crow, it should not be overstated. In the main the weight of white supremacy was enormous, and black people lacked political leverage to reverse the trend of racial oppression. Open confrontation invited swift punishment and retribution. Choosing to walk rather than ride segregated cars was an act of indirect resistance; grabbing the opportunity to steal a quick jostle on the street a spontaneous way to assert one's pride; but even such assertions were risky. Indeed, black people were lynched for as much.

Lynching was an old form of extralegal justice that had been practiced for many years, mainly against whites in the West and South; but in the 1890s it became both more widespread and increasingly aimed at black people. Between 1890 and 1917 at least two to three black southerners were hanged, burned at the stake, or otherwise murdered every week.

Lynching evolved as a sadistic and public ritual that involved death by prolonged torture, such as mutilation and burning, dismemberment, and the distribution of severed body parts as trophies and souvenirs. It was a gruesome public spectacle, a kind of cathartic blood sport that involved hundreds, even thousands, of cheering witnesses from all strata of southern white society. Mary Church Terrell called modern lynching a "wild and diabolical carnival of blood."

The extremity of the punishment was justified by the nature of the alleged crimes committed, notably the rape of white women by black men. During the era of segregation a climate of sexualized race hysteria engulfed the South, which imagined pure white southern womanhood under siege by the "black beast rapist." In truth, most lynching was not in response to sexual assault. Of nearly three thousand blacks lynched between 1889 and 1918, only 19 percent were accused of rape (and of these, many were falsely accused). Journalist and activist Ida B. Wells, who conducted the first in-depth investigation of lynching, pointed out that sexual liaisons between black men and white women were often consensual and initiated by the latter. If there was rape between the races, she said, it was the age-old practice of white men taking black women. Economic competition and resentment against the black middle class, argued Wells, was the real reason for lynching. White southerners cried the "beast," but lynching revealed more about the savagery of white racism than it did about the character of its victims.

Disfranchisement was the last, but by no means the least, major means of racial oppression to be imposed at the end of the nineteenth century. Enacted throughout the South between 1890 (Mississippi) and 1910 (Tennessee), disfranchisement was achieved mostly by state constitutional amendments that imposed property and literacy qualifications on the vote or by other devices, such as the poll tax.

Concern over widespread corruption in elections was the principal rationale for disfranchisement. Particularly in the black-belt areas, white minorities used myriad tactics to hold power, including vote purchasing, ballot stealing, bribery, intimidation, and violence. These tactics were used not only against black voters but between white factions as well. Many southern political leaders believed cheating at elections disgraced and demoralized southern politics.

Disfranchisement might seem like a paradoxical solution that punished the victims of voting fraud. But its logic was consistent with the view commonly held among white elites that black people were not intelligent enough to hold the franchise responsibly. At another level, some white leaders frankly argued for the economy of disfranchisement. "We are not begging for 'ballot reform'," explained an Alabama Democrat, "but we want to be relieved of purchasing the Negroes to carry elections. I want cheaper votes."

Conservative Democrats in the South believed that restoring power to the "intelligent and virtuous" propertied classes was also a solution to the expanding democratic vote of poor white people. White power per se was not threatened; at issue, rather, was which whites would have power. Disfranchisement was thus a strategy in diverse political calculations. Conservatives saw it as a solution to Populist challenges; in some states, white majority counties were willing to sacrifice universal manhood suffrage for better advantage against white-controlled black-belt counties.

Disfranchisement virtually eliminated black voting in the South. Although blacks had already been informally disfranchised in most states by intimidation, violence, and the gerrymandering of districts, the institutionalization of disfranchisement set in place a durable legal structure that would last for more than a half-century. In Louisiana, the number of black registered voters dropped from 130,000 in 1896 to 1,342 in 1904. In Alabama only 2 percent of eligible black men were registered to vote by 1906.

Southern lawmakers attempted to exempt poor white people from disfranchisement by creating various loopholes in the law. These included the "understanding clause," which allowed illiterates to vote if they could "understand" any section of the state constitution read to them, and the infamous "grandfather clause," which protected the franchise of all those who had been eligible to vote on January 1, 1867, as well as their sons and their grandsons. Nevertheless, the disfranchisement of whites was significant, owing in large part to the poll tax. In Louisiana, adult white male voter registration dropped from 96.3 percent in 1896 to 52 percent in 1904. Forrest G. Wood has estimated that from 97,000 to 108,000 white voters were disfranchised throughout the South.

For African Americans, Jim Crow was a dark period. An Alabama woman remarked, "There is no wonder that we die. The wonder is that we persist in living." Yet black people persevered and found ways to eke out a living, to school their children, to maintain their self-respect. Many avoided white people wherever possible, in order to avoid humiliation or trouble.

African Americans learned to "wear the mask," to act with deference in the presence of whites while hiding their true thoughts and feelings. As a blues refrain described, "Got one mind for white folks to see, 'nother for what I know is me." Accommodation to white supremacy was necessary for daily survival, but it did not mean submission. Resentment burned inside, especially among the "New Negroes," the generation born in freedom. Black people found ways to subvert the system passively, performed small acts of resistance, and occasionally challenged racism openly. Armed self-defense was rare but not unheard of, and at times even openly advocated in the black press. The Montgomery *Weekly News* advised blacks to "die like men [and] take two or three white devils along."

But in truth, the options were few. While during Reconstruction black people struggled for both political and economic independence, in the 1890s political action became impossible and the impulse for economic self-sufficiency turned inward, becoming individualized, even conservative. Jim Crow spurred the growth of a black middle class comprising businessmen, professionals, and clergy, who serviced the segregated community and market. In the 1880s and 1890s a conservative leadership that advocated accepting the Negro's subordinate status in the South emerged out of this stratum.

The most forceful and successful spokesman for this approach was Booker T. Washington, who founded the Tuskegee Institute, an agricultural and vocational school, in Alabama. Washington preached racial uplift through economic self-help and vocational education and counseled accepting segregation with "patience, forbearance, and self-control." While during the Reconstruction era, uplift meant the full rights of citizenship, in the 1890s, uplift ideology emphasized winning white people's acceptance by promoting the "better sort" of middle class Negro and blaming the lower classes of black people for their backward condition. Washington's strategy appealed to some African Americans as practical and realistic, even hopeful. But his leadership was also the creation of white society. Washington's message of quiescence and economic self-help resonated with the climate of industry, commerce, and laissez-faire that suffused both North and South and brought him white recognition and financial support.

Not all African Americans subscribed to the strategy of moderation and accommodation. In the early 1890s dissidents such as Ida B. Wells and T. Thomas Fortune, a Florida journalist, formed the Afro-American Council. The council condemned lynching, segregation, and disfranchisement and encouraged economic boycotts. W. E. B. Du Bois openly broke with Washington in 1903 because, he said, Washington "apologizes for injustice, . . . does not rightly value the privilege and duty of voting, belittles the emasculating effects of cast distinctions, and opposes the higher training and ambition of our brighter minds."

Yet, while Washington's critics hit at many truths, they too recognized that African Americans had few choices in the South. The Afro-American Council advocated out-migration; Wells herself went into exile in the North after racists burned down her Memphis newspaper, *Free Speech*. In fact, for many black people, leaving the South seemed to be the only alternative. Some sixty thousand black farmers migrated to the West during the 1870s and 1880s, and urban professionals, like Wells, began going north in the 1890s. As much as Du Bois emphasized political and civil rights, the thrust of his work in founding the Niagara Movement and the NAACP appealed to northern conscience to restore the nation's commitment to black political rights.

If southern race policy succeeded in disempowering black people and forcing them into conditions of near servitude, it failed to deliver on its promise to elevate poor whites. A new upper class of white planters, industrialists, and merchants thrived, of course. But for the lower classes of white southerners, the price of racial pride was high, including disfranchisement and the highest rates of illiteracy and poverty in the nation. Small white farmers fell into tenancy and debt, their decline feeding the growth of a low-wage labor force for the burgeoning southern textile industry. Thus while the New South built industries and became integrated into the national market, it remained a backward region based on a colonial economy and repressive labor relations for black and white laborers alike.

The nation's abandonment of racial equality and full citizenship for African Americans had implications beyond the South. The color line cast a long shadow across America, for it also radically foreshortened the possibilities for equality for other nonwhite peoples. Indeed, as white supremacy retook the South, race and racism were also reproduced in the Far West through campaigns of war and assimilation against American Indians and through the dispossession of Mexican-owned land.

THE WEST: MANIFEST DESTINY REALIZED

The Last Indian Wars

After the Civil War cheap land offerings by the government and the railroads and opportunities in mining and cattle ranching drew white settlers to the Great Plains. During the 1870s the white population west of the Mississippi grew from 7 million to 11 million. Increasingly, white settlers coveted American Indian land, both reservations and nonreservation (unceded) lands recognized and protected by treaty with the United States. Indeed, settlement and the integration of the West into the national market rendered impossible the old policy based on the isolation of Indians from whites and their removal to remote storage areas in the West. In the 1870s and 1880s Indian-white armed conflict reached its final and most desperate stage.

In 1874 George Armstrong Custer, a U.S. Army officer, led an illegal military expedition into unceded Sioux lands in the Dakotas that confirmed the presence of gold in the Black Hills. With white miners flocking to the area, the government moved against the Sioux. Although the treaty of Fort Laramie in 1868 had recognized unceded lands in the Powder River area as Sioux hunting grounds, in 1875 the government declared its intention to round up all nonreservation Sioux and bring them in by military force. Three military columns from the Missouri division of the U.S. Army launched a full-scale attack against the Sioux and their Cheyenne allies in the spring of 1876. But the Sioux were a formidable foe. Their most stunning victory took place at Little

Big Horn, where four thousand warriors led by Crazy Horse and Sitting Bull annihilated the entire Seventh Cavalry commanded by Custer. The Indians were defeated only after a prolonged U.S. military campaign of pursuit. Crazy Horse surrendered in 1877 and was immediately killed. Sitting Bull, who had gone to Canada with a small band, returned in 1881 and acquiesced, finally, to reservation life. But he, too, was murdered in 1890, as part of the massacre of the Lakota Ghost Dancers at Wounded Knee.

On the southern plains, the Comanche and Kiowas also resisted and lost. Although they had agreed to live on reservations in the Medicine Lodge Treaties, they were unhappy there. They frequently left and conducted raids into Texas and Mexico for livestock. As depredations increased in the 1870s, the government declared all Indians not on the reservations to be hostile. During the Red River War of 1874–1875, five army divisions pursued the Indians until they gave up in exhaustion. In the Southwest, the Apache also went off the reservations for raiding and resisted military control by guerrilla warfare into the 1880s. Geronimo was one of the last American Indian chiefs to accept defeat in 1886.

Historian Richard White has observed that the Indians nearly always won battles with U.S. military forces. They ultimately lost the war, however, because the U.S. Army practiced a kind of reverse guerrilla warfare, in which they pursued the Indians relentlessly, scattering and starving them until they surrendered. In 1877, after the government reduced the size of the Nez Perce reservation in Washington Territory, Chief Joseph attempted to lead his people to Canada, resisting U.S. Army attacks for months along a 1,321-mile-long flight. When he finally surrendered he said, "I am tired of fighting. The old men are all dead. . . . It is cold, and we have no blankets. The little children are freezing to death. My people, some of them, have run away to the hills. From where the sun now stands, I will fight no more forever."

The military campaigns of the 1870s and 1880s were accompanied by legal moves against American Indian sovereignty and tribal lands. In 1871 Congress formally abandoned the treaty system, declaring that the United States would no longer recognize or deal with Indians as sovereign nations. Indian policy shifted to an assimilationist strategy, which would last until 1930. Once the Indians had been militarily defeated, many white Americans pitied their destitute lives on the reservations. These included well-meaning reformers, who believed the Indians were ill served on reservations, which they likened to "pen[s] where a horde of savages are to be fed with flour and beef . . . [and] furnished with paint and gee-gaws by the greed of traders." The reformers believed that the Indians, small in number and widely dispersed, would become extinct unless they "flow[ed] in with the current of the life and ways of the larger [people]." Assimilation would thus "save" the Indians from extinction. But this was inherently a contradictory strategy because assimilation, which required extinguishing the Indians' way of life, was itself a kind of extinction.

One of the central features of assimilation was the cessation of Indian land according to a new federal policy called "allotment by severalty." This policy provided that Indians be "allotted" a fraction of their lands while the government and private interests assumed control of the rest. While the government had previously recognized Indian land as their birthright, it now regarded it as part of the public domain, to be used for the "permanent prosperity" of the West. Allotment was implemented on a tribe-by-tribe basis in the 1880s and in 1887 by the General Allotment Act (the Dawes Act), which committed the government to the allotment of all Indian lands.

The ostensible purpose of allotment was to induce Indians to become farmers on individually owned plots of land. By making Indians into yeoman farmers, allotment aimed to assimilate them into American society. As Secretary of the Interior Carl Schurz explained in 1881, allotment would "fit the Indians for the habits and occupations of civilized life, by work and education, to individualize them in the possession and appreciation of property." Of course, the Anglo-American method of farming required far less land than did the traditional Indian usufruct economies of hunting and casual farming. Anything more than 160 acres per household was surplus.

Assimilation also required the suppression of American Indian religious practices. In 1884 Congress banned the Sioux Sun Dance, and in 1888 it prohibited bundling, a ritual of preserving the spirits of the dead. These prohibitions hurt Indians deeply. A Blackfoot Indian said, "I do not understand why the white men desire to put an end to our religious ceremonials. What harm can they do to our people? If they deprive us of our religion, we will have nothing left. . . . We believe the Sun God is all-powerful, for every spring he makes the trees bud and the grass to grow. We see these things with our own eyes, and, therefore, know that all life comes from him."

Reformers also attempted to convert Indians to traditional Anglo-American gender roles and family structure. They believed the matrilineal kinship structure of many Indian tribes was evidence of sexual promiscuity and the foundation of Indians' supposed savagery. Elevating Indian women to the ideal of white middle-class womanhood, they believed, was central to civilizing the Indians. The Women's National Indian Association was founded by veteran women reformers and modeled on the "women's work for women" of the Protestant women's missions, which emphasized domestic work and Christian values of sexual and moral purity.

Finally, reformers sought to assimilate Indians through education. Between 1879 and 1895 the federal government increased its annual spending for native schooling from $75,000 to $2 million. It built some two hundred day schools on the reservations and twenty boarding schools. The most well-known institution was the Carlisle School in Pennsylvania, a boarding school founded by Henry Pratt in 1878. Pratt had experimented first with a program for American Indian students at the Hampton Institute, the first Negro college established after the Civil War and the alma mater of Booker T. Washington. Pratt's evangelical style, which emphasized instruction in reading, writing, manual skills, and Protestant values, so that the Indians would "rise to civilization," typified the approach to Indian education in the 1870s and 1880s.

If cultural arrogance marked the evangelical approach, it was tempered by an idealistic belief in the humanity—and the ultimate equality—of the Indian. By the 1890s, however, race pessimism had displaced idealism. The boarding school strategy had always been too expensive to be adopted as general policy, and critics questioned its efficacy, observing that the students "regressed" when they returned to the reservations by growing their hair long and wearing native clothing. The critique was part of a general view that doubted the Indians' racial capacity for civilization. Government officials and reformers, influenced by scientific race theories that arose in late nineteenth-century anthropology and ethnology, considered the Indians a hopelessly backward race, frozen in time and space. The American Indian was "an adult child," according to the commissioner of Indian education, Francis Leupp, who might be trained for a life of manual labor, but little more. By the turn of the century vocational schooling was the exclusive focus of Indian education. Indian policy makers invoked Booker T. Washington's model of limited education in the context of racial subordination. Washington, said Leupp in 1902, was successful because "the black man [was] to him a black man, and not merely a white man colored black."

Assimilation thus produced dubious results; just as education policy abandoned the goal of integrating Indians into American society as equal citizens, allotment failed to transform Indians into family farmers. That was a difficult goal to achieve in any event, since by the late 1880s the monopolization of agricultural land was well under way in the West. But the dispossession of the American Indians proceeded apace. Indian land ownership fell from 155,632,312 acres in 1881 to 77,865,373 acres in 1900. By the turn of the century the premise of the Dawes Act, that tribal land was American Indian private property, and the act's provisions requiring Indians' approval of the sale of their unallotted lands, were rendered moot. In 1900 the Jerome Agreement, a land cession rejected by the Kiowa and Comanche, was approved by Congress and then upheld by the U.S. Supreme Court. In *Lone Wolf v. Hitchcock* (1908) the Court declared that Congress held the "plenary [absolute] power" "to abrogate the provisions of an Indian treaty." All pretenses that recognized Indian sovereignty were gone. The American Indians were no longer nations, not even dependent nations. They were now individual wards of the state.

Mexicans: Strangers in Their Native Homeland

America's seemingly inexorable expansion to the Pacific Coast involved wresting territory not only from Indians but from Mexico as well. The Treaty of Guadalupe Hidalgo, which negotiated Mexico's defeat in the Mexican American War (1846–1848), gave roughly one half of Mexico—more than a half million square miles—to the United States, a territorial acquisition surpassed only by the Louisiana Purchase.

Yet it took several decades to consolidate American rule over the Southwest. In part this was because not Mexico but American Indians actually controlled large parts of it. The Mexican population in the Southwest—Californios, Tejanos, and Nuevomexicanos, and others descended from Spanish colonialists and Indians—numbered only about eighty thousand in 1848. Most lived and worked in a subsistence economy as small producers or on ranches characterized by *patron-peon* relations of mutual dependence and obligation. Sixty-one percent of the Californio population were landowners, although only 3 percent owned large *ranchos*.

The process of white settlement to the Southwest was uneven. In some areas white settlers rapidly outnumbered Mexicans. A rate war between rival railroads drove the cost of a ticket from the Missouri Valley to southern California down from $125 in 1886 to $1 in 1887; white migration to southern California skyrocketed, and whites soon outnumbered Mexicans ten to one. In other areas, however, Mexicans continued to dominate the population. Congress delayed statehood for New Mexico and Arizona until 1912 because the white population of those territories remained small through the early 1900s. Mexicans also continued to dominate the South Texas border region, between the Nueces and Rio Grande rivers. Still, racial suspicion and tension, dating to the founding of the Texas Republic and the Mexican American War and stoked by intruding Anglo-dominated market relations, suffused the border area. Historian David Montejano states that the border region remained "untamed" for fifty years after conquest, as local whites and the frontier battalion of the Texas Rangers, acting as a "military police of occupation," strived to consolidate Anglo power.

On occasion violent conflict erupted, as in the 1877 "salt war" in the El Paso area and the 1871–1876 "skinning wars" in South Texas. Both involved competition over economic resources. In the first instance, Mexicans resorted to arms when Anglos attempted to take over the salt lakes in the foothills of the Guadalupe Mountains, from which locals had developed a salt trade in northern Mexico. The skinning wars grew out of intense competition for cattle, whose hides carried a high market price. For over five years there were organized raids and counterraids on both sides of the Texas-Mexico border and armed conflict between Mexican cattle raiders and Anglo vigilance committees.

The old Spanish and Mexican land grants—some 15 million square miles of land theoretically protected by the Treaty of Guadalupe Hidalgo—posed an obstacle to white American settlers who sought opportunities in ranching and farming in the southwestern territories. From the 1850s to the 1890s, Mexicans were dispossessed of land through myriad strategies, including Anglo marriage into the families of elite Californios and Tejanos, fraud, and theft, as well as through legal means. Both California and Texas required all land titles from the Spanish and Mexican eras to be authenticated according to Anglo-American property law. Many members of the landed elite, whose deeds delineated property according to such markers as "a clump of trees" or whose deeds were long ago misplaced, lost their land. Still others simply could not afford the legal fees required to defend their claims. As a result of the California Land Act of 1851 Californios lost 40 percent of the land they had held in 1846. In

Texas, some whites occupied Mexican-owned land and then made legal claim based on their rights as squatters. Tejano-owned land ordered sold by county courts to settle tax arrears went to Anglos for suspiciously low bids. In June 1877, for example, the Hidalgo County sheriff auctioned three thousand acres of the Hinajosa land grant for $15. In New Mexico, a Court of Private Land Claims established in 1891 granted 80 percent of the Mexican land grants to Anglos.

The transfer of the land base to whites and the commercialization of the economy reduced most Mexicans in the Southwest to the status of landless wage labor. No longer could they work as small producers or find sympathetic *patrons* to attach themselves to. But there was plenty of work for Mexican laborers, dirty and difficult work that whites refused to do, such as railroad construction, copper and quicksilver mining, and "grubbing brush," which cleared the way for commercial agriculture. The changes in the nature of the labor market were oppressive to traditional Mexican family and life styles. Among the lower classes, traditional gender roles in the patriarchal household came under pressure, as women often had to do work intended for men. Dangerous and itinerant seasonal work created early widowhood or abandonment; by the 1880s nearly one-third of Mexican American households in California were headed by women.

In the context of conquest and the concomitant shifts in economic and political relations of power, Mexicans in the Southwest underwent a process of ethnic redefinition. Many Mexican Americans, especially among the working classes, withdrew into their own communities, both in towns and in isolated rural areas not yet dominated by Anglo settlers. In these spaces they developed what historian David Gutiérrez describes as a "distinct, if syncretic, variant of Mexican culture in what had become part of the United States." They spoke Spanish and sustained their own cultural and religious practices much in the same ways that they had before conquest. The extended family and the *mutualista*, or mutual aid association, provided networks of support and sustenance. On the other hand, many Californio, Tejano, and Nuevomexicano elites sought to distance themselves from the idea of being "Mexican" because that label carried increasingly negative racial connotations. Denying their mestizo heritage, these elites chose instead to identify as "Spanish" or "Castilian"—that is, white—in order to salvage their social status as the indigenous *gente de razón*, "people of reason." The strategy had limited success, however, for by the turn of the century the old upper classes, dispossessed of land and power, had dwindled in size and influence. But the impulse to claim whiteness remained strong. In part this was a sign of their diminished status. The appeal of whiteness derived also from the bifurcated black-white racial order of American society. Claiming whiteness was believed to be a way of avoiding the degradation of blackness. In fact, Mexicans were perceived in ambiguous racial terms; while some considered them a mixed race of two undesirable elements (Latin and Indian), comparisons to the Negro were also common. The Treaty of Guadalupe Hidalgo granted U.S. citizenship to the inhabitants of the ceded territory, which led a federal court to rule (*In re Rodriguez*, 1897) that Mexicans were "white" for purposes of naturalization, even if ethnologists considered them to be "Indian." Particularly in Texas, positioned geographically where the South and the Southwest intersect, Mexicans came to occupy an ethno-racial space in between white and black.

That trend was augmented when immigration from the Mexico interior to the Southwestern United States began in the 1880s and 1890s. Coincident with a labor shortage in the southwestern United States, the Mexican government of Porfirio Diaz was engaged in an aggressive campaign of modernization. That process opened the country to foreign capital and disrupted the traditional system of land tenure. In 1883 new land laws expropriated the *ejidos* (common lands), which would displace some five million people from their means of subsistence over the next twenty years.

Although the high tide of Mexican immigration would not occur until the 1920s, migration to the United States trebled during the Porfiriato. Anglo growers and employers favored Mexican labor because they seemed more tractable than black labor and because many returned home after one or two seasons of work. As an official of the U.S. Bureau of Labor explained in 1908, Mexican farm workers "do not occupy a position analogous to that of the Negro in the South. They are not permanent, do not acquire land or establish themselves in little cabin homesteads, but remain nomadic and outside of American civilization." Conquest had not only "thrown [Mexicans] among those who were strangers" but made them foreigners in their homeland.

Chinese Immigration and Asiatic Exclusion

Just as Mexican laborers were perceived as outsiders, so too were the Chinese who came to the Pacific coast during the second half of the nineteenth century. Americans who believed the West was a God-given gift to white civilization loathed sharing it with anyone else. Thus in 1850 California imposed a foreign miner's tax, which was aimed at excluding miners who came from Sonora, Mexico, and China to participate in the gold rush. But the labor needed to develop the West was considerable, and white labor was in short supply, especially for unskilled work that was dirty or dangerous. Employers thus recruited Chinese and Mexicans for railroad construction, for clearing and reclaiming land for agricultural production, and for other work critical to the early development of the West. But white Americans—themselves migrants from the eastern and midwestern U.S. and from Europe—welcomed neither group as permanent settlers or citizens. While Mexicans were tolerated to the extent that they were seasonal workers, Chinese soon earned the dubious distinction of being the only group to be legally excluded by name from the United States.

Chinese migration to the Pacific Coast was part of a larger exodus of some two million people from southern China in the nineteenth century. The "push" for emigration derived from a combination of factors that included population pressures and natural disasters, domestic political strife, and economic and social dislocations caused by Western intrusions. China's loss to Great Britain in the Opium War (1839–1842) was particularly damaging, as it was forced to open five ports to foreign commerce, to pay a $21 million indemnity, and to grant Westerners immunity from Chinese law.

In the mid-nineteenth century some 150,000 Chinese indentured laborers, or coolies, were recruited to replace African slaves on plantations in South America and the Caribbean after the abolition of slavery. Coolie labor was a form of semislavery. Chinese were often kidnapped or tricked into signing contracts and endured harsh conditions akin to slavery. Coolies who harvested guano off the coast of Peru, for example, did not always live long enough to finish their contracts.

By contrast, Chinese migration to North America and Australia was voluntary. Some half-million Chinese immigrated to these areas in the nineteenth century. With milder climates and waged labor—not to mention the discovery of gold deposits—they were favored destinations for Chinese migrants whose families were of modest or moderate means. Many Chinese laborers came to the United States on the credit ticket system and had to pay back the money advanced for their passage, but they were not bound by contracts and were not coolies. Admittedly, the difference may have seemed slight in practice. For example, the thirty thousand Chinese recruited to build the western portion of the transcontinental railroad from 1867 to 1871 faced arduous conditions and earned wages one-third less than that of white workers building the eastern section. An untold number of Chinese died in the high Sierras, some from working through the freezing winters, others from blasting dynamite while hanging from baskets suspended over the side of the mountain.

Yet, even as Chinese were a highly exploited labor force in the American West, the essentially voluntary nature of their migration had important consequences that encouraged the formation of communities. Because they were not coolies, Chinese more readily entered a range of occupations. As mining gave out, some Chinese became agricultural workers and tenant farmers. Chinese reclaimed the Sacramento-San Joaquin Delta and introduced the production of labor-intensive fruits and vegetables. Others came as or became merchants, who sold provisions and services to their coethnics, or commissioned and sold agricultural products in the general market. Still others became urban artisans and factory workers in San Francisco's nascent manufacturing economy.

Some Chinese started families in America, although relatively few women immigrated. Those who did comprised wives of merchants and, to a lesser extent laborers, servant girls, and prostitutes. As was the case with migrants from Mexico and Europe in the late nineteenth century, Chinese migrants were predominantly men of the laboring classes whose families sent them abroad to work and send money home. Approximately half of the two hundred thousand Chinese who came to the West Coast between 1874 and 1890 returned to China. Among those who stayed in the United States, many continued to maintain households in China. Most *huaqiao* (overseas Chinese) were not, in fact, bachelor sojourners but were members of extended transnational families. Outside of San Francisco, working couples were not uncommon in nineteenth-century fishing, farming, and small western towns. Despite the hardships facing many immigrants, Chinese wives improved their status in America. Free from the domination of their parents-in-law, many worked alongside their husbands and were, in effect, joint heads of household.

By 1870 the Chinese population in California numbered nearly fifty thousand; in San Francisco, Chinese accounted for one-quarter of the city's population in 1870 and 30 percent by 1880. Excluded by white skilled workers from high-wage markets (construction, transportation, metal work), Chinese worked in manufacturing, particularly in sectors

where new methods had shifted work from skilled labor to mass production and lowered wages, such as cigar making and shoe making. Economic
competition spurred whites' resentment, especially after the depression of
the 1870s, but more than jobs and wages were at stake. Race hostility
against the Chinese drew from the ideological traditions of Manifest
Destiny and free labor. White labor depicted Chinese as coolies, whom
they characterized as representing a racially based condition of servility, as
well as disease, moral depravity, and unchecked reproduction. The first
federal legislation restricting immigration, the 1875 Page Law excluding
prostitutes, was aimed at Chinese. In July 1877 a sandlot rally of the San
Francisco Workingmen's Party turned into a three-day rampage against
Chinese residents; later that year the party, running on the slogan "the
Chinese must go," swept the municipal elections. Anticoolieism became
a staple of Democratic Party politics on the Pacific Coast and Chinese
exclusion the West's principal demand in Congress. In 1882 Congress
suspended Chinese immigration for ten years. Exclusion was renewed in
1892 and 1902 and made permanent in 1904. Although Chinese ineligi-
bility to citizenship was already implicit in the nation's naturalization
laws, which provided the right to "free white persons" in 1790 and to
"persons of African nativity or descent" in 1870, the exclusion laws
explicitly barred Chinese from naturalization.

Exclusion, which legitimated the undesirability of Chinese, encouraged greater violence and discrimination. The worst violence in the
1880s occurred in the Mountain states and in the Pacific northwest,
where Chinese miners and railroad workers had settled. In 1885 and
1886 a string of riots and "deportations" took place in Seattle, Tacoma,
and Portland, in part in response to the depressed economic conditions
that followed the completion of the northern rail lines. In 1885 in Rock
Springs, Wyoming territory, a dispute between Chinese and white coal
miners led to a full-scale race riot. A mob of whites burned down the
Chinese quarter, shot and killed twenty-eight Chinese, wounded fifteen,
and drove the rest from town. Chinese were lynched or violently
expelled from other towns throughout the West. Few whites ever faced
criminal charges for their actions. In California, where the vast majority of Chinese resided, Chinese were pushed to the margins of society.
They were driven out of manufacturing and farming and segregated
residentially, their children segregated in a separate "Oriental School."
Exclusion also gave rise to illegal immigration, through smuggling and
through the use of fraudulent documents. Chinatown developed as a

segregated and insular community, with surname and place-of-origin associations and other protective societies adapted from China dominating its social organization. In a sense the marginalization of Chinese fulfilled nativist claims about Chinese difference and unassimilability.

Excluded from citizenship and the polity, Chinese challenged racial discrimination in the courts. A number of test cases organized by the Chinese Consolidated Benevolent Association (also known as the Six Companies) went to the U.S. Supreme Court. These cases not only delineated the boundaries of Chinese and Chinese Americans' rights in America but also decided important constitutional questions dealing with immigration and citizenship. These include Congress's plenary (absolute) power over immigration (*Chae Chan Ping v. United States,* 1889) and deportation (*Fong Yue Ting v. United States,* 1893), the applicability of the Fourteenth Amendment to all persons including noncitizens (*Yick Wo v. Hopkins,* 1886), and the universality of birthright citizenship (*United States v. Wong Kim Ark,* 1898).

As Chinese immigration declined in the 1890s, Japanese began coming to the West Coast. Some 118,000 Japanese immigrated between the mid-1880s and 1925. A large number came from Hawai'i, where they had worked as contract laborers on sugar plantations. In California and in other Western states Japanese labor replaced Chinese in farming and in railroad construction. Learning from the experience of the Chinese, some Japanese tried to deflect white hostility by demonstrating a commitment to join American society: they wore Western clothes, bought property, started families, joined Christian churches, and patronized white businesses. Nevertheless, by the turn of the twentieth century, Pacific Coast nativists began agitating for Japanese exclusion, invoking many of the Orientalist tropes that had been used against the Chinese. But anti-Japanese hostility differed in some important respects. Japan was not a backward, semicolonial nation like China but a modern imperialist nation that inspired both respect and anxiety in the West. If the Chinese "yellow peril" was imagined as an endless horde of coolies, the Japanese peril lay in imperialist Japan's alleged designs to take over America. In 1905 Japanese protests over the segregation of their children in San Francisco's Oriental School prompted a diplomatic crisis, which led to the negotiation of the "Gentleman's Agreement" in 1907. In an effort to forestall statutory exclusion, Japan agreed to restrict the emigration of laborers voluntarily. In a companion piece, President Roosevelt issued an Executive Order in 1908 that effectively barred the migration of Asians from Hawai'i—by then a United States territory—to the mainland. Thus by the first decade of the twentieth century Asiatic exclusion was established as national policy.

IMMIGRANTS FOR THE INDUSTRIAL AGE

The political and territorial consolidation of the South and West into United States speeded the completion of the country's industrial transformation. The same dynamic growth of capitalism that marked the United States was also evident in Europe, creating conditions there for emigration. As railroads and the capitalist market extended into rural areas, cheaper manufactured goods undercut the livelihoods of local artisans. The demand for agricultural produce in the cities encouraged the growth of large-scale commercial agriculture and the production of cash crops, threatening subsistence farming and small producers. These processes had shaped immigration from Europe to the U.S. since the 1820s, but in the last decades of the nineteenth century, when these dynamics reached deeper into Southern and Eastern Europe, a so-called new immigration began. While older migrant streams continued to flow to the U.S. (Germans were the third largest group of immigrants in this period), most immigrants were as yet unfamiliar to Americans. Italians and Jews from Russia and Eastern Europe were the largest groups, comprising 17 and 14 percent, respectively, of the total immigration from 1880 to World War I. In the decade before the war, the foreign-born comprised nearly 15 percent of the total population, the highest proportion in the nation's history.

Historian John Bodnar has argued against the image of the new immigrants as victimized peasants fleeing poverty. Rather, he describes emigration as a pragmatic choice made by families confronted with rapidly changing economic realities. In Italy, for example, the break up of the feudal land tenure system—which put nearly three hundred thousand parcels of land up for sale between 1861 and 1899—had different regional effects. In areas where farmers competed to buy small properties, as in southern Italy, emigration was a means for generating cash to buy land. In central and northern Italy, where land remained in the hands of large estates and was not for sale, peasant militancy, not emigration, was the strategy for improving one's condition.

In the late nineteenth century Italian migrants maintained strong ties to their home communities. They resisted the idea of permanent settlement in the United States; the annual return migration rate was greater than 45 percent. Few Italians were interested in buying land in America. "This [Italy] is the only true land," explained a Consenzan peasant. "We can live somewhere else for a while. But we can only buy land here."

In central and Eastern Europe, emigration was spurred by economic change as well as by religious persecution and political repression. Throughout the nineteenth century, Tsarist Russia isolated and oppressed Jews, requiring them to live in segregated communities (*shtetls*) within a "Pale of Settlement" along Russia's western border, from the Baltic to the Black Sea, encompassing present-day Byelorussia, Latvia, Lithuania, Moldova, Poland, Russia, and the Ukraine. Barred from owning or renting land outside of towns and cities, Jews worked as merchants and small craftsmen. Yet their occupational positions also came under pressure from increased competition from former serfs, who were emancipated in 1863. In the 1880s and 1890s Jews in Russia faced increased repression. They were expelled from Moscow, St. Petersburg, and Kiev, and faced frequent pogroms, or government-sponsored and inspired mob attacks. From 1880 to 1924, some 2.4 million Jews migrated to the United States.

A diverse population of Slavic peoples also migrated to America at the turn of the century. These included Ukrainians, Poles, Bohemians (Czechs), Slovaks, Slovenians, Croatians, and others who, for the most part, lived under Russian, German, or Austro-Hungarian rule. Most were Eastern Orthodox or Roman Catholic. Emigration became an option for Slavs in areas where landholdings were too small to be successful and alternative employment in industry was lacking. Many also chafed under political and ethnic repression. In the 1870s and 1880s, for example, many Poles left Prussia in response to chancellor Otto von Bismarck's forced assimilation policies, which included mandatory use of the German language and a state takeover of parochial schools.

The new immigrants were mostly unskilled workers—laborers, farm laborers, and domestic servants—with the exception of Jews, for whom tailoring was the largest occupational group. As with Mexicans and Chinese, a large percentage were unattached males—as many as 90 percent of Bulgarian and Serbian migrants, 87 percent of the Greeks, and 74.5 percent of the Italians. Those groups with a high percentage of males had a correspondingly high rate of return migration. Jews had a more balanced sex ratio and a lower rate of return because their migration tended to be family-based and because political repression in their homelands precluded return.

The many millions of laboring men who poured into the United States in the last decades of the nineteenth century and the first decades of the twentieth fed an explosive growth of urban construction and industrial production. Immigrant laborers erected the modern urban infrastructure: they built roads, dug sewers and subway tunnels, and laid streetcar tracks. They provided unskilled labor in mass production industries, creating and filling a new stratum in the workforce. For example, at the turn of the century the Carnegie steel plants in Pittsburgh employed some fourteen thousand common laborers, of whom more than eleven thousand were from Southern and Eastern Europe. The average wage was $12.50 a week, less than what a family needed for subsistence, and the accident rate averaged nearly 25 percent a year.

Immigrants' old-world cultures clashed with the requirements of factory discipline. Employers complained that workers frequently missed work for religious occasions and festivals—for example, the Greek Orthodox church had more than eighty festivals a year, and a Polish wedding could last from three to five days. Collective behavior in the workplace and in immigrant communities was often articulated in the language and rituals of premodern village culture like religious oaths, peasant parades, and food riots. Immigrant workers sometimes staged strikes for higher wages, but they were also used to break the strikes of native-born workers, as employers were adept at exploiting ethnic difference. Some labor unions reached out to immigrants, but others, particularly among the craft unions, remained suspicious of them. Among the latter were Irish Americans and German Americans, whose immigrant ancestors had toiled at the bottom rungs of the work force and faced ethnic and religious prejudice in the early and middle nineteenth century. By the late nineteenth century, however, these older immigrant groups had achieved a measure of economic and social incorporation, if not respectability. Irish Americans, for example, were prevalent in some of the skilled trades and in urban political "machines," which emerged in the late nineteenth century, such as New York's Tammany Hall and the Boston organization of Mayor James Curley.

The influx of immigrants in the 1890s and their concentration in poor urban communities elicited a variety of responses among Americans of older immigrant stock. New England elites as well as native-born craft workers considered the new immigrants to be unassimilable backward peasants from the "degraded races" of Europe, lacking the characteristics necessary for economic independence or self-government. The American Protective Association, formed in 1887, was anti-immigration and anti-Catholic, and boasted 2.5 million members at its peak in the mid-1890s. The Immigration Restriction League formed in 1893 with the goal of restricting immigration by means of a literacy test.

Anti-immigrant sentiment was not confined to politics. One of the most brutal anti-immigrant incidents involved the lynching of eleven Italians in New Orleans in 1891. Native-born whites blamed a growing population of Sicilian immigrants and a rumored Italian Mafia for the murder of the New Orleans police chief David Hennessy. After a jury acquitted nine Italians for the crime, a mob that included public officials and businessmen gathered to mete out "justice" on its own terms. Jewish immigrants experienced a growth of anti-Semitism, in Northern cities and in the South. Some of the first anti-Semitic demonstrations in the United States took place in the 1880s in the lower South, against Jewish supply merchants. By 1893 nightriders were burning farmhouses belonging to Jewish landlords. In northern cities, Jewish bankers and immigrants were scapegoated for the 1890s economic depression.

While some native-born Americans expressed hostility toward the new immigrants, others were more sanguine about the possibilities of assimilation. A new generation of college-educated middle-class Protestant women lobbied for factory reforms, formed settlement houses in immigrant neighborhoods, and promoted Americanization. Yet both the nativists and the social reformers condescended to immigrants and failed to appreciate the richness of their cultures. In fact, immigrant communities were not only sustained by ethnocultural and religious traditions but also comprised diverse political and ideological trends that were part of larger diasporas of exile. Polish immigrants, whose migration was inextricably linked to the division of Poland by its Great-Power neighbors, were keenly nationalist. Among Jews, religious orthodoxy, socialism, and Zionism were all prominent and divergent trends.

At the turn of the century European immigrants occupied an ambivalent and vexatious position in America's racial hierarchy, their place complicated by the demands of other racial categories under construction. While legally defined as "white" for purposes of naturalization, the native-born and older immigrants did not necessarily perceive the newer immigrants as "white," at least not as fully white as the "Anglo-Saxon race." Historians James Barrett and David Roediger have described the new immigrants as "in-between peoples, situated *above* African and Asian Americans but *below* 'white' people." Many immigrant workers, perceiving the disadvantage of being black in America, embraced whiteness as a strategy for economic and social advancement. But others, having experienced the sting of discrimination and group hostility both in their homelands and in America, identified with nonwhites. At the same time, Eastern and Southern European immigrants constructed their identities in ways that were not racial but ethnic, expressing national and religious ties. Over time, however, the process of becoming "American" was inextricably bound up with race.

THE IMPERIAL REPUBLIC

The racial hierarchies constructed in the last quarter of the nineteenth century were part of the United States' emerging modern national identity, and that identity was defined as much by its projections abroad as by its domestic relations. As the conquest of the West was consolidated and the frontier closed, the United States extended its horizons to the Pacific and to Asia.

Of course, expansion and conquest had been part of the nation's history and identity since its inception. Many of the arguments supporting earlier expansions were reiterated: commerce and trade, an outlet for class tensions, geopolitical considerations with regard to European nations, and providential design. But there were also important differences. Until the late nineteenth century, the nation had expanded into contiguous territory. (The exceptions were Alaska and the Midway islands, both acquired in 1867.) New territories were incorporated into the nation as areas for white settlement and for statehood. But could noncontiguous territories become states? What would it mean to make their colored inhabitants citizens? Could the United States, a democratic republic born of an anticolonial revolution, have colonies?

The Colonization of Hawai'i

The colonization of Hawai'i followed the recipe common to eighteenth- and nineteenth-century European colonialism—a succession of traders, Christian missionaries, merchants and planters, and soldiers; a decline of the native population through diseases introduced by Westerners; and the importation of racialized labor to produce cash crops for export.

At the time of contact in the late eighteenth-century, Hawai'ian society, which dated to the second century C.E., comprised highly stratified agricultural chiefdoms. Kinship groups worked the land for subsistence and for tribute to a hierarchy of lords and chiefs (*ali'i*). The "discovery" of the islands in 1778 by British sea Captain James Cook introduced Hawai'i to a market economy and into the nexus of the Euro-American trade in the Pacific and Asia.

In 1820 the first Christian missionaries arrived from the United States, strict Puritan Protestants from New England. In 1825 they converted Queen Ka'ahumanu and several high-ranking *ali'i*. The missionaries gained enormous political influence through their close relationship with Hawai'ian royalty. During the 1830s and 1840s American missionaries and lawyers wrote a Hawai'ian constitution and laws (the criminal code was virtually copied from Massachusetts law books) and even administered the state. The missionaries also pressured the Hawai'ians to change the system of land tenure, as they believed that individual land ownership would civilize the Hawai'ians by promoting industriousness and the nuclear family. The Great *Mahele* (land division) of 1848–1850 divided Hawai'i's land between the crown, the government, and the *ali'i*, and gave commoners the right to hold land in fee simple. By 1852 nonnaturalized foreigners were allowed to buy land.

The Hawai'ian elite has been called naive and passive for seemingly handing control of their sovereign nation over to foreigners. But in the context of rapid economic change and Western economic and military advantage, their actions may be better understood as efforts to stem the erosion of their power. For example, some anthropologists have argued that the *ali'i* may have seen Christianity as a countervailing force against the spread of the merchants' influence. Similarly, the Hawai'ian monarchy acceded to private property interests in the belief that economic prosperity would preserve the kingdom's political independence. The *Mahele* also attempted to keep land under Hawai'ian control, even as it made it alienable. However, few commoners held title to land and many were thrown off the estates, "left to wander in tears on the highway," according to a Hawai'ian contemporary, when *ali'i* leased their land to foreigners

The passage of land to foreigners was the critical element for developing the plantation sugar industry. The other necessity was labor, which was in short supply because the native Hawai'ian population was dwindling and, moreover, was averse to the arduous labor of cutting and hauling cane. The planters turned to imported contract labor, first from China and then Japan and Portugal; and, in the early twentieth century, from Korea, Puerto Rico, and the Philippines. By far the greatest number came from Japan in the last decades of the nineteenth century. Between 1875 and 1910, land devoted to sugar cultivation increased from 12,000 to 214,000 acres.

Indeed, sugar made the *haole* (white) elite ever more powerful. In 1876 the planters won a reciprocity agreement between Hawai'i and the United States, which gave their sugar duty-free access to the American market. Increasingly, *haole* leaders pressed for annexation by the United States. Annexation also had support among American military leaders, who coveted Hawai'i's strategic position in the Pacific Ocean and the deep-water port at Pearl Harbor. In 1893 members of the *haole* elite, including missionary descendents Stanford Dole and Lorrin Thurston, staged a coup, overthrowing Queen Lililuokilani (landing American Marines to face her down), and proclaimed a "Republic of Hawai'i." By any standard of international law it was an illegal takeover of a sovereign kingdom. President Grover Cleveland, however, resisted calls to annex Hawai'i, in large part because he believed it would exacerbate the Asiatic race problem. In 1898, when imperialist sentiment ran high in the United States, Congress approved the annexation of Hawai'i by a simple majority resolution, violating the two-thirds Senate ratification required by the U.S. Constitution. The colonization of Hawai'i may have been obscured by its territorial status, but the process of incorporation resonated with other processes of dispossession and conquest. Recognition by the United States of white territorial government over the sovereign Hawai'ian kingdom was analogous to its ignoring American Indian tribal governments in favor of the white-dominated Oklahoma Territory.

The Spanish American War and an Empire Without Colonies

Indeed, by 1898 American nationalism had reached a fever pitch. The press clamored for American intervention in Cuba, where Spain had been fighting a nationalist uprising in its colony since 1896. Notwithstanding widespread sympathy in the United States for the Cuban freedom fighters, Americans held significant economic interests in Cuba and Puerto Rico, another Spanish colony.

A proimperialist trend in the United States had grown since the 1880s, suffused with the language of Manifest Destiny and Anglo-Saxonism.

The evangelical Reverend Josiah Strong declared expansion to the Pacific was part of the inexorable westward march of Christian civilization. Naval Admiral Alfred Thayer Mahan argued in the language of Social Darwinism, applying the concept of "survival of the fittest" to international competition among nations.

The sinking of the *U.S.S. Maine* in Havana harbor in February 1898 gave the United States reason to declare war against Spain. In Cuba and Puerto Rico, American troops rather quickly defeated the already weakened Spanish. The "splendid little war" was won nearly too quickly, in fact, as Senator Henry Cabot Lodge instructed Theodore Roosevelt to prolong the fighting until Admiral Dewey's fleet reached the Philippines. In the Treaty of Paris in 1899, Spain ceded its colonial possessions to the United States for $20 million. The transfer of colonies was not so simple, however, because in liberating themselves from Spain, both Cuba and the Philippines had declared themselves independent republics.

Opinion in the United States was deeply divided. A contentious debate over the Senate's ratification of the Treaty of Paris raised questions about America's foundational beliefs. Anti-imperialist sentiment involved two lines of thinking. One view was overtly racist. Pointing to the nation's Negro and Asiatic race problems, this view opposed incorporating additional backward colored races into the nation. The other view opposed the acquisition of colonies as antithetical to American principles; as William Jennings Bryan stated, "Our nation must give up any intention of entering upon a colonial policy, such as is now pursued by European countries, or it must abandon the doctrine of consent of the governed." The expansionists argued that the inhabitants of Spain's former colonies were backward races incapable of self-rule, and that the United States had a moral duty to civilize and to protect them from European colonizers. Thus they claimed American interests were noble, unlike old-world colonialism. Alfred Beveridge, Jr., one of the most ardent expansionists in the Senate, declared expansion was "for the Great Republic, not for Imperialism." Many proimperialists frankly saw no problem, constitutional or moral, in ruling backward races without their consent, citing American Indian policy as precedent. A University of Chicago political scientist argued in 1899 that "uncivilized nations under tribal relations [in the Philippines] would occupy the same status precisely as our own Indians. They are, in fact, 'Indians'-and the fourteenth amendment does not make citizens of Indians."

In the end the expansionists won the day. President McKinley eschewed a formal annexation of Cuba, in part to avoid adding more black people to the nation and in part because the Cuban nationalist movement had gained considerable legitimacy in its fight against Spain. The Platt Amendment, passed by Congress in 1899 and added to the Cuban Constitution, made Cuba a "protectorate," an independent nation under the military protection of the United States.

Puerto Rico and the Philippines were annexed as "unincorporated territories"—that is, territories without the prospect of statehood—and organized as "insular (island) possessions" under the War Department. Puerto Ricans and Filipinos were given the status of "nationals"—that is, they owed allegiance exclusively to the United States but were not U.S. citizens. Each had a junior sort of republican government—for purposes of tutelage—but their affairs were subject entirely to approval by a Governor General appointed jointly by the president and by Congress. The U.S. Supreme Court ruled in the Insular Cases (1901) that the Constitution did not necessarily have to follow the flag. (The Jones Act of 1917 made Puerto Ricans citizens of the United States, although they had no representation in Congress and their affairs remained under U.S. authority.)

Notwithstanding President McKinley's claims of an American policy of "benevolent assimilation," Filipinos were wary about trading in one colonial oppressor for another. The Philippine revolution had militarily defeated Spain well before the Americans arrived and in 1898 had proclaimed an independent republic. When Spain transferred title to the islands to the United States, they occupied only the city of Manila. Thus, the United States had to impose benevolent rule by means of force. The Philippine American War (1899–1902) was brutal and bloody. The United States committed two-thirds of the Army to a guerrilla war that was led by generals with experience in the American Indian wars of 1870s and 1880s. U.S. troops committed atrocities, including burning villages, killing noncombatants, and torturing prisoners, which shocked Americans when details of the war leaked into the press. The Filipinos fought tenaciously before succumbing to the Americans' superior military force as well as their own internal divisions. Some seven thousand Americans and twenty thousand Filipinos were killed or wounded in the war, and hundreds of thousands of Filipinos—some estimates are as high as 1 million—died of war-related disease or famine.

In both Puerto Rico and the Philippines, the United States combined the use (or threat) of force with a policy of suasion that coopted
native elites by giving them economic advantages, including protected
access to the American market, political power over their own lower
classes, and promises of eventual self-rule. Yet, like Indian assimilation,
the strategy of civilizing uplift and self-rule was inherently contradictory, as cultural critic Vicente Rafael has explained, "the 'self' that rules
itself can only emerge when the subject has learned to colonize itself."

The policies of subordination and conquest that had developed as
solutions to the Negro and Indian questions, America's oldest race
problems, provided templates for race policy towards the nation's new
immigrants and the inhabitants of its new territorial acquisitions in the
late nineteenth century. When congressional leaders and other elites
debated taking the Philippines in the aftermath of the Spanish
American War, they often made reference to slaves and American
Indians to make the argument that democracy was not for everyone.
They understood that while various race policies differed in the specifics
there were certain important commonalities.

Most significant was the view that the "colored races" lagged far
behind whites on civilization's evolutionary scale. The doctrine of "consent of the governed," central to the Declaration of Independence did
not apply, it was argued, to "races of people adjudged incompetent for
self-government." A journalist asked in 1900, "Were the Negro slaves
canvassed and their consent obtained to their condition of slavery?
Were the Indians. . .? For that matter," he added, "has there been, until
today, any real opportunity given the . . . 35,000,000 of the female sex
to ascertain their opinion concerning the laws under which they live?"
Thus during the last quarter of the nineteenth century, American politics and culture infantilized former slaves, Indian wards, Chinese and
Mexican laborers, and Hawai'ian, Puerto Rican, and Filipino colonial
subjects in order to justify their exclusion from full citizenship.

At the same time, the Civil War and the Reconstruction amendments
to the U.S. Constitution had abolished slavery and established national
citizenship and civil rights. Racism had to be squared with these principles. Hence we see the emergence of myriad legal fictions like "separate
but equal" and "unincorporated territory" and pronouncements of
Congress's "plenary power" over immigration, Indian treaties, and insular
policy. America's "colored races" confronted a deep chasm between the

formality of equality and the reality of inequality. During the late nineteenth century, policies and practices of race evolved that would ensure, as W. E. B. Du Bois observed in 1903, that the most pressing question of the twentieth century would be that of the color line.

BIBLIOGRAPHIC ESSAY

Jim Crow South

On the transition from Reconstruction to the "New South," see C. Van Woodward, *Origins of the New South* (Baton Rouge: Louisiana State University Press, 1951). On Jim Crow segregation, see C. Van Woodward, *The Strange Career of Jim Crow* (New York: Oxford University Press, 1957); Leon Litwack, *Trouble in Mind: Black Southerners in the Age of Jim Crow* (New York: Knopf, 1998); Glenda E. Gilmore, *Gender and Jim Crow* (Chapel Hill: University of North Carolina Press, 1996). On convict labor, see David Oshinsky, *Worse than Slavery: Parchman Farm and the Ordeal of Jim Crow Justice* (New York: Free Press, 1996). On black politics, see Kevin K. Gaines, *Uplifting the Race* (Chapel Hill: University of North Carolina Press, 1996)

The West

For a general historical overview of the West, see Richard White, *"It's Your Misfortune and None of My Own": A History of the American West* (Norman: University of Oklahoma Press, 1991) and Patricia N. Limerick, *The Legacy of Conquest: The Unbroken Past of the American West* (New York: Norton, 1987).

American Indians

Frederick Hoxie, *A Final Promise: The Campaign to Assimilate the Indians, 1880–1920* (Norman: University of Oklahoma Press, 1984) and Brian Dippie, *The Vanishing American: White Attitudes and U.S. Indian Policy* (Middletown, Conn.: Wesleyan University Press, 1981) discuss changes in U.S. Indian Policy in the mid- to late-nineteenth century.

Mexicans

Douglas Monroy, *Thrown Among Strangers* (Berkeley: University of California Press, 1990), discusses the impact of white settlement on Indians and Mexicans in California in the nineteenth century. On Texas, see David Montejano, *Anglos and Mexicans in the Making of Texas* (Austin: University of Texas, 1987).

Asians

For an overview of Asian American history, see Sucheng Chan, ed., *Entry Denied: Exclusion and the Chinese Community in the U.S.* (Philadelphia: Temple University Press, 1991). On Japanese immigration, see Yuji Ichioka, *The Issei: The World of First Generation Japanese Immigrants 1885–1924* (New York: Free Press, 1988). On exclusion and other discriminatory laws against Chinese, see

Charles McClain, *In Search of Equality: The Chinese Struggle against Discrimination in Nineteenth-Century America* (Berkeley: University of California Press, 1994)

European Immigration

For an overview of late nineteenth-century migration from Europe to the United States, see John Bodnar, *The Transplanted: A History of Immigrants in Urban America* (Bloomington: Indiana University Press, 1985). Matthew Jacobson, *Whiteness of a Different Color: European Immigrants and the Alchemy of Race* (Cambridge: Harvard University Press, 1998), discusses the role of race in the process of immigrant assimilation.

Imperial Republic

On Hawai'i, see Sally E. Merry, *Colonizing Hawai'i: The Cultural Power of Law* (Princeton: Princeton University Press, 2000) and Rob Wilson, *Reimagining the American Pacific* (Durham: Duke University Press, 2000). On the Philippines, see Stuart Creighton Miller, *Benevolent Assimilation: The American Conquest of the Philippines* (New Haven: Yale University Press, 1982) and Vicente Rafael, *White Love and Other Events in Filipino History* (Durham: Duke University Press, 2000). Robert Rydell, *All the World's a Fair* (Chicago: University of Chicago Press, 1984) discusses the imperial self-image of the American nation as expressed at late nineteenth-century world's fairs.

6

THE CRITICAL PERIOD

*Ethnic Emergence
and Reaction, 1901–1929*

Andrew R. Heinze

The presidency of Theodore Roosevelt and the collapse of Wall Street form the most conventional endpoints of the 1901–1929 period. But we may also think of the era in terms of Louis Armstrong and Al Smith. Born in 1901 into a poor African American family in New Orleans, Armstrong emerged in the 1920s as America's most influential musician. Smith hailed from a poor family in New York City, and in 1928 he became the first man of Irish Catholic descent to run for the presidency on the ticket of a major party. Armstrong and Smith symbolized a new era in American life.

It was an era of emergence for ethnic minorities. Between 1900 and 1930, immigrants and their children continued to constitute roughly one-third of the U.S. population, as they had since the late 1800s. But their absolute numbers were impressive. During those three decades the number of people whom the Census Bureau classified as foreign-born white (mostly European and Canadian), or native white with at least one foreign-born parent, climbed from 26 million to 38 million. (America's total population increased from 76 million to 122 million in those decades.) In addition to this large population of immigrants, native-born African Americans increased from 9 million to 12 million between 1900 and 1930. The Native American (Indian) population, after three centuries of demographic catastrophe, stabilized at around 240,000 in 1900 and climbed to 340,000 in 1930. (Population figures are given in round numbers.)

The largest wave of immigrants in this period came from Eastern and Southern Europe: Jews, Slavs, and Italians. Together these three groups produced roughly 10 million immigrants, and more than half of these newcomers remained in the U.S. In addition, nearly 800,000 Mexicans entered the country, at least half of whom settled there. Approximately 350,000 French Canadians, 250,000 Greeks, and 170,000 Japanese came to stay between 1900 and 1930, as did tens of thousands of West Indians, Syrians, and Armenians. Smaller numbers arrived from other parts of Asia, Latin America, and Africa. Though not technically immigrants, Filipinos and Puerto Ricans also came to the mainland U.S. as members of the American commonwealth established in 1898. By 1930 approximately 100,000 Puerto Ricans were living in New York City, and no fewer than 45,000 young Filipino men dwelled in California, Oregon, and Washington. Large populations of Japanese and Filipinos also settled in Hawai'i. (The rates of reemigration varied enormously from group to group. Among Jewish and Irish immigrants, very few returned to the homeland, where they faced extraordinary religious persecution; immigrants from the Balkans, on the other hand, reemigrated at the very high rate of approximately 87 percent. For all immigrants, the median rate of return was probably around 25 percent.)

Immigrants from England, Scotland, Ireland, Germany, Scandinavia, and English-speaking Canada continued to arrive as well; more than 5 million from these lands settled in the U.S. between 1900 and 1930. However, these peoples were culturally much more similar to the American population than were the newcomers from Eastern and Southern Europe, Asia, Latin America and the Caribbean, most of whom were not English-speaking, not Protestant, and not at all familiar with the values and way of life of Americans.

One way of interpreting these statistics of immigration and race is to say that two out of five American residents were in a position of political or social disadvantage as a result of their ethnic or racial background. Who enjoyed which rights and privileges depended on a number of factors, especially skin color, citizenship, religion, and ethnicity.

Whether one was a man or a woman also mattered enormously. Before 1920 women lacked complete voting rights. This limitation circumscribed not only their citizenship but also the political power of the ethnic groups to which many of them belonged. In addition, immigrant women and black migrant women carried special burdens. The prejudicially low wages received by black men obligated their wives to work outside the home, which black women did in much higher proportions than white women. Most immigrant men came to America ahead of their families, and this created serious problems of desertion and marital estrangement. Husbands spent months and sometimes years adapting to America before the arrival of their wives, who suddenly seemed foreign to them. Japanese women crossed the Pacific as "picture brides," often to discover that their new husbands were much older than they expected.

All immigrants had to deal with the greater freedom enjoyed by women in America. Italians, for example, found this to be a nerve-racking challenge to their traditional way of life, which enshrined women in the home. On the other hand, Irish women and Eastern European Jewish women were accustomed to greater independence and thus adapted more easily to the ideal of modern womanhood. Because Jews and Irish Catholics came to America with the intention of settling down, unlike most immigrants who initially planned on repatriating, the women in these groups immediately played an important role as Americanizing agents. It was their responsibility to set up new homes as quickly as possible, which meant incorporating American goods and styles even as they maintained ethnic customs.

It is important to remember that in the families of all immigrants and black migrants, women faced the unique pressure of having to buttress husbands who were challenged by the rigors of work in a strange industrial world and by the loss of patriarchal authority over their Americanizing children. As mothers they were expected to transmit the culture of their native regions, but they also had to adapt home life to meet American standards (or Northern ones, for Southern blacks). Women living on Indian reservations west of the Mississippi, the domain of the once "Wild West," faced a unique type of culture shock, because their husbands and fathers were often traumatized by the loss of the physical mobility and independence they had formerly enjoyed.

In the years 1901–1929, ethnic minorities entered into American culture and politics more conspicuously than ever before. Given the universality of ethnic prejudice, it was probably inevitable that the emergence of such a wide variety of peoples provoked antagonisms. Southern whites tried to subordinate blacks with comprehensive laws of racial segregation and rituals of intimidation. Northern whites kept blacks at a distance with restrictive housing arrangements and by limiting their ability to advance in the workplace. Natives tried to control the number of newcomers by lobbying for federal laws to restrict immigration. Christians objected to the increase of Jews, Protestants to the increase of Catholics. Immigrants competed with one another, as well as with native whites and blacks, for control of jobs and neighborhoods. Despite these formidable antagonisms and tensions, "ethnic Americans" in this era established the cultural, political, and intellectual foundation for a cosmopolitan pluralist nation.

THE STRENGTH OF THE AMERICAN ECONOMY

Sandwiched neatly between the depression of the 1890s and the Great Depression of the 1930s, the 1901–1929 period was prosperous, except for short recessions in 1907–1908, 1913–1914 and 1921–1922. Prosperity attracted immigrants and also offered new opportunities to migrating groups within the nation's borders, such as the hundreds of thousands of Southern blacks who steadily moved north. Real wages of urban laborers remained much higher than in other countries, and much higher in the North and West than in the American South. By crossing the border into the United States, Mexicans could earn ten times what they received for field work at home. The leap in wages was comparable for immigrants from other lands. Letters from America back to the Old Country typically boasted of the finery enjoyed in the New World, and periodic visits from well-dressed emigrants proved to be a powerful advertisement of American wealth to those who had not yet come to "the Golden Land." "All of Ayn Arab rushed to America," a Syrian immigrant recalled, "It was like a gold rush."

In the hands of immigrants, American wealth had enormous impact on the home countries. Whether they intended to repatriate or settle in the United States, newcomers mailed millions of dollars a year to relatives back home. The comparative wealth of Americans turned immigrant communities into treasuries for humanitarian and political aid abroad. Immigrant leaders stressed the monetary obligations of the Americanized to their poorer and politically oppressed countrymen in the Old World. Furthermore, they emphasized the basic compatibility between loyalty to America and loyalty to the homeland. In the words of Ignace Paderewski, who personified the Polish national movement in America during World War I: "The Poles in America do not need any Americanization. . . . Be therefore the best Americans, but also help the Polish community." In 1912, after the outbreak of war between Turkey and Greece, hundreds of Greeks paraded in Los Angeles with Greek and American flags and with placards praising both American and Greek democracy: "Hail Sweet Land of Liberty." Greek immigrants not only contributed money for the war in the Balkans but tens of thousands left to fight, and then returned to the United States, believing that America, too, preserved the republican legacy of ancient Greece. The Irish and the Jews, who adjusted to American life fairly quickly, similarly equated Irish and Jewish nationalism with American ideals of freedom. Without the funds and encouragement of Irish and Jewish Americans, the struggles for an independent Ireland and a Jewish state in Palestine would have been far more difficult.

ECONOMIC AND POLITICAL CAUSES
OF IMMIGRATION AND BLACK MIGRATION

In addition to the attractiveness of the American economy, poor conditions abroad stimulated people to leave their homelands. Since the 1840s population explosions throughout Europe had given rise to a steady stream of emigrants, and overcrowding got worse as country folk with dwindling chances to live by the land moved to cities in search of a living as industrial laborers. Some kept to farm work by becoming seasonal migrants, crossing borders both within Europe and across the Atlantic in the off-season and returning to their native lands when planting time came again. Beyond the demographic problems that afflicted Europe, political oppression and chaos caused millions to seek a better fate elsewhere. The anti-Semitism of Tsarist Russia produced an exodus of more than 2 million Jews, most of whom came to the United States. Millions of Poles, Lithuanians, and other East Europeans also fled the Tsarist regime that had absorbed their countries in the eighteenth and nineteenth centuries. The Bolshevik Revolution of 1917 ended Tsarist oppression, and World War I reestablished the sovereignty of Poland and the Baltic states, but the Bolsheviks and the war created another set of human problems that hundreds of thousands sought to solve by coming to America in the early 1920s. Squirming under British rule, the Irish continued to emigrate in large numbers until they achieved a measure of sovereignty in 1921 with the creation of an independent state in southern Ireland. Mexicans suffered from the political chaos of their own government after the Revolution of 1910, which sparked an unprecedented flight north of the border into the American Southwest and California.

Within the boundaries of the United States, the Southern black population suffered afflictions that paralleled those of the Jews and the Irish abroad. Throughout this period, but especially after 1915, when war production created a great demand for labor in Northern factories, several hundred thousand black Americans fled the South hoping, very much as immigrants hoped, to find a "promised land" of new opportunities.

RACE AND THE LAW: DEGREES OF FREEDOM

The most important and disturbing legal development in the United States during this period was racial segregation. Between 1890 and 1914 every Southern state established laws that prohibited Negroes from attending the same schools; sitting in the same seats on trains, street-cars, and buses; and enjoying the same public services (from theaters to water fountains) as their white neighbors. This system of racial segregation, nicknamed "Jim Crow," created a degrading caste system. Laws determined who was "white" and who was "colored" based on bizarre ratios of white to black "blood" (often one thirty-second, meaning that one Negro great-great-grandparent marked a person as "black"). These dangerously absurd legal conceptions of race anticipated the notorious anti-Jewish laws of Nazi Germany.

Their purpose was somewhat different, however. Whereas Nazi law aimed at removing Jews from German society, American segregation law aimed at fixing Negroes in an inferior position as servants to whites. Jim Crow reminded Southerners every day in every social situation that "white" people were more moral, more refined, and more intelligent than "black" people. Black Americans understood the absurdity of this social system, but they could not protest for two reasons: terrorism and injustice. To violate the rules of racial deference (e.g., failing to step off the sidewalk when a white person approached, or looking defiantly at a white person) would invite swift punishment and possibly murder by an armed mob of angry whites, who usually attacked Negroes at night, burning their homes and assaulting and sometimes murdering men, women, and children. Second, Southern juries included only whites, which corrupted the entire justice system. Juries rarely convicted whites on the testimony of blacks, even in cases of cold-blooded murder. How was it possible for states like South Carolina, Georgia, Alabama, and Mississippi, with large black populations, to implement such a system? By eliminating the black vote. In this period, states passed laws with peculiar clauses designed to disqualify black voters.

RACE AND HEALTH:
LIFE EXPECTANCY AND INFANT MORTALITY

The rural South was the poorest region in the country, and racial discrimination made southern blacks poorer yet. At the turn of the century life expectancy at birth was 48 for white males and 51 for white females, compared with 32 for black males and 35 for black females. A white male who, in 1900, had already survived to age 20 could expect on average to reach 62, and a white female, 64; the corresponding figures for black men and women were 55 and 57. Life expectancy improved significantly for all Americans in the next three decades, but the racial gap persisted, with whites living about 10–12 years longer than blacks. White men and women born around 1930 could expect on average to live to 59 and 63; black men and women, to 48 and 50. Whites who reached the age of 20 by 1930 would live on average to the ages of 66 (men) and 69 (women); the corresponding figures for blacks were 56 and 57. Probably because so many black Americans moved North after 1915, their rate of infant mortality dropped more quickly than that of whites. Still, it remained 60 percent higher. By 1930 around sixty of every one thousand white infants died at birth, compared with one hundred of every one thousand babies classified as nonwhite.

CITIZENSHIP AND NATURALIZATION

Just as artificial but legalized distinctions of race framed the lives of black Americans, so did they affect aliens. Laws of American citizenship remained complicated and discriminatory throughout the 1901–1929 period. Two provisions were clear: (1) the Fourteenth Amendment to the Constitution (1868) guaranteed citizenship to everyone born in the United States (with the exception of certain Native Americans affiliated with tribes, to be discussed later), (2) after 1870 federal law made whites and people of African descent eligible for citizenship.

This legal code stigmatized Asians, making them the only group ineligible for citizenship until Congress reformed U.S. naturalization law in the 1940s and 1950s. (Local courts did naturalize a few thousand Asians despite the federal ban.) The odd stigma attached to Asians was highlighted by the 1923 Supreme Court decision in *Thind v. United States*, in which the plaintiff was a high-caste Hindu from northernmost India, and thus of Aryan descent. Frankly denying the biological and cultural subtleties of race, the Court argued that *white* meant whatever white people thought it meant: "the words of familiar speech, which were used by the original framers of the law, were intended to include only the type of man whom they knew as white."

Although Latin Americans were often viewed as nonwhite, the federal government granted them eligibility for citizenship. Immigrants from Western Asia, most of them Arabs and Jews from Syria and Palestine, or Armenians, generally attained citizenship. For a brief period (roughly 1910–1915) several contradictory rulings confused their situation, but the courts ended up classifying them as members of "the Semitic branch of the Caucasian race" and therefore eligible to become naturalized citizens.

As important as citizenship was for full civil and political equality, many immigrants disregarded or delayed the process of naturalization. With the conspicuous exception of the Jews and Irish, for whom America was a final haven from religious persecution, most newcomers intended to return to their native lands. Therefore, they initially had no intention of becoming U.S. citizens. By 1930 roughly 60 percent of white immigrants were naturalized citizens. According to the U.S. Census from that year, one of every two Italians, and one of every two Poles remained an alien. Mexicans had an extremely low rate of naturalization; in 1930 only 24 percent (about one in four) were citizens. Immigrants from the Balkans and Iberia, who had high rates of repatriation, also balked at citizenship. World War I accelerated the rate of naturalization, as immigrants felt tremendous pressure to show their loyalty to the nation and to conform to the credo of *100 percent Americanism* that dominated the wartime and postwar era. In the period 1907–1911, immigrants filed an average of 41,000 petitions for naturalization per year, whereas in the 1920s the annual average climbed to 188,430! The upsurge in citizenship after World War I meant millions of new voters who, as we shall see, changed the course of American politics.

The several hundred thousand members of the Native American tribes, the American Indians, endured a very complex and costly ordeal of citizenship. In the period between 1887 and 1934, federal Indian policy aimed to break up tribal lands and turn Indians into individualist citizen-farmers by assigning a standard homesteader's plot of land (160 acres) and full citizenship to the head of each household. This policy had dubious results. The tribes that cooperated with the government's plan lost 60 million of their 138 million acres of land to Congress (this was the "surplus" left over after the distribution of family allotments). Those Indians who became citizens by federal law sometimes found that individual states did not grant them voting rights, and tribes that voted against the individual-allotment plan stagnated on poverty-stricken reservations with virtually no legal rights. In 1924 Congress granted citizenship to all Indians born in the United States, but, like African Americans, they remained in many respects second-class citizens.

IMMIGRATION RESTRICTION

The most dramatic break in the history of American immigration occurred in the 1920s. After the Chinese Exclusion Act of 1882, Congress had begun to restrict and monitor immigrants, but after 1900 a campaign developed to close the country's borders to a whole range of nationalities. Anti-Asian sentiment in California, born out of a desire to ban Chinese laborers, spread virulently to the Japanese. In 1907–1908 public pressure led President Roosevelt and the State Department to conclude the Gentleman's Agreement with Japan, whereby Japan agreed to limit the emigration of its workers, especially to the American mainland. (Despite the new limits, well over one hundred thousand Japanese immigrants arrived in the next twenty years, many settling in Hawai'i.) Not satisfied with the sizable reduction of Japanese immigrants, Californians lobbied fiercely until the state government in Sacramento—in 1913 and again in 1920—produced laws prohibiting aliens from purchasing and leasing land. Confronted with an immigrant group, the Japanese, that admirably fulfilled the American work ethic and succeeded as farmers, Americans struck a devil's bargain. Logically, they should have lobbied for citizenship for these newcomers who helped build the rural economy of California. Instead they sought the opposite: total exclusion of the Japanese and all Asians. This movement in California merged with a national campaign directed against the great multitude of poor immigrants—most of them Catholic and Jewish—from Italy, Poland, Russia, Rumania, and Austria-Hungary. In 1921 and 1924 the restrictionists in Congress passed laws that drastically reduced the annual quotas of these targeted European groups and banned further immigration from Asia. Fueled by a nativist desire to restore America's "racial balance" and prevent the dilution of the so-called Nordic elements, these laws ended the national custom of welcoming European immigrants.

The two large immigrant groups not affected by the new law were the Canadians and the Mexicans, who continued to augment the American Catholic population. In the 1920s nearly a million Canadians, around a third of whom were French-speaking Catholics, and nearly five hundred thousand Mexicans emigrated to the Northeastern and Southwestern regions of the United States.

ETHNIC SELF-DEFENSE

In response to discriminatory laws and acts, a number of ethnic minorities created legal defense organizations that became a vital part of the American civil rights tradition. The first important associations were the American Jewish Committee (1906), the National Association for the Advancement of Colored People (NAACP, 1909–1910), and the Anti-Defamation League (1913). A number of well-established Jewish leaders formed the American Jewish Committee after an awful wave of anti-Jewish massacres in Tsarist Russia. The Committee organized public rallies and petitioned the U.S. government to make formal diplomatic protests against Russia's anti-Semitic policies. The Jewish fraternal organization B'nai B'rith formed the Anti-Defamation League (ADL) during the Leo Frank affair, in which a Jew was unfairly convicted of murder and later lynched by a bigoted mob in Marietta, Georgia. The ADL aimed to expose and combat racial and religious prejudice in America.

African Americans supported the National Association for the Advancement of Colored People, a biracial organization set up to protest and attack the Jim Crow system. The NAACP published a dynamic monthly, The Crisis, under the editorship of W. E. B. Du Bois. An impressive thinker and writer, Du Bois used this publication to lambaste lynching, segregation, and the hypocrisy of such customs within an allegedly free society. In addition to vocalizing the deep discontents of African Americans, the NAACP successfully attacked discriminatory laws in the courts. Participating in Supreme Court cases of the 1910s and 1920s, it helped overturn the use of "grandfather clauses" that disfranchised black voters in the South (Guinn v. United States, 1915), defeated a law enforcing racial segregation in the Louisville housing market (Buchanan v. Warley, 1917), and secured federal intervention against mob-dominated state trials (Moore v. Dempsey, 1923). The timeliness of the NAACP was proved by the fact that more than four hundred branches of the organization appeared in the first decade of its existence.

Other organizations followed these forerunners. In 1914, the Society of Syrian National Defense organized in Charleston, South Carolina, in response to a court's denial of citizenship to a Syrian immigrant. Its protest produced a successful legal appeal (*Dow v. United States*), authorizing citizenship for Arabs from Western Asia. In the 1920s Mexican Americans, their numbers enlarged by hundreds of thousand of immigrants and their confidence boosted by participation in the war effort, formed a number of political associations that merged into LULAC, the League of United Latin American Citizens (1929). Like other such organizations, LULAC maintained two mutually supportive goals: 1) the integration of Mexicans into American society through citizenship and voting, and 2) the defense of both the dignity and legal rights of Mexican Americans through protest of degrading stereotypes and discrimination in the use of public services and in the selection of juries. The 1920s also witnessed the first effective defense against the government's disreputable Indian policy. In 1923 the American Indian Defense Association, organized by a (non-Indian) reformer, John Collier, rallied enough humanitarian interest to stop the reckless exploitation of Indian lands and promote a new, more humane policy in the 1930s.

THE RISE OF ETHNIC COMMUNITIES AND "GHETTOS"

The new ethnic self-defense organizations were but one of many products of the ethnic communities that sprang up across America. Immigrants and black migrants from the South clustered in distinct regions of the country and neighborhoods of major cities. In the 1901–1929 period, more than 80 percent of America's foreign-born lived in the states of the Northeast and Midwest. Nearly three-fourths of the Irish immigrants concentrated in New England and the Middle Atlantic states. New England also housed roughly two-thirds of the French Canadians. More than one-third of the Germans settled in the eastern part of the Midwest (Ohio, Indiana, Illinois, and Missouri), and almost half of the Norwegians resided in the western part (Minnesota, Wisconsin, Iowa, and the Dakotas). The vast majority of the Jews concentrated in the middle Atlantic region and especially in New York City, where they comprised 28 percent of the population by 1915. Most Italians also gravitated to the New York-New Jersey-Pennsylvania area, and a third of them settled in the state of New York. Pennsylvania, Ohio, and Illinois became home to a large percentage of Polish and Slavic newcomers. Asians and Mexicans congregated in the West. Nearly half of the Chinese and more than three-fourths of the Japanese immigrants lived in California; nearly all Mexicans (88 percent) lived in Texas, New Mexico, Arizona, and California.

The new concentrations of immigrants altered the human geography of American cities. In 1910, 41 percent of the residents of New York City were foreign-born; in Chicago, 36 percent; Boston, 36 percent; Cleveland, 35 percent; Detroit, 34 percent; San Francisco, 34 percent; Providence, 34 percent; Newark, 32 percent; Seattle, 28 percent; Philadelphia, 25 percent. In the smaller Massachusetts city of Fall River, roughly four of every ten residents were French Canadians; in Milwaukee more than half of the city's population was of German ancestry. One of the most colorful demographic events of the early twentieth century was the appearance of ethnic neighborhoods in cities like these. The "Frenchvilles" or "Little Canadas" of Massachusetts, New Hampshire, Maine, and Rhode Island; the "Polonias" (Polish colonies) of Chicago and Buffalo; the "Little Italys" in cities throughout the Northeast; the Puerto Rican *colonias* of East and South Harlem and Brooklyn; the great Japantown of Los Angeles; and San Francisco's Chinatown stamped these places with a variety of languages, with the smells of ethnic markets and restaurants, and with the spectacle of public celebrations, honoring occasions such as the Chinese New Year and Catholic Saints Days. The Lower East Side of New York City, the densest urban neighborhood in the world, housed hundreds of thousands of Yiddish-speaking Jews; New York City was known as the New Jerusalem. The barrio of East Los Angeles had enough Mexican residents (more than ninety thousand in 1930) to rival cities in Mexico itself. On the upper part of Manhattan, Harlem emerged as the nation's most populous and distinctive Afro-American neighborhood. In the 1920s it became a kind of cultural capital, a gathering place for the rising stars of American jazz and blues, as well as the writers—Alain Locke, James Weldon Johnson, Langston Hughes, Zora Neale Hurston, to name a few—whose work earned the title "the Harlem Renaissance."

None of these areas were actually *ghettos*, a term that referred historically to parts of cities in Europe where Jews were literally locked in. Yet they harbored enough poverty and crime to seem like traps for neglected humanity. This was most true of black neighborhoods,

Chinatowns, and Japantowns, where racial prejudice prevented easy exit into surrounding neighborhoods. Despite the problems of inner-city ethnic neighborhoods, they usually nourished a rich cultural life, generating exciting fusions of ethnic and American music, theater, literature, and art.

RACE RIOTS

The convergence of different ethnic groups in American cities also produced serious conflicts between them. The teaching of native languages in schools, especially parochial schools, the nationality of priests and type of service in Catholic churches, and control over jobs, unions, and political positions all brought minorities into periodic power struggles. Immigrant memoirs are full of stories of "turf wars," in which gangs competed for control of the streets and youngsters ventured into "enemy" neighborhoods at their peril.

Without question, the most conspicuous and destructive form of conflict in the United States during this period was the "race riot." In addition to the gruesome practice of lynching, which ended the lives of more than one thousand black victims between 1900 and 1920, mob action against black Americans erupted frequently. Triggered by hysterical allegations or actual incidents of black-on-white crime, ugly crowds driven by deep fears of black power committed murders and burned buildings in Negro neighborhoods, In Statesboro, Georgia (1904), Springfield, Ohio (1904), Atlanta, Georgia (1906), Springfield, Illinois (1908), and East St. Louis, Illinois (1917), there were riots of varying severity, culminating in the "Red Summer" and Fall of 1919, when approximately twenty-five such outbreaks occurred. The worst such riot in American history took place in Chicago in July 1919. Sparked by the stoning of a black boy who had drifted into the "white" section of the beach on Lake Michigan, mobs of black and white men sprang up quickly and began a conflagration that lasted thirteen days. Fifteen whites and 23 blacks died in the conflict; 178 whites and 342 blacks sustained injuries. (Seventeen other murder victims were not racially identified.) Destruction of property left more than one thousand families, most of them black, homeless. Two years later Tulsa, Oklahoma, erupted, after an alleged assault upon a white woman by a black man. Nine whites and twenty-one blacks died, hundreds were injured and large tracts of the city were burned out and reduced to rubble.

The causes of these bloody events varied in each case. Sometimes, as in the Chicago riot, masses of blacks collided with white immigrants in labor battles in the city's huge meat-packing industry. Labor unions, which typically excluded or discriminated against black workers, appealed to the immigrants to stand as one against the "bosses," while black laborers often worked as strikebreakers, believing that big employers such as Armour and Swift would give them a better deal than the unions had to offer. Labor conflicts and racial antagonisms formed a volatile mixture, easily ignited by the summer heat of a crowded industrial city.

In the South, riots served less as an outlet for tension between competing ethnic groups and more as a means of maintaining a racial caste system. The Atlanta riot of 1906, the worst in the South prior to World War I, followed a campaign in the press against the rising aspirations of Negro residents. In one of the great works of American documentary journalism, *Following the Color Line* (1908), reporter Ray Stannard Baker traced the arc of tension in Atlanta, a city with a large black population that enjoyed rising levels of prosperity and education.

> On the afternoon of the riot the newspapers in flaming headlines chronicled four assaults by Negroes on white women. I had a personal investigation made of each of those cases. Two of them may have been attempts at assaults, but two palpably were nothing more than fright on the part of both the white woman and the Negro, As an instance, in one case an elderly woman, Mrs. Martha Holcombe, going to close her blinds in the evening, saw a Negro on the sidewalk. In a terrible fright she screamed. The news was telephoned to the police station, but before the officials could respond, Mrs. Holcombe telephoned them not to come out. And yet this was one of the "assaults" chronicled in letters five inches high in a newspaper extra.

Baker discovered a white community intent on separating themselves from blacks, and a black community that deeply resented the Jim Crow regulations being implemented against them. "The underman will not keep his place," Baker reported. "He is restless, ambitious, he wants civil, political, and industrial equality."

Baker suggested an interesting parallel between Southern hysteria about potential racial equality and Northern reactions against immigrants:

"Does democracy really include Negroes as well as white men? Does it include Russian Jews, Italians, Japanese? Does it include Rockefeller and the Slavonian street-sweeper?"

THE NATIVIST REACTION OF THE 1920S

These questions acquired special importance in the 1920s, when American nativism reached full tide. World War I precipitated an anti-German hysteria of surprising proportions. The nation's largest white ethnic group, German Americans, suffered severe persecution during 1917 and 1918, as their neighbors mobbed, harassed, and ridiculed them. A 1918 federal law required all states receiving federal funds to guarantee that English be the primary language of instruction in both public and private schools. Under intense pressure to show their loyalty, German Americans drastically curtailed their distinctive cultural practices. American fears of political subversion spread from Germans to radicals in 1919, when the federal government deported hundreds of foreign-born socialists and anarchists. The restrictive immigration quotas of 1921 and 1924 were part of a larger reaction against foreign "elements" that allegedly weakened the native stock of America.

There was a soft and a hard side to the national perspective on immigrants in the 1920s. The soft side came from Americans who were neither xenophobic nor nativist but wanted to see immigrants assimilate into the larger society as quickly as possible. During World War I, nearly one million immigrants of nearly fifty nationalities served in the American army. This mobilization combined with a massive patriotic campaign to encourage the foreign-born to put their native lands in the backs of their minds and cultivate an uncomplicated loyalty to America and its values. Since 1917, then, the country had been vigorously espousing an ideal of *unhyphenated Americanism.* However, the line between Americanism and chauvinism was never a clear one. On the other side of that line, the hard side of American public opinion included outright hostility toward ethnic minorities.

Revived in 1915, the Ku Klux Klan symbolized the ugly mood that waxed with the nation's isolationism and disillusionment after World War I. Unlike its predecessor of the 1860s, the new Klan combined anti-Negro racism with nativism and evangelical Protestantism. Branding Catholics and Jews as subversive foreign elements, terrorizing blacks who showed any signs of discontent with racial segregation, and punishing fellow white Protestants for adultery, gambling, drinking, and other licentious acts, the Ku Klux Klan enjoyed a brief period of social dominance in the early 1920s, especially in the Midwest and South. By the end of the decade scandal and internal conflicts weakened the Klan, state governments began to crack down on its vigilantism, and other Americans started to clash publicly with the white-robed bullies. In the summer of 1923, for example, a crowd of six thousand people, primarily Jews and Catholics, attacked and dispersed five hundred Klansmen who were meeting in the central New Jersey town of Perth Amboy. Despite the brevity of the Klan's terrorist reign, the notorious organization set an example of white supremacist militance for like-minded Americans in the decades after World War II.

The rough tactics of the Klan were complemented by the pseudoscientific racism of university professors and other members of the social elite. Relying on spurious theories of racial genetics, natural scientists, psychologists, and sociologists offered up evidence to support an idea that humankind broke down into several racially determined groups of varying intelligence. Nordics or Aryans, representing the Northern European, stood at the top of this hierarchy, Africans occupied the bottom tier, and everyone else fell somewhere in between. The founders and early advocates of intelligence testing, which became popular in the 1920s, subscribed to these genetic theories. Stanford psychologist Lewis Terman, who created the Stanford-Binet intelligence test; Harvard psychologist Robert Yerkes, who headed the U.S. Army's intelligence testing program during World War I; and Princeton psychologist Carl Brigham, author of the influential 1923 book *A Study of American Intelligence*, all added intellectual fuel to a nativist campaign whose most sensational books carried titles such as *The Passing of the Great Race* and *The Rising Tide of Color*. Elitist xenophobia hit Jews with particular force because Jews were entering prestigious colleges and universities in disproportionate numbers. To stem this academic tide, the nation's elite schools instituted quotas to minimize the number of Jewish students who were admitted. In some cases new psychological tests were used to support the claim that Jewish students were too intellectually intense and insufficiently balanced to mix in with the Ivy League set.

Although academic racism enjoyed a triumph in the passage of the highly restrictive immigration act of 1924, it faded away surprisingly quickly in the late 1920s and 1930s as a result of a powerful shift in American social science. Two of the most significant figures for that shift were professors at Columbia University: the philosopher John Dewey and the anthropologist Franz Boas. The most influential American philosopher of the era, the Vermont-born Dewey delighted in the excitement and ethnic diversity of New York City. His distinctive, future-oriented philosophy of *pragmatism* made no room for old-fashioned views of racial heredity; instead it emphasized the idea that all human beings were capable of dynamic growth and *self-realization*. The anthropologist Franz Boas attacked racist theories directly. More than any other scholar, Boas changed the way Americans thought about race by replacing it with the concept of *culture*. A German Jew who immigrated to the United States in the 1880s, Boas assaulted the myth of a "pure" European or American race and the corollary claim that intermixture with immigrants and blacks would cause some sort of national degeneration. Although he had been producing studies on the subject since the early years of the century, Boas and an impressive group of scholars who had been his students finally achieved a position of intellectual dominance in the late 1920s and 1930s. Their research suggested that ethnic traits (including intelligence as measured by tests) were determined primarily by environmental factors and not by collective genetic differences. By the late 1930s *culture* was well on its way to replacing *race* as the primary way of describing ethnic differences.

Nevertheless, in day-to-day life, prejudices remained strong enough to make the 1920s a decade of egregious stereotypes of Jews and Italians. As a result of notorious gangsters like Al Capone and headlines about crime families in American cities, Italians acquired the reputation of being criminals by nature. In the summer of 1920 mobs brutally attacked Italians in the southern Illinois town of West Frankfurt, on the pretext of crimes attributed to a Sicilian criminal association. The famous murder case of Nicola Sacco and Bartolomeo Vanzetti, two Italian anarchists who were convicted in 1921 and executed over mass protests in 1927, mixed the associations of Italian criminality and foreign radicalism and so made a fair trial nearly impossible. In the early 1920s the famous automaker Henry Ford shocked the country by publishing a series of anti-Semitic articles on "The International Jew" in his newspaper *The Dearborn Independent*. Reflecting both age-old prejudices and newer stereotypes of Jews as rootless revolutionaries, Ford disseminated the *Protocols of the Elders of Zion,* a notorious piece of Russian propaganda claiming that a Jewish conspiracy was busily achieving world-wide domination. On a more prosaic level, Jews had to deal with the fact that many white-collar jobs were closed to them—job adver-tisements frequently stipulated that applicants be Christian.

One of the most interesting responses to the intolerance of the 1920s was that of black nationalist Marcus Garvey, a Jamaican immigrant who settled in Harlem. Deeply moved by the plight of black people in Africa, Europe, and the Americas, Garvey dedicated himself to the cause of a grand return to Africa. There his people, like the Zionists who were settling in Palestine, would establish their own government and possess the dignity that went along with political independence. Garvey was a charismatic leader who appealed like no other to the masses of African Americans in northern cities. His Universal Negro Improvement Association included elaborate ranks, rituals, and regalia that generated feelings of pride among its thousands of members. With its belief in black superiority and racial separation, and its anti-Semitic and nativist undertones, Garvey's nationalism reflected some of the decadence of America's racial order. His Black Star Line, an ambitious shipping com-pany that was designed to prove both that blacks could successfully operate their own businesses and that they would one day return to Africa, ultimately failed because of Garvey's dubious business practices, for which he was arrested and deported. A model for later expressions of black nationalism, Marcus Garvey tapped a deep current in the psyche of African Americans. Though he misjudged the desire of people to return to Africa, Garvey ingeniously stimulated the collective pride that helped sustain life in America.

A NEW ETHNIC POLITICS

In light of the nativism of the 1920s, the unprecedented presidential candidacy of a Catholic, New York governor Al Smith, showed that pol-itics would be a primary means of dealing with the insecurity felt by immigrants and their children. In that election many immigrants sup-ported Smith (who wanted to repeal the Nineteenth Amendment) partly to oppose the Prohibitionists, who often linked immigrants with drunkenness and the corruption of American values.

The "new ethnicity" of American politics in this period had two primary elements, one symbolic and the other institutional. Symboli-cally, the rise of ethnic leaders to public importance and the celebration of ethnic holidays and occasions—such as the 1910 unveil-ing in Washington, D.C., of statues of Thaddeus Kosciusko and Casimir

Pulaski, Polish heroes who served in the American Revolution—gave minorities a feeling of pride and acceptance. Institutionally, the influx of minorities into the Democratic Party radically altered the political system.

Another institutional component that must be mentioned, at least in passing, was the disproportionate involvement of immigrants in radical political parties and movements. Many ethnic mutual-aid societies were socialist in spirit, as was the nation's largest foreign-language newspaper, the Yiddish *Forverts* (Forward). Many prominent socialists and anarchists were immigrants (especially German, Jewish, and Italian), and after World War I the two most important black leaders, aside from Garvey, were both socialists—W. E. B. Du Bois and A. Philip Randolph, who unionized Negro railway employees in the Brotherhood of Sleeping Car Porters. In the 1920s roughly 80 percent of the members of the American Communist Party were Jews and other East Europeans and Finns.

The new century started with a rush of political symbolism during the presidency of Theodore Roosevelt (1901–1909). One month after taking office, upon the assassination of William McKinley by a foreign-born anarchist, Roosevelt invited Booker T. Washington to luncheon at the White House, the first such invitation ever extended to a black American. Grasping the symbolic implications of this event, Southern racists exploded in anger over what they considered the president's irresponsible approval of "social equality" between the races. Roosevelt's political prudence led him to avoid repeating this kind of public act, and he later alienated many black Americans when he rashly dismissed several companies of Negro soldiers after the Brownsville (Texas) riot of 1906. But he did rely on Booker T. Washington as a key broker of political appointments in the South. Furthermore, even though he displayed a prideful bias toward the Anglo-American heritage, Roosevelt believed that individuals should be judged according to merit rather than race or religion. Cognizant of the political symbolism of the act, he appointed the first Jewish and Catholic cabinet members in the nation's history. Unlike most Americans at the time, Roosevelt believed that Asians should not be excluded from citizenship (a belief he expressed privately). He condemned the ignorant prejudice of those who abused Asian Americans, and he had a much more respectful attitude toward the Japanese than most Americans did, even though he felt that anti-Japanese prejudice was so strong as to make it necessary to limit immigration from Japan. Well traveled, internationally minded, and highly inquisitive, Roosevelt was the first cosmopolitan president of the modern era. In spite of his brusque patriotism and blunt roughrider persona, he inaugurated a new approach to ethnic minorities. He wanted to Americanize them as quickly as possible, but he recognized that they belonged to the body politic.

Of the presidents who came after Roosevelt in this period (Taft, Wilson, Harding, Coolidge, and Hoover), only Woodrow Wilson (1913–1920) had an important record vis-à-vis ethnic minorities, but one that was more ambiguous than Roosevelt's. The first Southerner to occupy the White House since the Civil War, Wilson originally displayed both nativist (anti-immigrant) and racist attitudes. In respect to race relations, he was culpable for allowing segregation into the federal government for the first time, in the departments of the Post Office and the Treasury, both of which were headed by Southern compatriots of his. In addition to importing the Southern caste system into the nation's capital, he accepted the invitation of Thomas Dixon, author of the viciously racist novel *The Clansman,* on which the famous film "Birth of a Nation" was based, to screen the movie in the White House. For Jews, however, the Wilson administration brought good tidings. Wilson succeeded in placing the eminent attorney Louis Brandeis on the Supreme Court, despite the opposition of anti-Semites both on and off the Court, and he supported the rising Zionist movement. Jews also appreciated Wilson's introduction of the Minorities Treaties at the Paris Peace Conference of 1919; these were designed to protect Europe's ethnic minorities from state-sponsored persecution. The Irish, however, rejected Wilson for his pro-British position; they helped thwart his campaign for the League of Nations and the Democratic Party's bid for the presidency in 1920. In sum, race, religion, and ethnicity played an important symbolic and practical role in national politics after 1900.

Accordingly, minorities began to deploy political strategies to affect both the policies and the symbolism that emanated from their government. The most important tactic was "getting out the vote" for candidates who supported various ethnic causes, especially in heavily immigrant cities such as New York, Chicago, Detroit, Cleveland, Boston, Philadelphia, Milwaukee, Buffalo, Pittsburgh, Baltimore, and Providence. Once sufficient numbers of immigrants became citizens and voters, political campaigns in American cities responded like barometers. St. Patrick's Day had long been an occasion for pro-Irish politicking, and in the early 1900s Italians lobbied successfully for Columbus Day. In these and other more local celebrations of ethnic heritage, politicians worked overtime amid the parades, extolling the virtues and achievements of immigrant Americans and suggesting how they might vote on the issues of the day.

Irish Americans were especially driven, as one of their leading historians explains, by an "addiction to and love of politics." By the 1890s they pioneered a distinctive style of urban politics, based on familiarity with the ethnic customs of city residents. Both takers of graft and givers of charity, ward politicians such as Big Tim Sullivan in New York City and Bathhouse John Coughlin of Chicago knew a smattering of foreign phrases, attended religious ceremonies different from their own, and gave their constituents a feeling of being protected and cared for in an impersonal and intimidating urban world. The diary of one day in the life of an Irish American boss, George Washington Plunkitt, included the following activities:

> 2 A.M. *Wakened by a boy with message from bartender to bail him out of jail.* . . . 6 A.M. Fire engines, up and off to the scene to see my election district captains tending the burnt-out tenants. Got names for new homes. 8:30 to police court. Six drunken constituents on hand. Got four released by a timely word to the judge. Paid the other's [sic] fines. 11 to 3 P.M. *Found jobs for four constituents.* 3 P.M. an Italian funeral, sat conspicuously up front. 4 P.M. *A Jewish funeral—up front again, in the synagogue.* . . . 8 P.M. Church fair. Bought ice cream for the girls; took fathers for a little something around the corner. . . . 10:30 a Jewish wedding. Had sent handsome present to bride. Midnight—to bed.

Generations of city politicians followed the Irish model, which combined an authoritarian and a cosmopolitan approach to the political order; inclusiveness, not exclusiveness, spelled victory at the polls.

To be sure, Irish domination of city politics generated conflicts with other ethnic groups, a striking example of which was the Italian challenge to Chicago potentate John Powers in the 1921 election for alderman. Three months after the election ended with a victory for Boss Powers, his opponent, Anthony D'Andrea, an alleged crime boss, was killed by a shotgun blast. We should also note the rise of a very different kind of politician from immigrant America, personified by Fiorello

La Guardia, whose father was Italian and whose mother was Jewish. A reformer who rebelled against machine politics and championed the underprivileged (who were exploited by the same ward politicians who helped them), La Guardia enjoyed one of the most brilliant careers in the history of American urban politics, serving with remarkable effect as Congressman (1917–1919, 1923–1933), President of the Board of Aldermen (1919–1921) and Mayor of New York City (1933–1945).

Like immigrants, black Americans entered a new world of urban politics after the Great Migration from the South and produced their own bosses and reformers. But they faced unique conditions as well. In cities and states with significant black populations, political parties often pandered to the "whiteness" of European immigrants. For example, in Baltimore in 1905 and 1909, politicians tried unsuccessfully to pass a law that would disfranchise Maryland's Negro residents. They lobbied for the immigrant vote by emphasizing the racial differences between immigrants and Negroes. The city's foreign-born population appeared to accept this racial categorization whether or not they voted for the legislation. The vast majority of newcomers did not live in the South and did not usually vote on such explicitly racist proposals. But even in the North and West, European immigrants quickly recognized that they had moved into a society divided along a color line. When that line appeared in elections they saw little benefit in siding with blacks and substantial rewards in identifying with the white majority.

Black Americans joined in the new urban politics despite the ever-present problem of racism, which made political power all the more vital to their future. While immigrants steadily gained political strength in the years before World War I, black residents of Northern cities had to deal with a *decline* in their position. As long as they had been a small percentage of a city's population, black Americans in the Northern states, despite racial prejudice, often lived in integrated neighborhoods and participated in municipal politics and society. Yet once their numbers swelled with thousands of Southern migrants, they faced two new realities: residential ghettos and more frequent discrimination in public places. In response to these unfortunate realities, black urban leaders developed a social and political philosophy of black self-sufficiency by promoting black businesses and politicians, so that the ghettoized population might gain economic and political power. Politicians built "little black Tammany Halls" that were part of a city's larger political machine but relied on the black vote and handled the problems of the black community. No different from their counterparts in immigrant neigh-borhoods, these machines benefited from the naiveté of poor, unedu-cated constituents and received a substantial amount of money from saloons, prostitution, and gambling rackets, all of which demoralized hard-working residents of the inner city. And yet, despite these blotchy trademarks of city politics, black Americans found their first nucleus of political power in the metropoles of the North. In Cleveland, for exam-ple, the black population increased from nine thousand to thirty-five thousand between 1910 and 1920 (an increase of nearly 300 percent compared to a 38 percent increase of the white population). Cleveland had its classic black "boss," a man named Thomas Fleming, but it also saw a new kind of political figure emerge in the late 1920s. As a result of dissatisfaction with the status quo in the black community, voters elected two new leaders, E. J. Gregg and Clayborne George, to join Fleming on the Cleveland City Council. Gregg and George refused to cozy up to a political party as Fleming had done with the Republicans. Instead, they held out until both political parties showed "a new respect for the Negro vote" by delivering valuable political appointments to black Clevelanders. On this political foundation Cleveland would elect the first black mayor of a major American city several decades later.

The new northern black electorate also made its presence felt in national politics during the 1920s. Traditionally partisans of the "party of Lincoln," Negro voters began to break ranks with the Republicans in 1924, when both the Democratic and the Progressive Party candidates for the presidency declared that race should not be a factor in American governance. The trend continued in 1928 when the Republican Party, in an effort to secure the Southern vote, refused to seat Negro delegates at their national convention. By 1932 the black vote swung to the Democratic Party and was not disappointed, as the Roosevelt adminis-tration gave a new prominence and dignity to African American leaders.

Nineteen twenty-eight was a turning point for another reason, too. For the first time since 1901 a Negro, Oscar de Priest of Chicago, won election to Congress. Like so many black Americans in this era, de Priest started life in the South (Alabama) and moved North. He arrived in Chicago in 1899 and instantly took to politics. Working his way up the Republican hierarchy, he became the first black alderman in Chicago. When he was sent to Washington as Representative of the First Illinois Congressional District, he leaped another hurdle, for no

Negro from a Northern state had ever sat in the U.S. Congress. Echoing what happened over the Booker T. Washington invitation to the White House in 1901, white Southerners flew into a rage when Mr. and Mrs. De Priest attended a tea for the families of Congressmen. (In Birmingham, Alabama, the Ku Klux Klan burned him in effigy.) On the other hand, an Afro-American newspaper spoke for millions when it said De Priest's election gave his people "new hope, new courage, and new inspiration."

In the presidential campaign of 1928, racial and ethno-religious issues loomed larger than at any time since the Civil War. The Democratic Party's unprecedented nomination of a Catholic, Al Smith of New York City, evoked strong anti-Catholic prejudices. Yet paradoxically, the large contingent of southern Protestants who disliked Smith's Irish Catholicism had to abandon the one political party—the Democrats— that fought for white supremacy in the South. In New York State, where Smith was governor, he had been building a coalition of immigrant and black supporters, and this new political mix would quickly become the national norm of a new, more urban Democratic Party. In 1900 the Democratic Party spoke for rural people, especially in the South. Yet throughout the 1920s, when millions of foreigners emerged as naturalized voters, the party appealed strongly to them. And as we have seen, urban black voters also began to leave the Republicans. By the election of 1932 the new coalition of urbanized ethnic minorities had remade the Northern wing of the Democratic Party in their own image. For the remainder of the century the Republicans lost the cosmopolitan flavor that Theodore Roosevelt had given them. His distant cousin Franklin, the Democratic nominee for president in 1932, inherited that legacy.

BEGINNINGS OF A COSMOPOLITAN CULTURE

If ethnic minorities reoriented politics in this period, they transformed culture. Since the rise of vaudeville in the 1870s, American popular entertainment offered an excellent medium for immigrant and ethnic talent. Many of the icons of popular culture were foreign-born or had clear ethnic roots. Prominent examples include movie stars and sex symbols Rudolph Valentino (Italian) and Mary Pickford (Canadian), magician Harry Houdini (Jewish), comedians Charlie Chaplin (English) and the Marx Brothers (Jewish), singer Al Jolson (Jewish), musician and singer Louis Armstrong (African American) and popular wit Will Rogers (Cherokee American).

American music developed from the dynamic interplay of native and immigrant and white and black talent. Some of this interplay grew out of pathetically racialized styles such as black minstrelsy, which thrived on white performers wearing blackface makeup ("blacking up"), grossly mimicking Negro servile gestures, and acting out with an emotionalism that was considered inappropriate in normal life. Around the turn of the century, however, the emotional excitement and spontaneity associated with African American music and dance started to appear in revolutionary new forms that reshaped Western music.

The blues-and-jazz revolution dates to the years before World War I. Although music styles rarely result from the genius of a single person, historians have found it convenient to recognize W. C. (William Christopher) Handy as the "father of the blues," because he was the first to publish and promote the music. In 1909, Handy wrote "Memphis Blues" as a campaign song for a mayoral candidate. The tune caught on like wildfire among whites and blacks, making Handy's band the top band in that city. In 1912 Handy wrote the classic "St. Louis Blues." A few years later the Alabama-born musician moved to New York City, where he became the primary popularizer of the blues and an influential creator of other popular songs. Handy's business partner, Harry Pace, went on his own to start the first Afro-American recording company; his first huge success came with the 1921 recordings of "Down Home Blues" and "Oh, Daddy" by Ethel Waters, who rose to stardom on Broadway and in Hollywood. As Handy's and Pace's careers illustrate, the rising music industry created an important new avenue of financial and artistic success for African Americans.

Further illustration may be found in the story of the discovery of Louis Armstrong in the 1920s. Fletcher Henderson, an accomplished musician who worked as an arranger for Harry Pace's record company, heard Armstrong play in New Orleans. Struck by the young trumpet player's virtuosity and stage presence, Henderson brought Armstrong to New York City to join his band at New York City's most prestigious dance hall, the Roseland Ballroom. That moment marked a turning point in the history of American music, for Armstrong turned out to be a musical pioneer, who popularized the solo and many of the nuances of singing and playing that defined the new music of jazz. Although a big-band music called *jazz* appeared before 1917, it was after World War I that "the Jazz Age" truly arrived, heralded by Louis Armstrong, blues singer Bessie Smith, and bandleader Duke Ellington. Radio, a new medium launched in the 1920s, brought these and other stars into living rooms across the country, and sales of phonograph records soared at the same time.

The formative role of African Americans in American popular music was matched by that of Jewish songwriters. During this era many of the nation's best-loved songs came out of Tin Pan Alley, the area in downtown Manhattan where a number of talented Jews, led by Russian-born Irving Berlin, busily worked at writing catchy melodies and lyrics. Such favorites as "White Christmas" and "God Bless America" flowed from Berlin's pen. The other towering figure to come out of Tin Pan Alley and a Russian Jewish background, George Gershwin, electrified the Broadway stage in the 1920s and created a powerful new fusion of jazz and symphonic music when he composed his brilliant *Rhapsody in Blue* in 1924.

Jewish immigrants also played an unusual role in the development of the American movie industry. After breaking a monopoly of early film companies that stultified the business, Jewish entrepreneurs founded the great Hollywood studios—Metro-Goldwyn-Meyer (MGM), Paramount, Universal, Columbia, and Warner Brothers. Although most movies did not focus on immigrant themes, it was more than a coincidence that the first successful "talking" picture, *The Jazz Singer* (1927), told the story of an immigrant cantor's son torn between the Jewish religious tradition of his father and the lure of stardom in American show business. The movie featured Al Jolson, who had made this very transition—from the world of his father, an immigrant cantor, to American stardom.

Even though most entertainment was simply entertainment, the huge presence of immigrants and minorities in American show business made for interesting challenges to social conventions that excluded them. In his silent pictures Charlie Chaplin portrayed the downtrodden but persevering "little guy," who might easily represent the ordinary immigrant, and who did so explicitly in the 1917 movie *The Immigrants*. Where Chaplin created poignant characterizations, the Marx Brothers introduced a distinctive kind of raucous comedy that shattered the snobbish pretensions of American patricians who disdained Jews and other outsiders. The groundbreaking musical and film *Show Boat* (based on Edna Ferber's 1926 novel) was authored, adapted, and produced by Jews, and it gracefully intertwined an indictment of racism and a conventional love story. Similarly, Louis Armstrong's stirring rendition of "Black and Blue" poignantly described the pain of racial prejudice.

More sentimental ethnic elements permeated American popular culture as well. The 1908 play *The Melting Pot*, by British Jewish writer Israel Zangwill, created one of the most enduring metaphors for America as a society of immigrants, *a melting pot* in which ethnic and religious differences disappear and a new American people emerges. The story is about two Russian immigrants, a Jew and a Christian, who fall in love despite severe family conflicts; it ends with their marriage and closes at the Statue of Liberty, with the lovers feeling sure that the varied races and nationalities in America will ultimately unite and create a new Republic of Man. *Abie's Irish Rose,* one of the longest-running plays of the 1920s, tells of another unlikely union, this time between a Jewish boy and an Irish girl. After predictable conflicts between the fathers, Solomon and Patrick, and bemused observation by their respective rabbi and priest, the couple weds in a Christian ceremony and has twins. This makes everyone happy, for the Jewish grandfather wanted a grandson and the Irish one a granddaughter! What made the sentimentality of these two popular plays particularly interesting was the fact that Jews had an extremely low rate of intermarriage. The dramas therefore reflected not a predominant fact but rather a grand vision of human compatibility and harmony across ethnic lines.

With the rise of radio in the 1920s a new genre of entertainment was born—the situation comedy—and some of the most popular early sitcoms focused on racial and ethnic themes. The groundbreaking show *Amos 'n' Andy*, launched in 1926 as *Sam 'n' Henry* but renamed in 1928, enjoyed unparalleled success and lasted through the 1950s. Played by two white entertainers, the characters Amos and Andy formed the nucleus of a daily story about African Americans from the South trying to make a life in New York City. Andy was unscrupulous, but Amos was sincere and portrayed with real humanity, despite the stereotyped buffoonery that marked most of the male characters on the show. African Americans split in their reactions to the show; some protested that it perpetuated degrading characterizations, while others appreciated the show as comedy, the only comedy featuring African American characters at all. Had African Americans possessed any real control over the content of radio shows, *Amos 'n' Andy* would have been a very different production, more akin to *The Goldbergs*. Launched in 1929, this sitcom about a New York Jewish family achieved almost as much success as *Amos 'n' Andy*, and without purveying objectionable stereotypes.

CONCEPTIONS OF RACE, ETHNICITY, AND AMERICAN IDENTITY

Virtually every ethnic minority in America experienced the dilemma of "dual identity." On the one hand, there was tremendous pressure to conform to the ways of the American majority, particularly during and after World War I, which brought nationalism to a fevered pitch. Yet inherited traditions and customs did not simply fall away like an old skin. Members of ethnic groups felt compelled to support the larger aims of their people. In *The Souls of Black Folk* (1903) W. E. B. Du Bois eloquently described the psychological condition of dual identity as it applied to African Americans:

> It is a peculiar sensation, this double-consciousness, this sense of always looking at one's self through the eyes of others, of measuring one's soul by the tape of a world that looks on in amused contempt and pity. One ever feels his twoness—an American, a Negro; two souls, two thoughts, two unreconciled strivings; two warring ideals in one dark body, whose dogged strength alone keeps it from being torn asunder. The history of the American Negro is the history of this strife—this longing to attain self-conscious manhood, to merge his double self into a better and truer self. In this merging he wishes neither of the older selves to be lost. He would not Africanize America, for America has too much to teach the world and Africa. He would not bleach his Negro soul in a flood of white Americanism, for he knows that Negro blood has a message for the world. He simply wishes to make it possible for a man to be both a Negro and an American, without being cursed and spit upon by his fellows, without having the doors of Opportunity closed roughly in his face.

The dilemma of dual identity affected every group in a distinctive way. Each one had its "assimilationists" and "traditionalists." the former promoted Americanization at the expense of many traditional customs, and the latter, though not necessarily rejecting Americanization, insisted that many ethnic customs be preserved. Yet within the general framework of new ways versus old, there were many nuances. Mexicans, for example, retained a very strong tie to Mexico, which was just over the border and easy to return to. As a result, and because of historic grievances dating to the Mexican American War, most Mexican Americans considered themselves "essentially Mexican." Nevertheless, they could not help but change many of their ways, as other immigrants did. The most settled Mexican Americans looked down on the new arrivals, whose foreignness, they thought, jeopardized their reputation among Americans. In turn, the newer immigrants disdained the condescension of Americanized Mexicans and criticized them for losing Mexican culture.

Most European immigrants, once they decided to settle in the United States, did not endure the intense ambivalence felt by Mexican Americans. Still, they oscillated between feelings of gratitude for the freedoms they enjoyed and feelings of nostalgia for their homelands. As the characters in Abraham Cahan's stories of Jewish immigrants were wont to say in moments of frustration, "a pox on Columbus." Such evocations did not imply distrust of America—the Jews, in particular, saw America as a kind of beloved homeland—but rather a sense of being caught between two worlds. In 1915 Horace Kallen, an American Jewish thinker, developed the concept of "cultural pluralism" as a resolution of the two-worlds problem. According to Kallen's theory, Americanization did not require ethnic minorities to reject their ethnic customs. Rather, those ethnic differences might enrich American society.

Indian voices sounded a poignant note in the problem of reconciling new and old, American and ethnic identities. A landmark event in the history of American Indian relations was the publication of Geronimo's autobiography in 1906. Although living as a prisoner of war from 1886, when the U.S. Army captured him, until his death in 1909, the Apache leader attained fame in the early years of the century. Once he ceased to be a military threat, Americans converted him into a celebrity. Geronimo toured regional expositions, appeared as a guest of honor at Fourth of July celebrations in Oklahoma (where he lived), and rode in Theodore Roosevelt's inaugural parade in 1905 at the President's invitation. Having secured the president's permission to publish his autobiography while he remained technically a prisoner of war, Geronimo gave a fairly candid critique of the U.S. government's treatment of his people. A pragmatic leader, Geronimo counseled the Apaches to adapt to American ways for their own benefit, but he also retained a proud attachment to the tribal homeland. "I think that my people are now capable of living in accordance with the laws of the United States," the old warrior stated, "and we would, of course, like to have the liberty to return to that land which is ours by divine right."

Will Rogers, of mixed Cherokee and white background, brought the Indian predicament into public view once he rose to become America's favorite humorist in the 1920s. "The Navajo Indians held a conference and decided that they could get along without the services of about twenty-five white office holders that had been appointed to help look after them. The Indians said they were doing it to save the white man money. Who said the Indians didn't have any humor?" This barb typified Rogers's wit, which reflected the irony of living simultaneously as a celebrity and a descendant of a tribe that had been tragically herded into Oklahoma two generations before his birth there. He was the first such public figure to remind Americans that even the "most native" among them were not quite as native as they liked to think. "My ancestors didn't come on the Mayflower," Rogers mused, "but they met the boat." Mapping out a new approach to the question of who belonged in America, Du Bois, Kallen, and Rogers pointed toward a more self-aware and cosmopolitan country than the one into which they had been born.

BIBLIOGRAPHIC ESSAY

The following bibliography is restricted to books that treat the 1901–1929 period in some detail. In listing studies of specific immigrant groups, I emphasize books that make extensive use of primary sources, especially foreign-language sources such as immigrant newspapers, correspondence, and memoirs.

An excellent visual starting point is Peter C. Marzio, ed., *A Nation of Nations: The People Who Came to America as Seen Through Objects and Documents Exhibited at the Smithsonian Institution* (New York: Harper and Row, 1976).

On the critical legal and constitutional questions of race and immigration, see the entries on "Race and Racism," "Native Americans," and "Alienage and Naturalization" in Kermit L. Hall, ed., *The Oxford Companion to the Supreme Court of the United States* (New York: Oxford University Press, 1992).

Valuable interpretations of ethnicity as a factor in this era of American history are offered by Philip Gleason, *Speaking of Diversity: Language and Ethnicity in Twentieth-Century America* (Baltimore: Johns Hopkins University Press, 1992); Werner Sollors, *Beyond Ethnicity: Consent and Descent in American Culture* (New York: Oxford University Press, 1986); Arthur Mann, *The One and the Many: Reflections on the American Identity* (Chicago: University of Chicago Press, 1979); and John Higham, *Send These to Me: Immigrants in Urban America* (Baltimore: Johns Hopkins University Press, 1975).

Reliable historical surveys of immigration, ethnicity, race and religious minorities include: Leonard Dinnerstein and David M. Reimers, *Ethnic Americans: A History of Immigration* (New York: Columbia University Press, 1999; orig. 1975); Alan M. Kraut, *The Huddled Masses: The Immigrant in American Society, 1880–1921.* (Arlington Heights, Ill.: Harlan Davidson, 2001); Thomas J.

Archdeacon, *Becoming American: An Ethnic History* (New York: Free Press, 1983); Roger Daniels, *Coming to America: A History of Immigration and Ethnicity in American Life* (New York: HarperCollins, 1990); John E. Bodnar, *The Transplanted: A History of Immigrants in Urban America* (Bloomington: Indiana University Press, 1985); and James Olson, *The Ethnic Dimension in American History* (New York: St. Martin's Press, 1999; orig. 1979). An older classic work, written in an epic rather than textbook mode, is Oscar Handlin, *The Uprooted* (Boston: Little, Brown, 1951). Another, older book that offers an interesting view of immigrant contributions is Carl Frederick Wittke, *We Who Built America* (Cleveland: Press of Western Reserve University, 1939).

Surveys on African Americans, Native Americans, and Asian Americans include the following: John Hope Franklin, *From Slavery to Freedom: A History of African Americans* (New York: Knopf, 2000; orig. 1947); Jacqueline Jones, *Labor of Love, Labor of Sorrow: Black Women, Work, and the Family from Slavery to the Present* (New York: Basic Books, 1985); Rayford W. Logan, *The Betrayal of the Negro: From Rutherford B. Hayes to Woodrow Wilson* (New York: Collier, 1965); Leon F. Litwack, *Trouble in Mind: Black Southerners in the Age of Jim Crow* (New York: Knopf, 1998); Francis Paul Prucha, *The Great Father: The United States Government and the American Indians* (Lincoln: University of Nebraska Press, 1984); John R. Wunder, *"Retained by the People": A History of American Indians and the Bill of Rights* (New York: Oxford University Press, 1994); Sucheng Chan, *Asian Americans: An Interpretive History* (Boston: Twayne, 1991); and Ronald T. Takaki, *Strangers from a Different Shore: A History of Asian Americans* (Boston: Little, Brown, 1989).

Specialized studies on racism, nativism, and anti-Semitism include John Higham, *Strangers in the Land: Patterns of American Nativism, 1860–1925* (New Brunswick: Rutgers University Press, 1955); Barbara Miller Solomon, *Ancestors and Immigrants* (Boston: Northeastern University Press, 1956); David M. Chalmers, *Hooded Americanism: The First Century of the Ku Klux Klan, 1865–1965* (Garden City, N.Y.: Doubleday, 1965); Kenneth T. Jackson, *The Ku Klux Klan in the City, 1915–1930* (New York: Oxford University Press, 1967); Kathleen M. Blee, *Women of the Klan: Racism and Gender in the 1920s* (Berkeley: University of California Press, 1991); Nancy MacLean, *Behind the Mask of Chivalry: The Making of the Second Ku Klux Klan* (New York: Oxford University Press, 1994); Leonard Dinnerstein, *Anti-Semitism in America* (New York: Oxford University Press, 1994); Allan M. Kraut, *Silent Travelers: Germs, Genes and the "Immigrant Menace"* (Baltimore: Johns Hopkins University Press, 1994); Frederick C. Luebke, *Bonds of Loyalty: German-Americans and World War I* (Dekalb: Northern Illinois University Press, 1974); Roger Daniels, *The Politics of Prejudice: The Anti-Japanese Movement in California and the Struggle for Japanese Exclusion* (Berkeley: University of California Press, 1962); Sucheng Chan, *Entry Denied: Exclusion and the Chinese Community in America, 1882–1943* (Philadelphia: Temple University Press, 1991); Matthew Frye Jacobson, *Whiteness of a Different Color: European Immigrants and the Alchemy of Race* (Cambridge: Harvard University Press, 1998); Ian F. Haney-Lopez, *White by Law: The Legal Construction of Race* (New York: New York University Press, 1996); Thomas F. Gossett, *Race: The History of an Idea in America* (Dallas: Southern

Methodist University Press, 1964); Elazar Barkan, *The Retreat of Scientific Racism: Changing Concepts of Race in Britain and the United States Between the World Wars* (Cambridge: Cambridge University Press, 1992); Michael M. Sokal, ed., *Psychological Testing and American Society, 1890–1930* (New Brunswick, N.J.: Rutgers University Press, 1987); and George W. Stocking, Jr., *Race, Culture, and Evolution: Essays in the History of Anthropology* (Chicago: University of Chicago Press, 1968).

Studies of specific immigrant and ethnic groups include the following, listed in chronological order of publication:

On the Irish and Germans, William V. Shannon, *The American Irish* (New York: Macmillan, 1963); Lawrence J. McCaffrey, *The Irish Catholic Diaspora in America* (Washington, D.C.: Catholic University of America Press, 1997; orig. 1976); Kerby A. Miller, *Emigrants and Exiles: Ireland and the Irish Exodus to North America* (New York: Oxford University Press, 1985); Timothy J. Meagher, ed., *From Paddy to Studs: Irish-American Communities in the Turn of the Century Era, 1880–1920* (New York: Greenwood Press, 1986); Phyllis Keller, *States of Belonging: German-American Intellectuals and the First World War* (Cambridge: Harvard University Press, 1979); and Frederick C. Luebke, *Germans in the New World* (Urbana: University of Illinois Press, 1990).

On East European Jews, Moses Rischin, *The Promised City: New York's Jews, 1870–1914* (Cambridge: Harvard University Press, 1962); Deborah Dash Moore, *At Home in America: Second Generation New York Jews* (New York: Columbia University Press, 1981); Andrew R. Heinze, *Adapting to Abundance: Jewish Immigrants, Mass Consumption and the Search for American Identity* (New York: Columbia University Press, 1990); Susan A. Glenn, *Daughters of the Shtetl: Life and Labor in the Immigrant Generation* (Ithaca: Cornell University Press, 1990); Ewa T. Morawska, *Insecure Prosperity: Small-Town Jews in Industrial America, 1890–1940* (Princeton: Princeton University Press, 1996); Daniel Soyer, *Jewish Immigrant Associations and American Identity in New York, 1880–1939* (Cambridge: Harvard University Press, 1997); and Arthur A. Goren, *The Politics and Public Culture of American Jews* (Bloomington: Indiana University Press, 1999).

On Italians, Virginia Yans-McLaughlin, *Family and Community: Italian Immigrants in Buffalo, 1880–1930* (Ithaca: Cornell University Press, 1977); John W. Briggs, *An Italian Passage: Immigrants to Three American Cities, 1890–1930* (New Haven: Yale University Press, 1978); Dino Cinel, *From Italy to San Francisco: The Immigrant Experience* (Palo Alto: Stanford University Press, 1982); Humbert S. Nelli, *From Immigrants to Ethnics: The Italian Americans* (New York: Oxford University Press, 1983); Donna R. Gabaccia, *From Sicily to Elizabeth Street: Housing and Social Change among Italian Immigrants, 1880–1930* (Albany: State University of New York Press, 1984); Robert A. Orsi, *The Madonna of 115th Street: Faith and Community in Italian Harlem, 1880–1950* (New Haven: Yale University Press, 1985); and Donna R. Gabaccia, *Militants and Migrants: Rural Sicilians Become American Workers* (New Brunswick: Rutgers University Press, 1988).

On East Europeans, Peter Paul Jonitis, *The Acculturation of the Lithuanians of Chester, Pennsylvania* (New York: AMS Press, 1986; orig. 1951); Victor R. Greene, *The Slavic Community on Strike: Immigrant Labor in Pennsylvania Anthracite* (Notre Dame, Ind.: University of Notre Dame Press, 1968); Victor R.

Greene, For God and Country: The Rise of Polish and Lithuanian Ethnic Conscious-
ness in America, 1860–1910 (Madison: State Historical Society of Wisconsin,
1975); Ewa T. Morawska, For Bread with Butter: The Life-Worlds of East Central
Europeans in Johnstown, Pennsylvania, 1890–1940 (New York: Cambridge University Press, 1985); M. Mark Stolarik, Immigration and Urbanization: The Slovak
Experience, 1870–1918 (New York: AMS Press, 1989); John J Bukowczyk, And
My Children Did Not Know Me: A History of the Polish Americans (Bloomington:
Indiana University Press, 1987); June Granatir Alexander, The Immigrant Church
and Community: Pittsburgh's Slovak Catholics and Lutherans, 1880–1915 (Pitts-
burgh: University of Pittsburgh Press, 1987); and Dominic A. Pacyga, Polish
Immigrants and Industrial Chicago: Workers on the South Side, 1880–1922 (Colum-
bus: Ohio State University Press, 1992).

On Mexicans, Albert Camarillo, Chicanos in a Changing Society: From
Mexican Pueblos to American Barrios in Santa Barbara and Southern California,
1848–1930 (Cambridge: Harvard University Press, 1979); Ricardo Romo, East
Los Angeles: History of a Barrio (Austin: University of Texas Press, 1983); George
Sanchez, Becoming Mexican American: Ethnicity, Culture, and Identity in Chicano
Los Angeles, 1900–1945 (New York: Oxford University Press, 1993); Camille
Guerin-Gonzales, Mexican Workers and American Dreams (New Brunswick:
Rutgers University Press, 1994); David G. Gutiérrez, Walls and Mirrors: Mexican
Americans, Mexican Immigrants, and the Politics of Identity (Berkeley: University of
California Press, 1995); Juan R. Garcia, Mexicans in the Midwest, 1900–1932
(Tucson: University of Arizona Press, 1996); and Douglas Monroy, Rebirth:
Mexican Los Angeles from the Great Migration to the Great Depression (Berkeley:
University of California Press, 1999)

On Japanese (see earlier periods for bibliography on the Chinese), John
Modell, The Economics and Politics of Racial Accommodation: The Japanese of Los
Angeles, 1900–1942 (Urbana: University of Illinois Press, 1977); Eileen Sunada
Sarasohn, The Issei: Portrait of a Pioneer: An Oral History (Palo Alto, Cal.: Pacific
Books, 1983); Evelyn Nakano Glenn, Issei, Nisei, War Bride: Three Generations of
Japanese American Women in Domestic Service (Philadelphia: Temple University
Press, 1986); and Yuji Ichioka, The Issei: The World of the First Generation Japanese
Immigrants, 1885–1924 (Urbana: University of Illinois Press, 1988).

On Greeks, Armenians, Syrians, Filipinos, and Puerto Ricans, Theodore
Saloutos, The Greeks in the United States (Cambridge: Harvard University Press,
1964); Robert Mirak, Torn Between Two Lands: Armenians in America, 1890 to
World War I (Cambridge: Harvard University Press, 1983); Alixa Naff, Becoming
American: The Early Arab Immigrant Experience (Carbondale: Southern Illinois
University Press, 1985); Antonio J. A. Pico, The Filipinos in America (New York:
Center for Migration Studies, 1986); and Virginia E. Sanchez Korrol, From
Colonia to Community: The History of Puerto Ricans in New York City (Westport,
Conn.: Greenwood Press, 1983).

Comparative studies of ethnic groups include Josef J. Barton, Peasants and
Strangers: Italians, Rumanians, and Slovaks in an American City, 1890–1950
(Cambridge: Harvard University Press, 1975); Thomas Kessner, The Golden
Door: Italian and Jewish Immigrant Mobility in New York City: 1880–1915 (New
York: Oxford University Press, 1977); Caroline Golab, Immigrant Destinations

(Philadelphia: Temple University Press, 1977); John Bodnar, *Lives of Their Own, Blacks, Italians, and Poles in Pittsburgh, 1900–1960* (Urbana: University of Illinois Press, 1983); Melvin G. Holli and Peter d' A. Jones, eds., *Ethnic Chicago* (Grand Rapids, Mich.: W. B. Eerdmans, 1984); Judith E. Smith, *Family Connections: A History of Italian and Jewish Immigrant Lives in Providence, Rhode Island, 1900–1940* (Albany: State University of New York Press, 1985); Gary R. Mormino and George E. Pozzetta, *The Immigrant World of Ybor City: Italians and Their Latin Neighbors in Tampa, 1885–1985* (Gainesville: University Press of Florida, 1987); and Hasia R. Diner, *Hungering for America: Italian, Irish, and Jewish Foodways in the Age of Migration* (Cambridge: Harvard University Press, 2001).

Studies of immigrants within the contexts of religion, education, and labor include Randall Miller and Thomas Marzik, eds., *Immigrants and Religion in Urban America* (Philadelphia: Temple University Press, 1977); James Hennesey, S. J., *American Catholics: A History of the Roman Catholic Community in the United States* (New York: Oxford University Press, 1981); Jay P. Dolan, *The American Catholic Experience* (New York: Doubleday, 1992); Bernard J. Weiss, ed., *American Education and the European Immigrant, 1840–1940* (Urbana: University of Illinois Press, 1982); Paula S. Fass, *Outside In: Minorities and the Transformation of American Education* (New York: Oxford University Press, 1989); James R. Barrett, *Work and Community in the Jungle: Chicago's Packinghouse Workers, 1894–1922* (Urbana: University of Illinois Press, 1987); and Gary Gerstle, *Working-Class Americanism: The Politics of Labor in a Textile City, 1914–1960* (New York: Cambridge University Press, 1989).

On black migration from the South, immigration from the West Indies, labor, the formation of "ghettos," and the Harlem Renaissance, see Nicholas Lemann, *The Promised Land: The Great Black Migration and How It Changed America* (New York: Vintage, 1991); James R. Grossman, *Land of Hope: Chicago, Black Southerners and the Great Migration* (Chicago: University of Chicago Press, 1989); Florette Henri, *Black Migration: Movement North, 1900–1920* (Garden City, N.Y.: Anchor Press, 1975); Ira de Augustine Reid, *The Negro Immigrant* (New York: Columbia University Press, 1939); Eric Arneson, *Brotherhoods of Color: Black Railroad Workers and the Struggle for Equality* (Cambridge: Harvard University Press, 2001); Kenneth L. Kusmer, *A Ghetto Takes Shape: Black Cleveland, 1870–1930* (Chicago: Illinois University Press, 1976); Allan H. Spear, *Black Chicago: The Making of a Negro Ghetto, 1890–1920* (Chicago: University of Chicago Press, 1967); Gilbert Osofsky, *Harlem, the Making of a Ghetto: Negro New York, 1890–1930* (New York: Harper and Row, 1966); Nathan Irvin Huggins, *Harlem Renaissance* (New York: Oxford University Press, 1971); and Jervis Anderson, *This Was Harlem: A Cultural Portrait, 1900–1950* (New York: Farrar Straus Giroux, 1982).

On aspects of cultural creativity, see Lawrence W. Levine, *Black Culture and Black Consciousness* (New York: Oxford University Press, 1977); Irving Howe, *World of Our Fathers* (New York: Harcourt Brace Jovanovich, 1976); Burton Peretti, *The Creation of Jazz: Music, Race, and Culture in Urban America* (Urbana: University of Illinois Press, 1992); James Lincoln Collier, *Jazz: The American Theme Song* (New York: Oxford University Press, 1993); James Lincoln Collier, *Louis Armstrong, an American Genius* (New York: Oxford University Press, 1993);

Jeffrey Melnick, *A Right to Sing the Blues: African Americans, Jews, and American Popular Song* (Cambridge: Harvard University Press, 1999); Richard M. Ketchum, *Will Rogers* (New York: American Heritage, 1973); Kenneth Aaron Kanter, *The Jews on Tin Pan Alley* (New York: Ktav, 1982); Neal Gabler, *An Empire of Their Own: How the Jews Invented Hollywood* (New York: Crown, 1988); Melvin Patrick Ely, *The Adventures of Amos 'n' Andy: A Social History of an American Phenomenon* (New York: Free Press, 1991).

On major political figures and trends, see Victor R. Greene, *American Immigrant Leaders, 1800–1910: Marginality and Identity* (Baltimore: Johns Hopkins University Press, 1987); Angie Debo, *Geronimo: The Man, His Time, His Place* (Norman: University of Oklahoma Press, 1976); Ronald H. Bayor, *Fiorello La Guardia: Ethnicity and Reform* (Arlington Heights, Ill.: Harlan Davidson, 1993); Thomas Kessner, *Fiorello H. La Guardia and the Making of Modern New York* (New York: McGraw-Hill, 1989); Oscar Handlin, *Al Smith and His America* (1958); David Levering Lewis, *W. E. B. Du Bois* (New York: Henry Holt, 1993, 2000), 2 vols.; Judith Stein, *The World of Marcus Garvey* (Baton Rouge: Louisiana State University Press, 1986); Jervis Anderson, *A. Philip Randolph* (New York: Harcourt Brace Jovanovich, 1973); David Burner, *The Politics of Provincialism: The Democratic Party in Transition, 1918–1932* (New York: Knopf, 1967); James J. Connolly, *The Triumph of Ethnic Progressivism: Urban Political Culture in Boston, 1900–1925* (Cambridge: Harvard University Press, 1998); Gwendolyn Mink, *Old Labor and New Immigrants in American Political Development: Union, Party, and State, 1875–1920* (Ithaca: Cornell University Press, 1986); John M. Allswang, *A House for All Peoples: Ethnic Politics in Chicago, 1890–1936* (Lexington: University of Kentucky Press, 1971); Edward R. Kantowicz, *Polish-American Politics in Chicago, 1888–1940* (Chicago: University of Chicago Press, 1975); Paul Avrich, *Sacco and Vanzetti: The Anarchist Background* (Princeton: Princeton University Press, 1991).

There are no complete analyses of the complicated racial and ethnic politics of Theodore Roosevelt and Woodrow Wilson. Thomas G. Dyer, *Theodore Roosevelt and the Idea of Race* (Baton Rouge: Louisiana State University Press, 1980) approaches the subject but misses the complexity of Roosevelt's attitudes, as does the otherwise excellent comparative biography by John Milton Cooper, Jr., *The Warrior and the Priest: Woodrow Wilson and Theodore Roosevelt* (Cambridge: Cambridge University Press, 1983). The reader should consult the leading biographies of these presidents.

For a sample of the many illustrative primary sources relevant to the 1901–1929 period, see Hutchins Hapgood, *The Spirit of the Ghetto* (Cambridge: Harvard University Press, 1902); W. E. B. Du Bois, *The Souls of Black Folk* (Chicago: A. C. McClurg, 1903); Thomas Dixon, *The Clansman: An Historical Romance of the Ku Klux Klan* (New York: Doubleday, Page, 1905); S. M. Barrett, ed., *Geronimo's Story of His Life* (New York: Duffield, 1906); Upton Sinclair, *The Jungle* (New York: Doubleday, Page, 1906); Ray Stannard Baker, *Following the Color Line* (New York: Harper and Row, 1908); Israel Zangwill, *The Melting Pot* (New York: Macmillan, 1909); Emily Greene Balch, *Our Slavic Fellow Citizens* (New York: Charities Publication Committee, 1910); Margaret F. Byington, *Homestead: The Households of a Mill Town* (New York: Charities Publication

Committee, 1910); United States Immigration Commission, *Reports* (1911); James Weldon Johnson, *The Autobiography of an Ex-Colored Man* (Boston: Sherman, French, 1912; Reissued by Dover Publications, 1995); Mary Antin, *The Promised Land* (Boston: Houghton Mifflin, 1912); Edward Alsworth Ross, *The Old World in the New* (New York: Century, 1914); Madison Grant, *The Passing of the Great Race* (New York: Scribner's, 1916); Abraham Cahan, *The Rise of David Levinsky* (New York: Harper and Brothers, 1917); William I. Thomas and Florian Znaniecki, *The Polish Peasant in Europe and America*, 2 vols. (Chicago: University of Chicago Press, 1918–1920); Robert F. Foerster, *The Italian Emigration of Our Times* (Cambridge: Harvard University Press, 1919); Philip Davis, *Immigration and Americanization* (Boston: Ginn and Company, 1920); Anzia Yezierska, *Hungry Hearts* (Salem, Mass.: Ayer Company, 1920) and *Bread Givers* (Garden City, N.Y.: Doubleday, 1925); Robert E. Park and Herbert A. Miller, *Old World Traits Transplanted* (New York: Harper, 1921); Robert E. Park, *The Immigrant Press and Its Control* (New York: Harper, 1922); Chicago Commission on Race Relations, *The Negro in Chicago: A Study of Race Relations and a Race Riot* (Chicago: University of Chicago Press, 1922); Jean Toomer, *Cane* (New York: Boni and Liveright, 1923); Horace Kallen, *Culture and Democracy in the United States* (New York: Boni and Liveright, 1924); Edith Abbot, *Immigration: Select Documents and Case Records* (Chicago: University of Chicago Press, 1924); Alain Locke, *The New Negro* (New York: A. and C. Boni, 1925); Louis Wirth, *The Ghetto* (Chicago: University of Chicago Press, 1928); Emma Goldman, *Living My Life* (New York: Knopf, 1931); Manuel Gamio, *The Mexican Immigrant: His Life-Story* (Chicago: University of Chicago Press, 1931); Yamoto Ichihashi, *Japanese in the United States* (Palo Alto: Stanford University Press, 1932).

Several films provide unique insight into the racial and ethnic dynamics of the era: *Birth of a Nation* (1915), about the Ku Klux Klan as a redeemer of the nation; *The Immigrants* (1917), Charlie Chaplin's comic portrayal of a newcomer; *The Jazz Singer* (1927), about the painful conflict between ethno-religious tradition and American stardom, featuring Al Jolson; *Broken Blossom* (1919), a poignant, groundbreaking film about the relationship between a white woman and a Chinese man. Although it falls outside the period covered in this chapter, we should note the 1936 version of *Show Boat*, featuring singer Paul Robeson, which dramatized the themes of racial mixture and prejudice in the 1926 novel by Edna Ferber.

7

CHANGING RACIAL MEANINGS

Race and Ethnicity in the United States, 1930–1964

Thomas A. Guglielmo and Earl Lewis

In the early 1940s, as Nazi theories on Jewish inferiority received greater attention and censure worldwide, a small controversy was fast developing around the U.S. government's own racial categorization of Jews. It became clear at this time that some immigration officers were instructing Jews wishing to naturalize to fill in "Hebrew"—and not "white," as some applicants wished—in response to the race question on naturalization forms. Such directives rankled some members of American Jewish organizations like the Anti-Defamation League of B'nai B'rith and individuals like Arthur Hays Sulzberger, publisher of the *New York Times*. Formal letters of protest to leading government officials followed, setting off confusion within the federal government. Immigration and Naturalization Services (INS) Chief Earl G. Harrison commissioned a report specifically on whether the "Hebrews" are a race, while the Secretary of Labor, Frances Perkins, was forced to admit that such questions were extremely difficult to answer, since most scientists "don't agree what a race is, nor what races there are."

In time, and no doubt in part as a result of the pressure of the protesters and the vehement anti-Nazi context of the moment, the federal government revised its forms eliminating "Hebrew" (among many other groups) as an acceptable answer on the race question. As far as naturalization forms were concerned, racial identification for a wide range of people was greatly simplified. Instead of over fifty races—from Finn to Flemish, South Italian to Syrian—the government whittled its list down to six: White, African or African descent, Filipino, Indian, Eskimo, and Aleutian. Those groups who had been excluded from naturalization for years—namely most Asian groups—were not included on the list. In making these revisions, INS officials noted that "scientific opinion with regard to race has changed," and therefore their racial classifications had to comport better with "contemporary opinion."

This example speaks to the malleability of race; the ways in which power and politics—rather than biology or genetics—define race; the transformation of and resulting confusion with the race concept during the interwar and war years; and the ways in which race powerfully shaped people's opportunities, as in the case of naturalization rights and Asians.

This essay explores these issues and more. The first part of the essay examines the changing scientific meaning of race. The second and longer section of the essay addresses how the social and political meanings of race in people's everyday lives changed over time, in part as a result of shifts in race science. We explore how Americans encountered race and the nation's racial structure, with some Americans attempting to dismantle that structure to gain greater equality and others attempting to shore it up to protect their own privileges. Finally, we will discuss the wartime emergence of "ethnicity" as a new social scientific category as a result of changing conceptions of race.

We argue that between 1930 and 1965 both the scientific and sociopolitical meaning of race changed dramatically. The race concept, in these years, came to mean a much more specific set of human groupings and lost virtually all of its scientific legitimacy as a natural, unchanging biological essence. Similarly, and in part as a result of these paradigmatic shifts in race science, the social and political meaning of race—that is, its power to shape people's everyday lives and opportunities—underwent important changes. In 1930, race meant that African Americans, Asian Americans, Latino/Latina Americans, and Native Americans were often restricted by legal or other means from many if not all of the following resources—a quality home, a quality education, a quality job, union membership, citizenship rights, the ability to marry exogamously, the right to be tried by a jury of one's peers, and the right to own land. At this time, race also meant that certain European groups, while generally accepted as white and therefore greatly privileged relative to nonwhite groups or the "colored races" mentioned above, still faced their share of racial discrimination and prejudice. This was particularly the case for the races of Southern and Eastern Europe, whose immigration to the United States had recently been drastically reduced by the federal government on racial grounds. Together these inequalities—along with a set of ideologies (i.e., "racisms") that both explained and helped constitute them—made up the racial structure of the United States in 1930.

By 1965 this structure had changed dramatically. All racial divisions among Europeans had disappeared, leaving groups such as Italians, Poles, and Jews—now considered "ethnic groups" rather than races—facing no societal disadvantage whatsoever on account of their race (i.e., their whiteness). Indeed, an Irish Catholic, John F. Kennedy, became president of the United States in 1961. As for the "colored races," they had, by 1965, through an increasingly powerful set of social movements, forced the federal government to abolish virtually all legal barriers to racial equality (e.g., Jim Crow segregation, disfranchisement, immigration exclusion, naturalization restrictions, restrictive covenants, and alien land laws). By the mid-1960s racial discrimination still pervaded the United States, of course, but the American racial structure—in large part because of vigilant activism from below—had been profoundly and forever transformed.

THE CHANGING SCIENTIFIC MEANING OF RACE

The scientific meaning of race underwent several critical changes in the interwar years. First, there was what historian Elazar Barkan has called the "retreat of scientific racism." Although social scientists such as Franz Boas and Robert Park had for years been raising serious questions about the validity of the race concept, it was really in the 1930s and 1940s that a significant and powerful group of scientists, responding in part to the rise of Nazi racialism abroad, consciously rejected essentialist understandings of race. They argued instead that culture, and not some natural essence, was the most significant determinant of human behavior and capabilities. Exemplifying this shift were scholarly works such as Ruth Benedict's *Race: Science and Politics* (1940), Ashley Montagu's *Race: Man's Most Dangerous Myth* (1942), and especially Gunnar Myrdal's landmark *An American Dilemma* (1944), all of which gained a wide, popular audience during the war years. This shift in scientific race thinking culminated in the early 1950s with the publication of the United Nations Educational, Scientific, and Cultural Organization's (UNESCO) *The Race Concept*. A series of statements written by leading scientists from all over the world, it simply restated, reinforced, and lent great legitimacy to the fact that unity much more than difference characterized humanity; that no evidence suggested that race was connected in any way to intelligence, psychology, culture, or character; and that "pure" races did not exist.

Second, the Depression and war years witnessed not only the "culturalization" of race, but its simplification as well. For much of the early twentieth century, race was used to describe the widest variety of human groupings, from large populations like whites, Negroes, Latins, and Anglo-Saxons to very small groups like the Manx and Moravians, Syrians and Serbians. In the interwar and war years, as a result of immigration restriction, African American migration from the South to the North and West, and the rise of Nazism abroad, scientists and other intellectuals became less interested in delineating the racial divisions of Europeans and more concerned with the "major branches of mankind." These branches varied, depending on the scientist, yet they almost always included at least the "big three": Caucasian, Mongoloid, and Negroid. An example of the simplification of race on the government's naturalization forms opened this chapter. But there were numerous other examples, particularly in the realm of science, where even UNESCO's work conceded that there were only three great races—the ones mentioned above. Certainly this shift was not instantaneous; nor was it necessarily always reflected at the popular level or present uniformly across the country. For instance, in wartime Los Angeles, the idea that Mexicans were a distinct race "became even more clearly defined and firmly entrenched." Still, when talking broadly about America's scientific and intellectual community, this shift was real.

Indeed, compelling proof of this fact is the wartime emergence of "ethnicity" as a new social scientific concept. A review of major academic journals in a wide range of disciplines—economics, history, anthropology, sociology, political science, and literature—reveals that only in the postwar years did "ethnicity" and "ethnic" become common scholarly terms or categories of analysis. This was so because of the changing meaning of race in these years. As the race concept was simplified to exclude peoples like Magyars and Montenegrins from its purview, something new was needed to refer to such groupings. *Ethnic* fast became the category of choice. Other possible options like *nationality* were no doubt ruled out because Magyars and Montenegrins, for example, did not fit neatly into any one nation.

These scientific changes had a complicated set of meanings that made it hard to predict how they would affect everyday social relations. On the one hand, these new scientific ideas certainly aided the cause of groups denied equal rights on the basis of scientifically discredited race thinking. It also, of course, made it more difficult for segregationists, racialists, and exclusionists to continue to rely upon the word of science to support their racial projects. On the other hand, the new simplification of race, as historian Matthew Jacobson has argued, did tend to consolidate many Greeks and Germans, Moravians, and Magyars into the white or Caucasian category and, in so doing, encouraged these groups to think of themselves as such. Moreover, "as scientists asserted over and over that 'Aryans,' 'Jews,' 'Italians,' 'Nordics,' and the like were not races, their myriad assertions themselves all buttressed an edifice founded upon three grand divisions of humankind—'Caucasian,' 'Mongoloid,' and 'Negroid'—whose differences by implication *were* racial." In the end, the political and social ramifications of the shift in race thinking were unclear. Therefore, it is only through social history that we can discern what the changing meaning of race meant to various people in their daily lives—when they sought to buy a house, enter a restaurant, join a union, get a job, immigrate to the United States, marry a partner, and so forth.

THE CHANGING SOCIAL AND POLITICAL MEANING OF RACE

The Great Depression

The stock market crash of October 1929 and the ensuing decade-long Great Depression brought incalculable loss and despair to millions of Americans. In the industrial North and Midwest, unemployment and eviction rates soared, while employers drastically reduced the hours and wages of those few people lucky enough to work. Southern and western ports, meanwhile, faced a dip in exports and a rapid increase in unemployment. In rural America conditions were just as bleak. With farm incomes declining by 60 percent between 1929 and 1932, one third of all farmers lost their land in these years. All the while, state and local relief systems, to say nothing of private charities, were wholly unequipped to deal with the magnitude of the Depression.

But Depression-era deprivation cannot be explained by or appreciated fully through economic statistics alone. Race mattered a great deal. How else could one explain the fact that African Americans, for example, suffered the sting of the Depression so much more severely than many other groups? For example, in one survey of 106 cities, the Urban

League reported "with a few notable exceptions . . . the proportion of Negroes unemployed was from 30 to 60 percent greater than for whites." In certain sections of Chicago, for example, African Americans' jobless rate had climbed as high as 85 percent. As a result, while making up less than 8 percent of the city's population, African Americans comprised over 30 percent of those on relief. And relief rarely amounted to much. The federal government's New Deal was often more like a raw deal for many African Americans: the Civilian Conservation Corp lodged them in segregated camps; the National Recovery Administration ignored job discrimination and pay disparities; the Tennessee Valley Authority excluded them almost entirely; and the Agricultural Adjustment Administration greatly favored white farmers. As writer Langston Hughes poignantly put it in his "Ballad of Roosevelt" (1934):

> the pot's still empty,
> And the cupboard's still bare,
> And you can't build a
> bungalow
> Out o' air—
> Mr. Roosevelt, listen!
> What's the matter here?

These facts are a smaller part of a much larger story, however: the inequities of the U.S. racial structure, which varied some from one region to the next, but in which African Americans were always located close to if not on the bottom. In the South, African Americans were denied the right to vote, made subject to an extensive system of Jim Crow segregation, often lynched with impunity, and forced to comply with a range of racial etiquette rules that reinforced subordination daily. And things were not always radically better in the North and West, where restrictive covenants, real estate practices, financial institutions, neighborhood violence, and "improvement" organizations all worked to segregate African Americans residentially; where many unions barred them from membership and employers refused to hire them for high-paying, skilled jobs; and where, as in the South, equal access to public accommodations was rarely the rule.

African Americans were not the only group poorly positioned in this structure. Ethnic Mexicans, too, (all people of Mexican origin, citizens and noncitizens alike), throughout the Southwest, suffered from

widespread segregation in schools, public accommodations, and neighborhoods; they were often excluded from serving on juries; and they
were given the most menial jobs at the worst pay. The Depression era,
moreover, brought a state-sponsored repatriation program, which sent
hundreds of thousands of ethnic Mexicans (many American citizens
among them) "back home" to Mexico, often involuntarily.

For Asians and Asian Americans things were no better. On the West
Coast, for instance, widespread job discrimination forced groups like
Japanese Americans and Chinese Americans to find work in their own
ethnic enclaves; alien land laws robbed them of their right to own property; and antimiscegenation laws (which also targeted African
Americans and Native Americans in many states) prevented them from
marrying any partner they wished. In addition, by the 1930s immigration and naturalization laws excluded all Asians from immigrating to
the United States and deemed all immigrants making it to the U.S.
prior to these laws ineligible for citizenship. As for Native Americans,
their racial status had long made them exceedingly vulnerable to white
aggression, landgrabs, and treaty violations. Indeed, by the time of the
crash, and in large part because of the Dawes Act of 1887 (which instituted a new program of land allotment without any say from Native
Americans), Indians were becoming increasingly a landless and destitute
people. Virtually half of Native Americans who lived on reservations and
who were subject to allotments had lost their land, while a slightly larger
percentage earned on average less than $200 a year.

Even certain European groups suffered from racial discrimination.
The racialist theories behind the Immigration Act of 1924 still circulated freely around the United States and continued to cause problems
for some Europeans. Jews, for instance, continued to face restrictive
covenants in certain cities, a rising Depression-era anti-Semitism
reflected in the popularity of Father Coughlin and grassroots organizations like William Pelley's Silver Shirts and the Christian Front, and
discrimination in college admissions at elite universities like Harvard.
Other European groups encountered similar discrimination. In one
extensive study of Italians in New Haven conducted in 1938, sociolo-
gist Irvin Child found that "there is . . . a widespread prejudice against
Italians which makes it difficult for people of Italian descent to obtain
the better jobs in the community." Similarly, in Chicago, for well into
the 1930s Italians met with some degree of resistance from other
European immigrants and some native-born whites when moving into

certain neighborhoods. In his classic and highly influential text, *One Hundred Years of Land Values in Chicago* (1933), Homer Hoyt reproduced a list made by a West Side realtor that ranked "races and nationalities with respect to their beneficial effect upon land values." Southern Italians were eighth on this list of ten groups, just above African Americans and Mexican Americans.

Still, it must be stressed that all Europeans—even the putatively inferior groups—were largely accepted as whites from the moment they arrived in the United States by "the widest variety of people and institutions—naturalization laws and courts, the U.S. census, race science, newspapers, unions, employers, neighbors, realtors, settlement houses, politicians and political parties, and so forth." Generally speaking, this acceptance meant most concretely that all immigrants from Europe could become citizens of the United States, vote with no problems, join virtually any union once they became citizens, and move to virtually any neighborhood without any serious or organized resistance. This acceptance varied somewhat by religion and region most notably. Regardless, for certain groups their racialness as Italians, Poles, or Greeks mattered when it came to rights and resources; but their color status as whites mattered infinitely more. As Matthew Jacobson has aptly put it, whiteness was the key that opened the Golden Door.

The U.S. racial structure, then, just as surely conferred advantage as disadvantage. Whoever was accepted as white in this system received access to better jobs, better housing, more powerful unions, better incomes, citizenship, and voting rights. And these privileges often transcended class and gender lines, such that, as Dana Frank has recently shown, "white working-class women entered a labor market in which they were below white men, but they were above women of color and—in many but not all cases—above men of color." For women who worked at home, privileges were just as numerous and striking. Residential segregation meant not only better housing but also better amenities, like electricity and running water, which made housework and child care incomparably easier. Moreover, white women of all class backgrounds, often because of the superior wages of their husbands, were much more likely than nonwhite women to hire domestic servants. Predictably, these servants were almost always women of the "colored races." Taken together, whiteness conferred great privilege on all who could lay claim to it—irrespective of one's gender, class, or *European* race.

Because of these great inequities, groups disadvantaged by the U.S. racial structure fought hard to make sense of it, restructure it, reform it, or eliminate it. This was particularly true during the Depression years, when many Americans lost faith in an economic system that was collapsing all around them and a political system that, at least initially, could do little about it. Efforts to change the U.S. racial structure were undertaken by a wide array of groups, in the name of a diverse range of ideologies, political projects, and social identities. African Americans all across the country, for instance, joined a range of groups and movements like the Communist Party, the Urban League, the CIO, and the NAACP. During this period blacks turned to the federal courts for protection, began the slow shift to the Democratic Party, organized to vote, and took part in massive studies to expose the underbelly of racism and discrimination as a blight on democracy. Away from the glare of the media they told stories and encouraged their children to fight for a better tomorrow. Through activism, they fought for better relief provisions, better jobs, better housing, anticolonialism in Ethiopia and antifascism in Spain, and antilynching and anti-poll tax legislation here in the United States.

Meanwhile, many ethnic Mexicans, deeply troubled by repatriation and a Depression era rise in anti-Mexican hysteria, responded in a variety of ways. Some Mexican Americans joined new organizations such as LULAC, which stressed assimilation as the solution to Mexican American problems in the United States. Others joined and built *mutualistas*, unions, and important umbrella organizations like Confederacion de Uniones Obreras Mexicanas. They encouraged cultural preservation and blamed Americans, not unassimilated immigrants, for the plight of *la raza* (the people).

Battles for greater racial justice in the 1930s did not always unfold within strict racial boundaries, however. Indeed, as Michael Denning has argued, much of the activism outlined above was part of a larger whole—"the Popular Front . . . the insurgent social movement forged from the labor militancy of the fledgling CIO, the anti-fascist solidarity with Spain, Ethiopia, China, and the refugees from Hitler, and the political struggles on the left wing of the New Deal." And African Americans, Mexican Americans, Asian Americans, and various European groups all became centrally involved in this movement as artists, writers, musicians, and workers. Many of these groups, as well, through their activism in the movement, attempted to restructure the U.S. racial order in whichever way they could—through poetry, plays, marches, union drives, strikes, and movements for the unemployed.

Naturally, all of this activism against the racial structure attracted its share of resistance—particularly during the Depression years when competition over scarce resources only increased. A great example of this comes from within the Popular Front itself or, more specifically, the CIO unions. Many white CIO workers, their "culture of unity" notwithstanding, never fully accepted the official union line of racial equality, whether this was in the workplace, in the union hall, or in social events like picnics and bowling. Instead, while many racial groups insisted on using their unions to work for greater social justice, many white workers—some of whom were of Southern- and Eastern-European origin—fought to maintain the racial status quo through the 1930s and well into the '40s. Speaking about Memphis's CIO unions, Michael Honey has argued that there was "a stormy and continuing confrontation . . . over the meaning of trade unionism—with blacks wanting to use the union to batter down segregation and whites wanting it to keep segregation in place." And, of course, resistance occurred in other places as well: in scores of AFL unions and railroad brotherhoods that excluded various non-Europeans from membership; in boardrooms, where corporate leaders devised and enforced racially stratified pay scales and job structures, and in workplace cafeterias and bathrooms; in homes where parents taught their children the importance and location of the color line; in neighborhoods and public accommodations where color boundaries were fiercely defended; through radio shows, movies, and other forms of popular entertainment that reinforced the place of whites and nonwhites daily; and—in the South—through lynchings and southern Democrats' tight control over Congress, among many other means.

The state, during the Depression, largely sided with those groups fighting to maintain—not undermine—the racial structure. Of course, this was not always the case. FDR hired a significant number of second-tier African American bureaucrats to his cabinet; protected the labor movement that proved so beneficial to many "colored races"; and made real progress with regard to Native Americans by appointing John Collier as Commissioner of Indian Affairs and by ending the disastrous allotment program. Moreover, some members of FDR's cabinet like Harry Hopkins and Harold Ickes, not to mention his wife Eleanor, fought hard (if ultimately in vain) to ensure equal access to relief for all groups; and, particularly in the case of the latter, spoke out vigorously and frequently against racial injustice.

Still, larger problems remained. We have already discussed New Deal shortcomings when it came to African Americans' relief. In addition, FDR, in large part because he did not wish to alienate the powerful southern Democrats in Congress, did little to disturb the racial status quo of the South (i.e., its deep racial inequality). He refused to pass anti-poll tax or antilynching legislation, and his New Deal programs largely strengthened the hand of Black Belt planters, "the bulwark of the solid, segregationist South." Ethnic Mexicans too were often excluded from receiving relief because of rampant discrimination at the local level and were, as noted, victims of state-sponsored forced repatriation. Moreover, at the height of anti-Mexican hysteria, the state did not help matters when it reclassified Mexicans as nonwhite for the first time on the U.S. census in 1930. Finally, regarding Asian groups, the state continued to refuse them naturalization rights or immigration quotas of any kind. And for some Asians things only got worse during the 1930s. With passage of the Tydings-McDuffie Act in 1934, for example, the state reclassified Filipinos as aliens, making them no longer eligible for New Deal relief benefits and setting their annual immigration quota at a paltry fifty. For all of these groups, crucial reforms like the Social Security and Wagner Acts were disappointments. The former excluded domestic, agricultural, and common laborers—many of whom were African American, Latino, and Filipino; the latter did not protect the organizing rights of these same workers.

For some groups, however, the New Deal was nothing less than transformative. For Southern and Eastern Europeans, programs created and legislation enacted during the Depression—the Home Owners Loan Corporation, Federal Housing Administration loans, the Social Security Act, and the Wagner Act—provided them with enormous advantages over non-European groups in the housing and labor markets and when it came to state insurance benefits. It was these programs more than anything else that transformed so many working-class racially suspect "new" European immigrants into respectable middle-class "white ethnic" suburbanites. This transition really occurred during World War II and beyond; but its origins lay in New Deal programs created during the Depression.

And this point is really the theme of the era. For the "colored races" as well, little changed in the U.S. racial structure in these Depression years. However, just as the seeds for future transformations were sown for Southern and Eastern Europeans in these years, so too was this the case for groups like Mexican Americans and African Americans, who were beginning to join unions, civil rights groups, and other Popular Front organizations. Through expanded involvement in a broad array of organizations and institutions, many members of the "colored races" were building foundations for future social movements that ultimately transformed the U.S. racial structure.

World War II

The pace of change to America's racial order increased significantly during the war years. Massive wartime production created millions of new, better-paying industrial jobs for women and men, while union strength was on the rise; organized labor added 7 million new members during World War II. Perhaps more important, however, was how the war was represented and understood. In battling totalitarianism and Nazism abroad, American propaganda machines worked overtime to portray the U.S. nation as antithetical to its enemies. This meant that if totalitarianism demanded conformity, mocked freedom, and preached racial hatred, then Americans were pleasantly plural and instinctively democratic. Popular films and novels during the war never tired of celebrating American racial diversity. As John Hersey wrote in the preface to his best-selling novel, *A Bell for Adano* (1944), "America is an international country. . . . No other country has such a fund of men . . . who understand the ways and have listened to their parents sing the folk songs and have tasted the wine of the land on their palate of their memories. This is a lucky thing for America."

And yet despite these lofty ideals, the rise in wartime job opportunities and paeans to pluralism did not magically transform the U.S. racial structure. As in the past, if real change were to occur on this front, "colored races" would have to demand it. And this is precisely what happened, as activism by African Americans and Mexican Americans came of age. Using wartime democratic propaganda for their own purposes and building on Depression-era activism, these groups turned Roosevelt's war for "four freedoms" into what W. E. B. Du Bois called "the War for Racial Equality." The result was a restructuring of the racial order by the 1960s.

Asian Americans, Native Americans, African Americans, Mexican Americans, and some European Americans all shared some similar strategies of democratizing the U.S. racial structure at this time. Large numbers of men and women of all groups, for instance, served in the armed forces, invested in war bonds, participated in scrap metal drives, and worked in war production plants, all of which can be seen, at least in part, as an attempt to prove to their compatriots that they too were patriotic Americans deserving of equal rights. Native Americans provide a particularly striking example of these efforts. So many Native Americans served in the armed forces during the war (twenty-five thousand total, including eight hundred women) that the *Saturday Evening Post* remarked, "we would not need the Selective Service if all volunteered like Indians."

But battles in the "War for Racial Equality" certainly occurred on other fronts as well. African Americans were active from the start, in part because the gap between wartime democratic rhetoric and their everyday experiences was so intolerably enormous. For example, while booming wartime production brought higher-paying jobs to so many Americans in the early years of the war, many of these industries barred African Americans outright. In 1940 African Americans comprised only "0.2 percent of workers in aircraft production." In addition, they had to serve in segregated military units and received only the most menial positions in the Armed Forces, while the Red Cross segregated their blood.

In response to these injustices, African Americans took action in a variety of ways. Labor leader A. Philip Randolph organized the March on Washington Movement, which ultimately forced FDR to sign Executive Order 8802. This established the Fair Employment Practices Commission (FEPC), which sought to eliminate racial discrimination in government defense jobs. African American newspaper editors launched a "Double V" campaign to push for victory over the Axis abroad and over racial discrimination at home. Meanwhile, old civil rights groups swelled in size—the NAACP increased its membership ninefold—and new organizations like the Congress Of Racial Equality (CORE) were born; African American workers continued to battle within a growing and strengthening labor movement, becoming active leaders in CIO (and some AFL) locals and internationals across the country; African American social scientists at institutions like Howard University conducted groundbreaking research into the meaning of race and the nature of race relations in the United States; activists, public officials, intellectuals, and artists worked to harness the national mass medium of radio to fight racial segregation and discrimination. Finally, and perhaps most important, 2 million African Americans from the South moved northward and westward in the 1940s to find, if not a promised land, at least a place with greater possibilities for freedom. There they voted, exchanged favors with bosses of urban political machines, built new community-based institutions, transported and transformed elements of a rural folk culture such as the blues into new expressions, and struggled against other forms of discrimination and racial hostility. Capturing this moment of promise, Margaret Walker wrote in her poem "For My People" (1942): "For my people . . . trying to fashion a world that will hold all the people, all the faces, all the adams and eves and their countless generations; Let a new earth rise. Let another world be born. . . . Let the martial songs be written, let the dirges disappear. Let a race of men now rise and take control."

For Mexican Americans, too, the war years produced an upsurge in political activism aimed at restructuring the U.S. racial order. Their history in Los Angeles is instructive. As historian Edward Escobar has argued, ongoing police harassment of Mexican Americans, coupled with the outbreak of the "Zoot Suit" Riot in 1943 (in which hundreds of "Anglo" servicemen attacked and viciously beat scores of Mexican American youth), forever transformed Mexican Americans' "narrow political focus into . . . community-wide activism." Of course, this new activism had its roots in the civil rights and labor politics of the previous decade. Still, it was during the war years that Mexican Americans (particularly members of the second generation), mobilizing around the activities of community institutions like mutual aid societies, newspapers, and volunteer groups, built a new and assertive civil rights movement. As Escobar writes, "Mexican Americans [in Los Angeles] emerged from the wartime experience with a confidence and sophistication that exemplified a new political identity and a new political style. Simply put, they would no longer be ignored."

For groups like Japanese Americans, however, battling against racial injustice became even more challenging during the war years. Shortly after the bombing of Pearl Harbor and the U.S. declaration of war on Japan, anti-Japanese American feeling, always strong on the West Coast, reached a fever pitch among local and state politicians, farming interests, the press, labor unions, and everyday people. The *Los Angeles Times* noted, for instance, that "A viper is nonetheless a viper wherever the egg is hatched—so a Japanese American, born of Japanese parents—grows up to be a Japanese, not an American." Operating within this context of growing race hysteria, FDR ordered the internment in February 1942 of more than 110,000 Japanese and Japanese Americans living on the West Coast. General Dewitt, who oversaw the whole operation, justified it by stating that even among second- and third-generation Nisei "the racial strains are undiluted" and "racial affinities are not severed by migration."

Japanese Americans responded to the pains of war and internment in a variety of ways. Some sued the federal government all the way to the United States Supreme Court for violating their constitutional rights, with none gaining the relief desired. Others turned to traditional community institutions such as Christian churches and Buddhist temples, which "acted as racial-ethnic centers of protest" during the incarceration period. A few newspaper men and women, who avoided internment, continued publishing Japanese-American papers and in some cases fearlessly critiqued the government's treatment of Japanese Americans, encouraging the latter to use their rights to resist state oppression. Incensed by their treatment, and refusing to see themselves as other than loyal Americans, some organized protest movements in concentration camps to resist enlistment into the military until the government upheld Japanese Americans' civil rights. At the same time, some thirty-three thousand Japanese Americans joined the armed forces and pinned their hopes for future racial justice on their continued demonstration of patriotism and loyalty to America.

That attempts to restructure the racial order pervaded wartime America is perhaps best exemplified by the fierce resistance such attempts elicited. Pop culture's picture of pleasant pluralism notwithstanding, home-front America seethed with racial tensions. The Department of Labor reported that between July 1943 and October 1944, seventy-one race-related strikes had occurred throughout the country involving over sixty thousand female and male workers. Two impulses caused these strikes: either African Americans, sometimes with help from integrated unions, were demanding greater racial equality in the workplace or whites were demanding less.

Neighborhoods were another critical battle site. Due to restrictive covenants, discriminatory lending and real estate practices, and grass-roots neighborhood resistance, African American communities in the urban North, South, and West were already severely crowded prior to the war. Thus, when war finally broke out, and larger and larger numbers of African Americans poured into these communities, a crisis fast developed. In Chicago, the Metropolitan Housing Council reported in 1943 that "[t]he Negro district, prevented from expanding by restrictions on all sides, housing an already overlarge population in 1940, and housing that population in deteriorated, inadequate, indecent accommodations, is today bursting at the seams. . . . An explosive situation exists." The MHC proved prophetic as full-scale race riots and/or disturbances plagued scores of cities and towns across America. The worst of these occurred in Detroit in June 1943, where battles between African Americans and whites swept through the city uncontrolled for three days, leading to hundreds of injuries and thirty-four deaths. In the end, six thousand national troops were required to quell the violence.

White riot and strike protagonists were sometimes of "new" European immigrant origin—that is, Poles, Italians, Hungarians, Russians, and Jews, among others. Their involvement speaks to another wartime transformation: the increasing salience among these groups of a white racial identity. Though much more research needs to be done on the subject, it appears that it was during the war years that Southern and Eastern Europeans began to mobilize most consciously and more frequently than ever before as whites. Why exactly this was the case— particularly when these groups were accepted as "white on arrival" in the United States—is an important and complicated question on which we can only speculate now. And certainly a compelling answer would vary some from one group to the next. It would seem, however, that for all Southern and Eastern Europeans the salience of a white racial identity had something to do with the simplification of racial discourse, which also simplified and limited Europeans' racial identity options; the northward and westward migration of "colored" groups, particularly African Americans, creating numerous housing and workplace battles around which a white identity could be both mobilized and constructed; and the increased feeling among immigrants and their second-generation children of belonging to America, which, as Arnold Hirsch has aptly noted, "seemed organically linked" to a sense of whiteness.

And indeed it was during the war years that many Southern and Eastern Europeans felt most American. To be sure, discrimination and prejudice still persisted. Fearing an anti-Semitic backlash, FDR refused in the late 1930s and early 1940s to alter immigration quotas to allow for the entry of thousands of European Jews wishing to escape Nazi terror. Indeed, at the height of the Holocaust, 40 percent of Americans, according to one opinion poll, still believed Jews had too much power.

Meanwhile, employers across the country—particularly during the early years of the war when intense labor shortages were still rare—attempted to restrict their hiring to "Nordics only."

Still, a transformation in the general treatment of European Americans was well underway. Only twenty years prior they were widely condemned as biologically inferior and unassimilable. Now they were seen as the very definition of a democratic America. If African Americans, Latinos, Native Americans, and Asian Americans were sometimes featured as members of America's exalted melting pot, it was really the European groups who appeared over and over as indispensable to it. As one character in Sinclair Lewis's best-selling novel *Cass Timberlane* (1945) remarks, "the new America is not made up of British stock and Irish and Scotch, but of the Italians and Poles and Icelanders and Finns and Hungarians and Slovaks." And to appreciate this fact was to "speak the American language." Similarly, one *Time* article, in describing a U.S. army raid in France, noted that the names of the GIs "sounded like the roster of an All-American eleven. . . . There were Edward Czeklauski of Brooklyn, George Pucilowski of Detroit, Theodore Hakenstod of Providence, Zane Gemill of St. Clair, Pa., Frank Christensen of Racine, Wi., Abraham Dreiscus of Kansas City. There were the older, but not better, American names like Ray and Thacker, Walsh and Eaton and Tyler. The war . . . was getting Americanized." Indeed, the concept of Americanization had come a long way since the days of Anglo-conformity in the World War I era. By World War II, Americanization seemed more like ethnicization, the process by which ethnics did not become more American, but rather Americans became more ethnic (i.e., *European* ethnic).

And *ethnic* is the right word here. These groups had become so accepted at this time that the differences between them and "Old" Americans ceased to be considered racial at all. It was for this reason that, as we saw at the outset of this essay, ethnicity emerged as a critical social scientific concept. When racial lines no longer separated a Magyar from a Moravian, ethnicity appeared as a term to describe their differences.

When war finally came to an end in Europe, in May 1945, and in the Pacific several months later, some important changes had certainly occurred to the U.S. racial structure. Foremost, there was a change in expectations across the board. As one Mexican American put it in 1942, "This war . . . has shown those 'across the tracks' that we all share the same problems. It has shown them what the Mexican Americans will do, what responsibility he will take, and what leadership qualities he will demonstrate. After this struggle, the status of the Mexican Americans will be different." Returning veterans joined with others in their communities to fight for basic civil rights in the next two decades. Among whites the war highlighted the underlying tension implicit in creating a truly democratic country. For those ethnics who identified more and more as white, they proved as hardened as southern whites in their opposition to close interactions with "colored" groups. Thus, while the war created greater opportunity for social and geographic mobility for all groups, it also placed the nation on a collision course with its existing racial order.

The Cold War and Early 1960s Activism

If World War II marked a turning point in the efforts of certain racial groups to demand equal rights, then the postwar era marked a new chapter in the nation's long history with race. Many nonwhites did not waste much time in seeking to affect change. Japanese Americans, for instance, fresh out of wartime concentration camps, got right to work to eliminate racial restrictions against them on the West Coast. Japanese Americans such as Kajiro and Kohide Oyama and organizations such as the Japanese American Citizens League fought alien land laws in the courts and through public initiatives, and scored major victories. In 1948, in *Oyama v. California,* the U.S. Supreme Court declared that such laws were unconstitutional; eight years later, California voters passed Proposition 13, banning these laws forever.

But not all Asian Americans were as successful at pushing for equal rights. Chinese Americans had to concentrate more on protecting the rights they already had. The rise of Cold War anticommunism, the fall of China in 1949, and the outbreak of the Korean War a year later all contributed to a growing suspicion of Chinese Americans in the United States. In 1950, Congress passed the Internal Security Act, which permitted the federal government to intern Communists during times of national emergency. In the mid-1950s the government instituted the "Confession Program," which allowed undocumented Chinese immigrants to report themselves, and everyone else they knew to be in the United States illegally, to the INS; in exchange the INS granted these immigrants citizenship so long as they were innocent of any involvement in subversive activities. Scores of Chinese immigrants came forward—ten thousand in San Francisco alone—and gained citizenship in the process. However, through this program the federal government increased its surveillance of Chinese American communities, using information they received through "confessions" to find and deport Chinese immigrants suspected of communist activities or sympathies.

As for Mexican Americans in the 1950s, in response to state repression—especially the so-called Operation Wetback of 1954, in which the federal government swept through ethnic Mexican communities, apprehended undocumented immigrants, and deported more than 1 million of them—a "new, broader-based civil rights movement" among Mexican Americans emerged. At the heart of this movement was a wide range of organizations, from the GI Forum and LULAC in Texas to El Congresso, the Community Service Organization (CSO), and the Los Angeles Committee for the Protection of the Foreign Born in California. In 1949 in Los Angeles, the CSO registered fifteen thousand voters to help elect Edward Roybal to the Los Angeles City Council; while five years later, thanks in part to LULAC's legal strategy and organizing, the Supreme Court, for the first time, extended fourteenth-amendment protection to Mexican Americans in the landmark *Hernandez v. Texas* decision.

The most powerful and influential of postwar movements, however, came from African Americans. And despite a real lack of historiographical attention, this movement may have begun in the North, "partly due to the greater access to the ballot and freedom to organize without violent retaliation." In New York, for instance, as historian Martha Biondi has recently shown, "in the first decade after the war . . . [African Americans] fought for better jobs, an end to police brutality, new housing, Black representation in government, and college education for their children. Their battles . . . pushed New York City and state to pass landmark anti-discrimination laws in employment, housing, public accommodations, and education, that inspired similar laws in dozens of other states, and became models for national legislation." And African Americans were active in the West too. In 1958, blacks in Oklahoma launched a six-year campaign to end segregation in restaurants, while African Americans in Denver staged a sit-in at the Governor's office to protest racial discrimination.

And yet this movement, for all its success, ran into massive resistance on a wide range of levels. First, the rising Cold War climate of anticommunism, as Mary Dudziak argues, did offer activists added leverage in their fight for equal rights, as the U.S. government became ever more committed to polishing its global image. Still, this climate also severely restricted the boundaries of acceptable antiracist protest. In addition, many African American activists lost their most committed allies in labor unions and civil rights organizations because of anticommunist purges. Second, resistance came in the urban North and parts of the urban West, from African Americans' white neighbors and coworkers. Through neighborhood improvement organizations, local politics, wildcat strikes, union activism, and violence, they resisted the integration of "their" workplaces and neighborhoods with everything in their power. Indeed, in Chicago, "between 1945 and 1950, some 485 racial 'incidents' were reported to the Chicago Commission on Human Relations" many of which were major disturbances in which thousands of white women, men, and children destroyed property and assaulted African Americans. The formerly "inferior races" of Southern and Eastern Europe were big actors in these dramas.

Finally, the most powerful force for resistance was the federal government, particularly in the realm of housing. The federal government, of course, was central to the Cold War purges, but they opposed African Americans in other, more insidious ways as well. As historian Arnold Hirsch has argued, "With the emergence of federal supports for the private housing industry, public housing, slum clearance, and urban renewal . . . government took an active hand, not merely in reinforcing prevailing patterns of segregation, but also in giving them a permanence never seen before. The implication of government in the second ghetto was so deep, so pervasive, that it virtually constituted a new form of de jure segregation." The most disastrous of government programs was no doubt its FHA loan program, which because of its highly discriminatory appraisal methods, channeled billions of dollars in home loans away from African American and other "colored" neighborhoods and toward white suburbia. As historian Kenneth Jackson has shown, "the main beneficiary of the $119 billion in FHA mortgage insurance issued in the first four decades of FHA operation was [white] suburbia." Thus, the government in these years was intimately involved not just in making the second ghetto but in making the first all-white, multiethnic, middle-class suburb, as well. In the end, this suffocating housing discrimination, coupled with equally powerful obstacles in the labor market (deindustrialization, discrimination, etc.), went a long way in explaining the outbreak of African American revolts in hundreds of cities and towns across the country between 1965 and 1968.

Meanwhile, in the South, things developed a bit differently. In the immediate postwar years, African Americans, often led by returning World War II veterans, stepped up their drive to restructure the racial order in the South and had some success. In cities such as Winston-Salem, Greensboro, and Atlanta thousands of African Americans registered to vote for the first time, leading to the election in Winston-Salem of the first black alderman in 1947, and to the creation of black political machines in all three of these cities. Most impressively, "as a result of these efforts, the number of Negroes registered to vote in the south increased from 2 percent in 1940 to 12 percent in 1947." As historian C. Vann Woodward noted, "For the first time since the beginning of the century Negroes reappeared in elective and appointive office, largely in the upper South, on school boards, city councils, and other minor posts." Complementing these activities at the national level was the NAACP's ongoing legal strategy that continued to pay off in important ways. The Supreme Court outlawed segregation in interstate travel in 1946; segregation at state-funded graduate and law schools in 1950; and in 1954, in its landmark *Brown v. Board of Education*, reversed the Plessy decision of 1896, declaring that "in the field of public education the doctrine of 'separate but equal' has no place."

In these battles, however, the executive branch was decidedly less helpful. President Truman had his moments of rhetorical flourish when it came to African American civil rights; he also spoke out in favor of a permanent FEPC, desegregated the military, and created a Committee on Civil Rights which, after an extensive report on race in the United States, called for, among other things, the establishment of a civil rights division of the Justice Department and the passage of antilynching and anti–poll tax legislation. Still, when it came to following through on these recommendations or on his more inspired civil rights addresses, Truman did very little.

But if Truman, thanks in part to the power of Southern Democrats, was ineffective, Eisenhower was worse. When the Supreme Court handed down its momentous Brown decision and he was asked to comment, Eisenhower equivocated publicly and denounced it privately. Furthermore, when brutal anti-African American violence spread throughout the South, the President refused to do anything in word or deed about it. His sending troops into Little Rock, Arkansas, was too little too late, and his Civil Rights Act of 1957 was, according to one Southern segregationist, "in the main . . . a victory for the South."

Eisenhower's inaction sent a clear message to the white segregation-ist South—resist Brown if you wish; and this message was well received and very quickly acted upon. Throughout the region individuals and institutions organized a massive resistance against integration of any kind: the Southern white press vehemently and vocally denounced the Supreme Court decision; grass-roots resistance movements, like the White Citizens' Council, which claimed a membership of half a million people in the mid-1950s, emerged throughout the South; state legisla-tures passed scores of new prosegregation legislation; and 101 of the South's congressmen signed a manifesto in 1955 that, in the words of Anthony Lewis, made "defiance of the Supreme Court and the Consti-tution socially acceptable . . . [and gave] resistance to the law the approval of the Southern Establishment." The result of these varied efforts were staggering. By 1955, in eight southern states no school integration had taken place at all.

These events, taken together, taught many African Americans a lesson they had in fact learned many times before: that if progress were to be made, they would have to rely on their own actions and their own pressure from below. We have already seen that this activism had been steadily rising for several decades. It reached a new mass direct-action phase in the late 1950s and early 1960s with the Montgomery Bus Boycott of 1955–1956 and especially the sit-in movement that spread throughout the South in the early 1960s.

Beginning in Greensboro, North Carolina, black college students used the power of their wallets and purses to draw attention to the ugli-ness of segregation. Students borrowed a chapter from the annals of American labor, which had mounted effective sit-down strikes during the 1930s. At North Carolina A&T, Fisk, and other campuses, disci-plined corps of black students descended on local restaurants and lunch counters, quietly but defiantly demanding to be served. On many occa-sions they encountered hostile whites, determined to see the black youth obey the laws and practices of segregation. These students used these gatherings to galvanize adults and remind all that segregation could be attacked if blacks organized.

And so organize they did—in well-established civil rights groups such as the NAACP, the Urban League, and the National Colored Women's Association—and in newer ones like the Congress for Racial Equality (CORE), the Student Nonviolent Coordinating Committee (SNCC), and the Southern Christian Leadership Conference (SLCC).

It should be pointed out, however, that despite popular emphasis upon the role of organizations like SCLC and leaders like Martin Luther King, this was first and foremost a movement of African American "local people." As historian David Garrow has noted:

> What the carefully scrutinized historical record shows is that the actual human catalysts of the movement, the people who really gave direction to the movement's organizing work, the individuals whose records reflect the greatest substantive accomplishments, were not administrators or spokespersons, and were not those whom most scholarship on the movement identifies as the 'leaders.' Instead, in any list, long or short, of the activists who had the greatest personal impact upon the course of the southern movement, the vast majority of names will be ones that are unfamiliar to most readers.

And it was these unfamiliar African Americans who, despite massive and violent resistance and a long apathetic federal government, built a movement that secured major civil rights legislation in 1964 and 1965: the Civil Rights Act of 1964 ended de jure segregation for good and the Voting Rights Act of 1965 finally returned the franchise to southern African Americans. Also coming out of this movement, if less directly, was the equally momentous Immigration Act of 1965. This abolished all racial quotas and excised all references to race in U.S. immigration policy and law. This would lead to new immigration waves from Latin America and Asia that would, like African American migration from the South several decades earlier, forever alter the demography, racial politics, and racial structure of the United States.

BIBLIOGRAPHIC ESSAY

The history of race and ethnicity in the United States between the Great Depression and the passage of the Civil Rights Act of 1964 is characterized by profound and transformative changes in social relations and in the ideologies used to understand and shape these relations. For a general overview of these changes, read Ronald Takaki, *A Different Mirror: A History of Multicultural America* (Boston: Little, Brown, 1993) and Gary Gerstle, *American Crucible: Race and Nation in the Twentieth Century* (Princeton: Princeton University Press, 2000).

By the late 1930s the harsh realities of racist thinking as social policy found full form in Nazi Germany. At about the same time, new scholarship critical of scientific racism emerged. Eventually this scholarship served to undermine the logic of racism and segregation in the United States. See, for example, Gunnar Myrdal, *An American Dilemma: The Negro Problem and Modern Democracy* (New York: Harper, 1944); Ashley Montagu, *Race: Man's Most Dangerous Myth* (New York: Columbia University Press, 1942); Ruth Benedict, *Race: Science and Politics* (New York: Viking, 1943); UNESCO, *The Race Concept: Results on an Inquiry* (Paris: UNESCO, 1952); and Elazar Barkan, *The Retreat of Scientific Racism: Changing Concepts of Race in Britain and the United States Between the Wars* (Cambridge: Cambridge University Press, 1992).

For other work on race/ethnicity in the ideological and cultural realm during the prewar and/or postwar eras, see Lee D. Baker, *From Savage to Negro: Anthropology and the Construction of Race, 1896–1954* (Berkeley: University of California Press, 1998); Michael Denning, *The Cultural Front: The Laboring of American Culture in the Twentieth Century* (New York: Verso, 1997); and Elizabeth Grace Hale, *Making Whiteness: The Culture of Segregation in the South, 1890–1940* (New York: Pantheon, 1998).

For work on the racialization of various European immigrant groups, see Eric Arnesen, "Whiteness and the Historians' Imagination," *International Labor and Working-Class History* 60 (Fall 2001): 3–32; James R. Barrett and David R. Roediger, "In-between Peoples: Race, Nationality, and the 'New Immigrant' Working Class," *Journal of American Ethnic History*, 16 (spring 1997): 3–44; Thomas A. Guglielmo, *White on Arrival: Italians, Race, Color, and Power in Chicago, 1890–1945* (New York: Oxford University Press, 2003); Matthew Frye Jacobson, *Whiteness of a Different Color: European Immigrants and the Alchemy of Race* (Cambridge: Harvard University Press, 1998); and George Lipsitz, "The Possessive Investment in Whiteness: Racialized Social Democracy and the 'White' Problem in American Studies," *American Quarterly*, 47 (September 1997): 369–387.

For other important work on European groups and race/ethnic issues in these years, see Ronald H. Bayor, *Neighbors in Conflict: The Irish, Germans, Jews, and Italians of New York City, 1929–1941* (Baltimore: Johns Hopkins University Press, 1978); Lizabeth Cohen, *Making a New Deal: Industrial Workers in Chicago, 1919–1939* (New York: Cambridge University Press, 1990); and Gary Gerstle, *Working-Class Americanism: The Politics of Labor in a Textile City, 1914–1960* (New York: Cambridge University Press, 1989). Materials in the files of the Immigration and Naturalization Services, Record Group 85, National Archives I, underscore the federal government's own role in reclassifying European immigrant communities in ethnic rather than racial terms.

Members of the "colored races" played pivotal roles in restructuring the U.S. racial order. There is a voluminous literature on these histories up to and through World War II. On African Americans, see St. Clair Drake and Horace Cayton, *Black Metropolis: A Study of Negro Life in a Northern City* (New York: Harcourt, Brace, 1945); Robin D. G. Kelley, *Hammer and Hoe: Alabama Communists During the Depression* (Chapel Hill: University of North Carolina Press, 1990); Earl Lewis, *In Their Own Interests: Race, Class, and Power in Twentieth-Century Norfolk, Virginia* (Berkeley: University of California Press, 1991); Ronald H. Bayor, *Race and the Shaping of Twentieth-Century Atlanta* (Chapel Hill: University of North Carolina Press, 1996); and Barbara Dianne Savage, *Broadcasting*

Freedom: Radio, War, and the Politics of Race, 1938–1948 (Chapel Hill: University of North Carolina Press, 1999).

On Mexican Americans, see Edward J. Escobar, *Race, Police, and the Making of a Political Identity: Mexican Americans and the Los Angeles Police Department, 1900–1945* (Berkeley: University of California Press, 1999); Neil Foley, *The White Scourge: Mexicans, Blacks, and Poor Whites in Texas Cotton Culture* (Berkeley: University of California Press, 1997); Vicki Ruiz, *From Out of the Shadows: Mexican Women in Twentieth-Century America* (New York: Oxford University Press, 1998); and George J. Sanchez, *Becoming Mexican American: Ethnicity, Culture, and Identity in Chicano Los Angeles, 1900–1945* (New York: Oxford University Press, 1993).

On Native Americans, see Jere Bishop Franco, *Crossing the Pond: The Native American Effort in World War II* (Denton: University of North Texas Press, 1999); and Peter Iverson, *We Are Still Here: American Indians in the Twentieth Century* (Wheeling, Ill.: Harlan Davidson, 1998). On Asian Americans, see Sucheng Chan, *Asian Americans: An Interpretive History* (Boston: Twayne, 1990); Alice Yang Murray, ed., *What Did the Internment of Japanese Americans Mean?* (Boston: Bedford, 2000); Ronald Takaki, *Strangers from a Different Shore* (Boston: Back Bay Books, 1989); David Yoo, *Growing up Nisei: Race, Generation, and Culture among Japanese Americans of California, 1924–1949* (Urbana: University of Illinois Press, 2000); Nayan Shah, *Contagious Divides: Epidemics and Race in San Francisco's Chinatown* (Berkeley: University of California Press, 2001); and Judy Yung, *Unbound Feet: A Social History of Chinese Women in San Francisco* (Berkeley: University of California Press, 1995).

The literature on the postwar struggles of these same groups and on the resistance they faced is also large. On the urban North and African Americans, see Arnold R. Hirsch, *Making the Second Ghetto: Race and Housing in Chicago, 1940–1960*, 2nd ed. (Chicago: University of Chicago Press, 1998); Martha Biondi, *To Stand and Fight: Black Radicals and the Struggle for Negro Rights in New York City, 1945–1955* (Cambridge: Harvard University Press, 2003); and Thomas J. Sugrue, *The Origins of the Urban Crisis: Race and Inequality in Postwar Detroit* (Princeton: Princeton University Press, 1996).

On the West and its more complicated set of race/ethnic groups, see David G. Gutiérrez, *Walls and Mirrors: Mexican Americans, Mexican Immigrants, and the Politics of Ethnicity* (Berkeley: University of California Press, 1995); Peggy Pascoe, "Race, Gender, and the Privileges of Property: On the Significance of Miscegenation Law in the U.S. West," in Valerie J. Matsumoto and Blake Allmendinger, eds., *Over the Edge: Remapping the American West* (Berkeley: University of California Press, 1999), pp. 215–230; Chris Friday, "'In Due Time': Narratives of Race and Place in the Western United States," in Paul Wong, ed., *Race, Ethnicity, and Nationality in the United States: Toward the Twenty-First Century* (Boulder: Westview Press, 1999); and the works previously cited by Ruiz, Chan, Takaki, and Iverson.

The literature on the southern freedom struggle is, of course, enormous. For a sample of excellent works, see Taylor Branch, *Parting the Waters: America in the King Years* (New York: Simon and Schuster, 1988); Clayborne Carson, *In Struggle: SNCC and the Black Awakening of the 1960s* (Cambridge: Harvard

University Press, 1981); Mary L. Dudziak, *Cold War Civil Rights: Race and the Image of American Democracy* (Princeton: Princeton University Press, 2000); Charles Payne, *I've Got the Light of Freedom: The Organizing Tradition and the Mississippi Freedom Struggle* (Berkeley: University of California Press, 1995); Belinda Robnett, *How Long? How Long?: African-American Women in the Struggle for Civil Rights* (New York: Oxford University Press, 1998); and Harvard Sitkoff, *The Struggle for Black Equality, 1954–1992* (New York: Hill and Wang, 1993).

For the role of the state in the struggles over the U.S. racial order during the prewar and postwar eras, see especially Desmond King, *Making Americans: Immigration, Race, and the Origins of the Diverse Democracy* (Cambridge: Harvard University Press, 2000); Daniel Kryder, *Divided Arsenal: Race and the American State during World War II* (Cambridge: Cambridge University Press, 2000); Harvard Sitkoff, *A New Deal for Blacks* (New York: Oxford University Press, 1978); and Patricia Sullivan, *Days of Hope: Race and Democracy in the New Deal Era* (Chapel Hill: University of North Carolina Press, 1996).

On organized labor, in addition to the many works already cited, see Michael K. Honey, *Southern Labor and Black Civil Rights: Organizing Memphis Workers* (Urbana: University of Illinois Press, 1993); Bruce Nelson, *Divided We Stand: American Workers and the Struggle for Black Equality* (Princeton: Princeton University Press, 2001); and Bruce Nelson, "Class, Race and Democracy in the CIO: The 'New' Labor History Meets the 'Wages of Whiteness'," *International Review of Social History* 41 (1996): 351–374.

On gender and the U.S. racial order, see especially Dana Frank, "White Working-Class Women and the Race Question," *International Labor and Working-Class History*, 54 (Fall 1998): 80–102; Ruth Feldstein, *Motherhood in Black and White: Race and Sex in American Liberalism, 1930–1965* (Ithaca: Cornell University Press, 2000); and Gwendolyn Mink, *The Wages of Motherhood* (Ithaca: Cornell University Press, 1995).

8

RACIAL AND ETHNIC RELATIONS IN AMERICA, 1965–2000

Timothy J. Meagher

On March 21, 1965, Martin Luther King, Jr. led a march across the Pettus Bridge in Selma, Alabama, on the road to Montgomery, the state's capitol. The march capped a brutal battle between police and black protesters, including a vicious assault on marchers on this very bridge by local and state police just weeks before. As with other demonstrations of the era, most notably in Birmingham, Alabama, in 1963, the whole world was watching this confrontation on television. Black protesters may thus have been bloodied, but ultimately, they, not the police, the city of Selma, nor the state of Alabama would triumph. On August 6, 1965, President Lyndon B. Johnson would sign the Voting Rights Act of 1965, the second major piece of civil rights legislation passed in little over a year. Solid majorities in Congress for this new civil rights act and rapidly rising support for the civil rights movement suggested that race relations in the United States had reached an historic pass.

Over the next thirty-five years, from the march across the Pettus Bridge to our own time, racial and ethnic relations, boundaries, and identities in the United States were entirely transformed. A new configuration of ethnic and racial relations, a new structure of thinking about ethnicity and race—a new discourse—emerged. Before the 1960s, white privilege and power had kept African, Asian, and Latino Americans out of the arena of real political and economic competition. African Americans were still disfranchised in their heartland of the American South and only slowly and painfully beginning to move up economic and political hierarchies in northern cities. Native Americans were a forgotten people, most wasting away in desultory and desperate poverty on reservations or in the poorest neighborhoods of western cities. Asian Americans were a tiny minority, only 0.5 percent of the population as late as 1960, because restrictive immigration laws had choked off their entry into the United States. Latinos, made up largely of a Mexican American lumpen proletariat in the Southwest and impoverished Puerto Ricans in eastern cities, were, if anything, even more marginalized than African or Asian Americans.

Only whites competed among each other for important economic and political stakes or cultural recognition. Divisions among whites were still important—economically, socially, and politically—as late as the early 1960s. Ethnic divisions appeared to have collapsed into a religious "triple melting pot" of Protestant, Catholic, and Jew by the 1950s, but the boundaries separating those religious groups still seemed durable, and religious group identities still seemed charged at the end of that decade. Widely acclaimed studies of ethnic and racial relations in the early 1960s by Gerhard Lenski on Detroit and Daniel Patrick Moynihan and Nathan Glazer on New York predicted, as Moynihan and Glazer stated, "Religion [as well as race] seem to define the major groups into which American society is evolving as the specifically national aspect of ethnicity declines."

In the period after 1965 a new kind of ethnic and racial relations would emerge. Not only ethnic but even religious divisions among whites would weaken, as boundaries separating Catholics, Protestants, and even Jews grew porous. This process had origins long before 1965 and by the millennium even yet would remain incomplete. Nevertheless, the merging of white ethnic and religious groups—by any measure, residential integration, the diversification of the economic elite, or intermarriage—accelerated rapidly after 1965. At the same time, African, Native, Asian, and Latino Americans entered into arenas of political and economic competition and struggles for cultural recognition with a heretofore unknown power and confidence. Together these groups remade understanding of American racial and ethnic relations. In the case of Native, Asian, and Latino Americans, this was quite literally true, for all of them not only began to assert claims for equality and recognition with a new vigor, they also began to invent pantribal Indian or panethnic Asian or Latino American identities that had hardly existed before. As dynamic as those groups were, however, it was African Americans who took the lead in asserting minority claims most aggressively and consistently, and African Americans who were most responsible for the new configuration. By the 1980s, all of these groups had invented a new conception, a new language of American social and ethnic relations, a language of "minorities" and "multiculturalism" that set African, Asian, Latino, and Native Americans apart against an undifferentiated white America. How much that conception has fit the realities of racial and ethnic boundaries, identities, and relations, and whether it, too, will soon dissolve into a new configuration is difficult to judge or predict at this time, the beginning of a new millennium.

The civil rights movement that reached its peak in 1965 had been dedicated to eliminating Jim Crow—the state impositions of racial inferiority and discrimination that existed throughout much of the South. Buoyed by the discrediting of scientific racism that followed the defeat of the Nazis, by the American government's sensitivity to third-world nations during the Cold War, by the Democratic Party's recognition of black voters in northern cities, and by the decisions of an activist Supreme Court, the civil rights movement waged a steady, heroic, and successful "war" of nonviolent protest against Jim Crow from the mid-fifties to the mid-sixties. The Civil Rights Acts of 1964 and 1965 broke forever state-enforced Jim Crow in the South, and made deliberate, transparent state racism forever impossible.

Yet even as King and his followers crossed the Pettus Bridge in triumph, African Americans were already rethinking the place they sought in American life and how they expected to get there. Though the mainstream civil rights organizations, the NAACP, and King's own Southern Christian Leadership Conference, remained committed to the goal of integration and tactics of nonviolent protest and legal challenge, new voices and new leaders emerged to question both, even as the movement was reaching its zenith. The most articulate new leader was a former Nation of Islam minister named Malcolm X, a man of stunning rhetorical gifts and charisma, who became a powerful influence on young black activists. Disturbed by its corruption, Malcolm X had left the Nation of Islam in 1964, but he carried with him its emphases on black solidarity, suspicion of whites, and openness to violent resistance. In the year between his departure from the Black Muslims and his assassination in 1965, Malcom X attempted to broaden and deepen that ideology with a critique of capitalism and identification with other colonized peoples.

Malcolm X's powerful personality, sharp rhetoric, and dramatic murder has made him a legendary figure for young blacks to this day, but he had a profound impact in his own time. In the early 1960s, while still a member of the Black Muslims, Malcolm X's influence spread through chapters of the Congress of Racial Equality (CORE) throughout the North. In 1965, he also had a powerful impact on Student Nonviolent Coordinating Committee (SNCC) activists when he delivered an electrifying speech to SNCC workers on the eve of the Selma protests. In 1963, CORE's members ousted James Farmer in favor of Floyd McKissick, and in 1965, Stokely Carmichael took over SNCC. Both new leaders were militants and sympathetic to appeals to black solidarity. Carmichael quickly became the spokesman for a new vision of Black goals and strategies. In June of 1966, in a Greenwood, Mississippi, schoolyard Carmichael talked not of integration or nonviolence but "Black Power." The next year Carmichael wrote a book with the political scientist Charles Hamilton that defined Black Power as "a call for black people in the country to unite, to recognize their heritage, to build a sense of community . . . to define their own goals, to lead their own organizations, and to support those organizations." Yet, as Manning Marable notes, meanings of Black Power quickly came to vary across a wide political spectrum. Some on the left understood Black Power as a clarion call to a political and economic revolution and perhaps even the creation of a separate black state. Yet black Republicans—with Richard Nixon's blessing—also seized on the phrase to suggest that Black Power could best be translated as Black Capitalism. If left and right sometimes stretched the meaning of Black Power beyond recognition, the phrase was not hollow. Its emergence marked a major turning point in racial and ethnic relations in the United States. Tamar Jacoby contends that by the spring of 1967, less than a year after Carmichael's Black Power speech in Mississippi, the protest movements of the early 1960s seemed a "distant memory." Jacoby asserts: "Activists' clothes, their talk, their image, their very body language had changed completely. The word 'Negro' was virtually dead, so was the phrase 'civil rights' and the idea of a multiracial crusade."

Jacoby exaggerates, but it was clear that African American understandings of their place in America were changing, and not just at the elite level of activists and intellectuals, but also below, among young African Americans living in northern cities. Beginning in Harlem in 1964 and rising to a crescendo in Detroit and Newark in 1967, African American ghettoes in cities across the United States erupted in riots. The eruption in Los Angeles of the Watts ghetto in 1965 cost thirty-four lives and forty million dollars in property damage. In Detroit forty-three people died, almost two thousand were injured, and fires ravaged fourteen square miles. Even the nation's Capital was not spared. In April of 1968, Washington's black ghettoes exploded. Martin Luther King's assassination touched off the Washington conflagration, but many of the other riots erupted after confrontations between blacks and white police officers. In Harlem in 1964, for example, residents rioted after a white police officer shot a fifteen-year-old black youth while trying to stop a fight. In Detroit, too, the spark came after police raided an after-hours nightclub in a black neighborhood. In all, the race riots from 1964 to 1972 resulted in more than 250 deaths, 10,000 serious injuries, and 60,000 arrests.

The riots suggested that the new militancy summed up in the phrase Black Power had deep and broad roots in the African American community. This new militancy was not all-pervasive among African Americans; indeed, polling data right up until King's death suggested broader support for him and his integrationist goals among blacks than for the newer Black Power advocates. Nevertheless, there was a palpable shift in sentiment even among those who continued to pay homage to King.

In large part, this was because of the very success of the civil rights movement. Julian Bond has described Black Power as "a natural extension of the civil rights movement . . . from the courtroom to the streets . . . [to the] ballot box to the meat of politics, the organization of votes into self interest units." In practical terms, the Voting Rights Act had finally guaranteed blacks political rights and permitted them to compete for political power anywhere in the United States. Black Power was the new slogan of that competition. In a less tangible but meaningful way, the civil rights movement and its successes had also aroused African Americans everywhere, helped them to shed fears born of years of savage repression, and raised their expectations of equality. Yet the civil rights movement, having accomplished those goals, could not move into the next phase. Civil rights protest tactics worked effectively in the South to provoke third parties, sympathetic whites in the North, and the federal government to put pressure on the southern states. There was strong white support in the North for the crusade to sweep away state legislated discrimination. Yet when the movement turned to the North itself, to cities like Chicago, it foundered among the rising expectations of black ghetto dwellers and the ambivalence or outright hostility of many northern whites. A change in tactics and attitude, a new militancy, had been brewing among members of northern CORE chapters, particularly in San Francisco and Brooklyn, long before the movement's final great southern victory after Selma.

Whatever the reasons, the changes in black strategies and attitudes summed up in Black Power had clearly been made, and they manifested themselves quickly in African American life. Instead of protest politics and the quest for rights, electoral politics and the drive for political office, substantive legislation and patronage began to dominate the black community. The results were impressive. Between March of 1969 and May of 1975, the number of black elected officials tripled from a little less than one thousand to nearly three thousand. In the South, the number of black office holders rose from less than one hundred in 1965 to one thousand in 1975. This was clearly the result of the Voting Rights Act, as the number of blacks registered to vote skyrocketed. In Mississippi it grew from 6.7 percent before 1965 to 59.8 percent of age-eligible blacks by 1969. Many of the newly elected, particularly in the South, won only minor posts—councilmen or school commit-teemen in small towns or cities. Yet almost every major city in the country would elect an African American mayor between 1965 and 1990, beginning with Carl Stokes in Cleveland and Kenneth Gibson in Newark, and ultimately including Coleman Young of Detroit, Maynard Jackson of Atlanta, Harold Washington of Chicago, Tom Bradley of Los Angeles, Wilson Goode of Philadelphia, David Dinkins of New York, and Kurt Schmoke of Baltimore. The number of black congressmen also rose from three in 1961 to thirteen in 1971 and to thirty-nine in 1993.

Black Power was not just a commitment to political mobilization; it was also a call for cultural revival and recognition. The two were not unrelated; black pride and solidarity undergirded the push for political power. In 1972, Imamu Baraka, the poet; Richard Hatcher, Mayor of Gary, Indiana; and Charles Diggs, a congressman from Detroit, presided over a black political convention in Gary that drew more than twelve thousand participants who made that link explicit. Yet Black Power's cultural program was, in many ways, far more successful than even the new Black politics. Beginning in the late 1960s Black Power advocates launched an attack on accepted American ideals of assimilation and Anglo-American cultural supremacy. As Stokely Carmichael's and Charles V. Hamilton's *Black Power* flatly stated, "we reject the goal of assimilation into middle class America." Native, Asian, and Latino American activists, and even some white ethnic leaders, would take up this rhetorical assault on Anglo-American culture and it would have critically important consequences for American racial and ethnic relations.

Yet of course it had revolutionary consequences for the black community too. It prompted changes in African American life, from new hairstyles and clothes to new holidays—Kwanzaa—to changes in names—personal names drawn from Islamic or African sources—and changes in the name of the race, substituting black or African American for Negro. Manufacturers, sensitive to this new market of racially conscious Blacks, made their own adjustments, producing everything from Black GI Joe and Barbie dolls to African-theme greeting cards. The most important, visible, and often controversial impact of the Black Power cultural revival was on the curricula of colleges and school systems. Before the late 1960s, the historian John Blassingame estimated, only five graduate history programs in the United States offered African American history courses and all of these were historically black colleges. By the middle 1970s, one observer estimated, there were Black Studies programs or courses in hundreds of colleges and universities across the country. These programs were often born in controversy; strikes and protests took place at schools as diverse as San Francisco State and Cornell University, and these schools would remain embattled throughout the 1970s and 1980s. By the latter decade, the numbers of Black Studies programs had begun to decline, but Black Studies and its offshoot, Afrocentric curricula, remained popular not only among many black college and university students and professors, but in the school departments of predominantly black cities like Detroit and Atlanta. Moreover, even most blacks who rejected what they perceived as the militant Afrocentrism of scholars like Molefi Asante remained fiercely committed to black pride and cultural recognition. Black Power may not have worked a political revolution, but it had worked a cultural one.

The black revolution that began in the 1960s reverberated far beyond the African American community. Native, Latino, and Asian Americans, inspired by the black example, also began to assert themselves and helped African Americans transform American ideas about race and ethnicity. Yet they did more as well. They "made" new panethnic groups that had never existed before—Native, Latino, and Asian American peoples, out of existing constituent tribal or national groups. With blacks, then, they worked to try to forge a new multicultural nation defined by the four major minorities set against a white majority. Once boasting millions of people in tribes stretching across a North

America that they had once ruled alone, the census counted but 523,391 Native Americans in the United States in 1960. The intent of Federal policy in the twentieth century was to encourage Indian assimilation; however, it also unwittingly laid the groundwork for the panethnic Indian identity that emerged in the 1960s. Federally funded Indian boarding schools may have tried to suppress Indian cultures among their charges, but because they drew students from a variety of tribes they also acted as little intra-Indian "melting pots." Policies aimed at terminating tribes and encouraging exodus from the reservation had the same effect. As Indians from all tribes gathered in the cities, they found each other there, discovered common grievances, and forged common organizations and institutions. Between 1952 and 1972, the federal government helped to relocate an estimated hundred thousand Indians to cities where they joined thousands more who had migrated to urban areas on their own.

As it would for other minorities (Latinos and Asian Americans), the black-led civil rights crusade and its successor, the Black Power movement, sparked a Native American movement that would transform the meaning of being Indian in America. Indian activism had little direct connection with either the black-led civil rights movement or later Black Power organizations, but both clearly inspired and helped shaped the new Native American protest. As Joanne Nagel states, "Red Power borrowed from civil rights organizational forms, rhetoric, and tactics but modified them to meet the specific needs and symbolic purposes of Indian grievances, targets, and locations." Political stirrings were noticeable in the Indian community as early as 1961, when representatives from sixty tribes met at the University of Chicago to organize and lay out a common political strategy. The National Indian Youth Council (NIYC), formed out of that meeting, became a kind of nursery for later activists. In the mid-1960s, several tribes sponsored "fish-ins" to assert their claims to special treaty rights in disputed waters and territories. In 1966, Indians from several tribes gathered to protest and ultimately disrupt a meeting between the Secretary of the Interior, Stewart Udall, and the staff of the Bureau of Indian Affairs in Santa Fe, New Mexico. That same year, it appears, Vine Deloria, Jr., used the phrase Red Power for the first time in a speech he made to the National Congress of American Indians.

It was, however, the occupation of Alcatraz Island in the middle of San Francisco Bay by scores of Indians on November 20, 1969, that sparked a new Red Power movement into life. The Alcatraz protesters pointed to a clause in an 1868 treaty between the Federal government and the Sioux to justify their occupation. That clause allowed Indians to claim unused federal property (in this case, the abandoned prison) on land that once had been tribal property but had been ceded to Federal authorities. The occupiers demanded that the island be remade into a center for Native American studies, an Indian Center for Ecology, and a training school. They stayed on the island for nineteen months, held news conferences, convened powwows and even launched occasional bow and arrow assaults on passing boats. The protest did not end until June 11, 1971, when Federal marshals removed the last fifteen remaining activists from the island. Alcatraz was a turning point in American Indian history, a decisive act giving birth to a Red Power movement. Indian activists like Deloria, Frances Wise, and George Horsecapture all agreed that Alcatraz "was a master stroke of Indian activism," and "a major turning point." Another veteran of Indian protest later told Joanne Nagel, "it started with Alcatraz; we got back our worth, our pride, our dignity, our humanity." Alcatraz not only sparked the Red Power movement to life; it embodied the movement's new panethnic identity. The activists who took over the island were largely urban Indians. They included Sioux, Navajo, Cherokee, Mohawks, Yakimas, and Omahas. As significantly, they self-consciously celebrated a new panethnic identity, calling themselves the "Indians of All Tribes," who stated in their initial press release, "We the native Americans re-claim the land known as Alcatraz island in the name of all American Indians."

Alcatraz touched off nearly a decade of Red Power protests across the country. Most were, like Alcatraz, "supratribal," drawing on, and enacted in behalf of, a wide and various range of Native American peoples. Many were coordinated, or at least inspired, by a new Indian organization, the American Indian Movement (AIM), founded in Minneapolis in 1968 to fight for Indian civil rights and made up largely of urban Indians of diverse tribes. In 1970 and 1971, Indians occupied Fort Lawton and Fort Lewis, in Washington State, and Ellis Island, the old immigration depot in New York harbor, and tried to "invade" the Bureau of Indian Affairs in Washington, D.C. In 1972 caravans of Indians crossed the country in a well-publicized descent on the BIA's offices. After 1972, protests took on a more violent tone and turned from civil rights to treaty rights issues. From February to May of 1973, activists took over the village of Wounded Knee, the site of the last great conflict in the Indian wars on the Pine Ridge reservation in South

Dakota. Two Indians were killed and many more Indians and whites wounded in that protest as gun battles broke out between activists and federal officials. The last major protest event in the decade was the "Longest Walk," another march on Washington in 1978.

By the time the Red Power protest movement had fizzled out in the late 1970s it had helped make Indians a far more powerful force in American politics than at any time in their twentieth-century history. The Indian population was too small to produce the kinds of gains in elected or appointed officials that marked African Americans' rising political power. Yet Indians' political clout was evident in the favorable legislation they wrung from Congress in the 1970s: the Self-Determination Act of 1975, the Health Care Improvement Act of 1976, and the Indian Child Welfare Act of 1978. Federal spending on Native Americans also skyrocketed, rising 22 percent a year from the 1960s until the late 1970s. Money for urban Indians alone rose from $8.5 million to $95.6 million over the same period. The Red Power protesters helped this cause by stoking Native American solidarity and making Indian issues more visible. They may also have acted as a radical foil that more moderate, conventional organizations, like the National Congress of American Indians and the National Tribal Chairman's Association, used to their advantage in negotiating with Congress and federal administrators. However they won their gains, Red Power produced tangible results.

Like Black Power, perhaps even more so, Red Power was as much a cultural clarion call as a battle cry for political struggle. Red Power's call for a renewal of Indian pride was electric. One Native American remembered that this new spirit of Indian pride swept his reservation like a "tornado" in the late 1960s and early 1970s. Yet, as with Black Power, Red Power was not just in the air; it worked a revolution in Indian culture, spawning new institutions and organizations dedicated to a revival of Native American culture. Over the last thirty years tribes across the United States, for example, have set up their own museums to interpret their cultures and traditions to their own people and visitors alike. In 1998, there were over one hundred and fifty such museums listed in the Smithsonian Institution's Tribal Museum Directory, and they meet regularly in a museum association known as the "Keepers of the Treasures." As that name suggests, Native Americans have been as concerned with regaining control of their culture as with educating their own people and others about it. Native Americans have thus sought to retrieve sacred objects and ancestral remains from white-run institutions that had collected them for study and display. In 1990, Native Americans helped push through the Native American Graves Protection and Repatriation Act to ensure such retrievals. In addition to museums, Indians have established their own radio shows, language classes, and tribal colleges. Today thirty-three tribal colleges, scattered from Michigan to California and Washington State to New Mexico, are members of the American Indian Higher Education Consortium. At the same time a number of major colleges and universities, including Arizona, California at Berkeley, Nebraska, Dartmouth, and Montana, have established Native American studies programs and many more offer courses in Native American history or literature.

These efforts did not merely revive specific tribal cultures and loyalties, however; Red Power political and cultural movements began to define a new people, a pantribal Indian people. In this way Red Power differed significantly from Black Power, which built on an existing race-wide consciousness of kind. Red Power emerged out of the Indian communities of the cities where tribal distinctions had blurred and intertribal marriage was common. From the beginning, organizations like AIM or NIYC pushed agendas that "emphasized the rights of all tribes and all Indians." In part such pantribalism was simply a pragmatic recognition of how Indians could operate most effectively within the American political system. Leaders understood they could make a more powerful impact on the Federal government as a broad national Indian people than as local tribes. Deloria has argued, "Pan-Indianism . . . accepted the definition of Indians as an American minority group and sought to make the group an identifiable constituency with recognizable influence, a group to whom successful white politicians owed favors. Thus today, we often talk about the Indian vote . . . we hardly ever . . . speak of the tribal vote." Yet through the Red Power movement, Pan-Indianism has become more than a political strategy; it has become a racial identity, emotionally felt and marked by distinctive "Indian" cultural customs. These included some rituals originally rooted in the cultures of specific tribes, like the sweat lodge, that eventually came to transcend their tribal origins and became "one of the things [all] Indians did." "By the 1970s," Deloria suggests, "it was possible to find wholly new kinds of behavior generally accepted as Indian." Indeed, as early as 1973, a survey of Arapahoe and Shoshone high school students in Wyoming found that almost all of them identified themselves "supratribally" as well as tribally—as Native Americans or American Indians as well as Shoshone or Arapahoe. The results of the political and cultural mobilization of Native Americans were nothing short of revolutionary. Indians, pounded into passivity and hounded towards extinction in the 1950s, became confident, aggressive, and often successful political players by the 1970s. As important, buoyed by political protest, they regained pride in their heritage and helped black Americans challenge older American conceptions of assimilation. The revival of Indian pride had a remarkable effect on the Indian population. Dwindling down through the first part of the twentieth century, the Native American population began to grow after 1930, initially slowly, but by the 1960s and 1970s very rapidly. Indeed, between 1960 and 1990, the Indian population grew from a little over 500,000 to nearly 1.9 million. Natural increase did not account for this skyrocketing growth; it involved nothing less than the "deassimilation" of hundreds of thousands of Americans; once ashamed of or indifferent to their native roots, they were now eager to re-claim their native past.

Latinos had lived within the continental boundaries of the United States before Anglo- or African Americans, but it was not until the twentieth century that migration from Mexico, Puerto Rico, Cuba, and other Latin American countries began to make Latinos a formidable force. Integration into world markets provoked economic dislocations throughout much of Latin America and many of the same countries suffered from the disruptions of war and revolution. Meanwhile, American economic growth accelerated, and improved communications raised awareness of the contrast between North America's apparent promise and Latin America's plight. By the 1970s and 1980s the urgency to migrate grew so strong that thousands crossed the southern border of the United States surreptitiously, and millions settled into a permanent illegal status after such secret crossings or after their visas for temporary stays ran out. Migration from Latin America to the United States, legal and illegal, thus boomed in the late twentieth century. Migrants from Mexico numbered less than fifty thousand in the 1910s, increased significantly in the 1920s, but fell back during the depression when some Mexican immigrants were even forced to return home. In the 1950s Mexican migration began to pick up again, rapidly accelerating by the 1970s. In the 1950s, about 250,000 Mexicans came to the United States, but by the 1970s the number increased to 650,000, and by the 1980s to over 1.5 million. Puerto Rican migration first reached significant size in the 1940s, and by

1950 there were about 300,000 first- and second-generation Puerto Ricans in the United States. By 1970, because of migration and natural increase, that population had quadrupled to almost 1.4 million and by 1980 had risen to over 2 million. Cubans had nineteenth-century roots in Florida, but the vast majority of today's Cuban Americans or their parents or grandparents came to the United States after Fidel Castro took over Cuba in 1959. From that year to 1990 an estimated eight hundred thousand Cubans fled to the United States. Finally, civil war and economic depression sent Salvadorans and Guatemalans to the United States in the 1970s and 1980s. In 1986, 138,000 Salvadorans, 51,000 Guatemalans and 15,000 Nicaraguans applied for amnesty under the terms of the new immigration law that went into effect that year. By 1990 there were an estimated 22 million Latinos in the United States and the number was rising so quickly that some experts predicted that there would be well over 40 million by 2010.

Like African Americans, Latinos lived on the margins of American economic, political, and cultural life until the 1960s, and, as with African Americans, a revolution in Latino life in the United States began in that decade. Mexican and Puerto Rican struggles for civil rights extended back into the early twentieth century, but the successes of the black-led civil rights movement inspired and energized Latinos as never before. Cesar Chavez and his United Farmworkers Union were among the most successful of the new organizations. Engaging in its first strike in 1965 and winning its first contract battles in 1966, Chavez's UFW was more like a social movement than a union. Learning from King and the black civil rights movements, the UFW did not launch a single strike but a series of continuous strikes blending into a single struggle on behalf of Mexican American farm workers. Chavez also pledged the UFW to nonviolence, a major break from Mexican traditions, and deliberately cultivated the sympathies of a broader public, reaching it through television and tying it to the movement through boycotts and volunteerism. Employing the same tactics as King's SCLC, the UFW's strikes began to blend into a broader civil rights struggle. The UFW would have a checkered subsequent history, but, as Geoffrey Fox has said, "from this period [the late 1960s and afterward] in part, because of Cesar Chavez's strategic discoveries, and in larger part because of the structural changes that had made the movement possible, the history of Mexican American political consciousness ceases to be a separate story from that of other protesting groups in the United States."

In the turbulence of the 1960s, trends of growing group assertion and solidarity in the Latino community paralleled the rise of Black Power among African Americans. As in the black community the new militancy appealed first to younger activists. In 1969, the National Chicano Youth Liberation Conference met for the first time in Denver and endorsed the idea of a national Chicano political party. Shortly thereafter, students in San Antonio founded La Rada Agnate (the United People) to contest local elections. The conference also heard the Chicano poet Aurita proclaim the Spiritual Plan of Aztlan, a vague claim to the American Southwest as the original homeland of the Mexica, Aztec, and other ancient Mexican peoples. In Los Angeles another group, the Brown Berets, emerged out of a church youth group, seeking to pull young Mexican Americans together into a coherent political force. Halfway across the country in Chicago, Illinois, a Puerto Rican gang called the Young Lords began to move from fights over street turf to community organizing. Jose Jiminez, their leader, had been impressed by black protest and inspired by Malcolm X while serving time in jail. By 1969, the Young Lords had established branches in New York and later Philadelphia. Like SNCC or CORE, these organizations led the shift to a more militant Latino politics in the late 1960s and early 1970s, a politics of group solidarity, pride, and self-assertion— "Brown Power."

Yet just as importantly, they saw themselves as members of more than just their own national groups—Mexicans or Puerto Ricans, for example. There were, of course, the black models that they saw as allies in their liberation struggle. Yet they also began to see the even closer links that potentially bound Puerto Ricans and Mexican Americans as Latinos—speakers of the same Spanish language. A riot in the Puerto Rican neighborhood of Chicago, provoked by conflicts with the police, eventually sparked the creation of a Spanish language community organization that served both the city's large Puerto Rican and Mexican American communities. In 1969, Jiminez and the Young Lords moved further afield, traveling to Los Angeles to link up with the leaders of the National Chicano Youth Liberation Conference and the Brown Berets. These were only small groups of young people, but they were pulling out of the radical rhetoric and ideology of the era and using a language of solidarity and liberation to forge a new panethnic identity for the Latino community in the United States. Geoffrey Fox suggests that "it was in the name of solidarity that various Chicano, Puerto Rican, and other

Latino groups began exploring the alliances that would become key to building a wider Hispanic identity."

As in the African American community, Latino political mobilization followed quickly upon the emergence of group consciousness. Several groups emerged in the 1970s to encourage Latino voter registration—including, for example, the Southwest Voter Registration and Education Project (1974) and the National Puerto Rican Coalition (1977). The success of such groups is hard to measure. On the one hand, the percentage of Latinos of voting age registered to vote did not increase between 1972 and 1988. Indeed, it fell from a little over 44 percent to 35 percent in that time. Nevertheless, the absolute number of Latinos registered and participating in the election process rose significantly, simply because the volume of Latino migration to the country was so huge. These numbers and a new Latino self-confidence paid off in an increase in elected officials and significant political appointments. By 1993, there were 196 Hispanic mayors in the United States and more than fourteen hundred municipal officials. The latter figure represented a gain of 45 percent from 1983. Progress was, however, most clearly visible at the Federal level. The number of Latino congressmen rose from three in 1961 to seventeen in 1993. Many of the gains came in the 1980s and 1990s when Latinos picked up eleven seats. As early as 1979, Latino politicians of all backgrounds had created their own organization: the National Association of Latino Elected and Appointed Officials. This increasing electoral strength in turn prompted an accompanying surge in federal appointments. While President Johnson appointed only three Latinos to the federal bench, President Carter selected nine Latino justices.

Again, as for Blacks and Native Americans, Latino or Hispanic Power, or its constituent elements—"Brown," Chicano or "Borriqueno" (Puerto Rican) Power, was as much a cultural movement as a political one. Latinos, like African Americans, challenged prevailing notions of assimilation, attempted to construct or preserve the integrity of group culture, and demanded recognition and respect for their cultural difference. Also as with African Americans, this effort created and drew strength from Hispanic or Latino ethnic studies programs in universities around the United States. In 1984, one survey estimated that 23 percent of higher education institutions in America offered courses in Hispanic studies and 6 percent permitted undergraduates to major in Hispanic or Latino Studies. Frank Bonilla, founder and longtime director of one

such Latino Studies Center at the City University of New York, contended that such programs were necessary to rectify the distortions and
demeaning stereotypes of standard accounts of Latinos, to help create a
Latino intelligentsia, and to maintain a Latino "perspective" in the
study of American life and community. In some universities, particularly
in California, such programs were Chicano Studies, in the northeast,
Puerto Rican Studies, and in the Southeast, at Florida International
University, for example, Cuban Studies. Yet some programs broadened
to encompass the cultures of a variety of nationalities within the broad
framework of Latino Studies.

As with African Americans, Indians, and Latino Americans, a new
Asian American solidarity and self-confidence emerged in the critical
years of the late 1960s and early 1970s. The Asian American "movement" of that era differed from the other three in a number of ways.
The battlegrounds for Asian Americans were more likely to be
campuses than neighborhood streets, for example. The initial major
battles were the Third World Strikes, at San Francisco State College in
the fall and winter of 1968 and 1969 and the University of California
at Berkeley in the winter of 1969. William We suggests, "probably
more than any other single event, the Third World Strike at San
Francisco State symbolized the potential of Asian American activism."
The critical organizations in these early battles, the Intercollegiate
Chinese for Social Action, the Asian American Political Alliance in
California, and Asian Americans for Action on the East Coast drew
heavily from college students. This did not mean that the movement
had no links to local Chinatowns and other Asian American communities, or that students were not interested in making those links.
Indeed, in 1970, members of the AAA established the Asian American
Community Center in New York's Chinatown and began work to preserve the neighborhood. Still, the initiative in the Asian American
movement came largely from the campuses. Another important difference was the importance of the antiwar movement in provoking the
new Asian American consciousness. In part, this reflected the movement's campus roots, but it also reflected the special significance of a war
in Asia and its racial consequences for Asian people in the United
States. Nevertheless, as We notes, "Although the antiwar movement
politicized a generation of Asian Americans, the Black Power movement moved them toward the goals of racial equality, social justice,
and political empowerment." At the "Asian American Experience in

America—Yellow Identity Conference" held in Berkeley in 1969, Isao Fujimoto talked about the need "to shatter the myth of assimilation and to prove how the racist, colonialist majority exploited the minorities."

If the Asian American movement was inspired by Black Power, however, it undertook the same kind of effort as the Latino movement did to raise the consciousness of Asian Americans from various groups and simultaneously knit them together into a single panethnic entity, The names of student organizations suggested this deliberate attempt to forge a new group. Indeed, the Asian American Political Alliance may have been the first organization in American history to use the term Asian American. The choice of the name suggested both the rejection of the western "Oriental," as blacks had rejected Negro, and the recognition, as Yuji Ichioka argued, that "If we rallied behind the Asian American banner . . . we could extend our influence."

While young Chinese, Japanese, and Filipino Americans caught the spirit of a new "Yellow Power," dramatic changes in immigration to America promised to make that rallying cry more than an empty slogan. Asian immigrants had been all but excluded from the continental United States since the turn of the century. Grudging acknowledgment of Cold War constraints allowed a small trickle of Chinese and other immigrants to enter the United States in the 1950s. In 1965 Congress completely overhauled the immigration laws. Inspired by the civil rights movement, the historic new law did away with the old noxious racist quotas that favored northwestern Europeans. Nevertheless, few believed that the new law would produce any significant changes in the origins of immigrants. While signing the bill, President Johnson remarked, "The bill we sign today is not a revolutionary bill," and Congressman Emmanuel Celler argued that abolition of nationality quotas would not end continued European dominance among the immigrants. Yet taking advantage of the new law's opportunities for educational, occupational, and family reunification exemptions, immigrants poured into the United States from Asia. In the 1970s, millions of Laotian, Cambodian, and Vietnamese refugees fleeing the debacle in Indochina added to this already surging immigrant tide from Asia. The number of Asian Americans thus rose more than 140 percent in the 1970s and more than 100 percent in the 1980s.

These numbers gave the Asian American community more political heft than they had ever enjoyed before. That heft, and the new sense of political consciousness among the Asian American leadership, translated into some important political gains for Asian Americans. By 1992, for example, there were nine Asian American congressmen. Asian Americans also won local offices in Monterey Park, Gardena, Cerritos, and Torrance, California, in the 1980s as well as the governorship of Washington in 1996. Hawai'i is the heartland of Asian American politics, however. In 1990, the Governor, Lieutenant Governor, and fifty-four state legislators were Asian Americans—largely Japanese Americans—in Hawai'i. Despite recent gains, the Asian American population has not increased enough to give the group the kind of voting power that African or Latino Americans can boast of in many states. Furthermore, Asian Americans, particularly the new immigrants, have been, if anything, even less likely to register to vote than members of the other two groups. A survey of California voters in 1990 found that only 39 percent of Asian Americans were registered to vote, compared to 65 percent for whites, 58 percent for blacks and 42 percent for Latinos. On the other hand, Asian American politicians have some advantages the other groups do not. If they cannot tap as many votes, such politicians can and have tapped the rich financial resources of upwardly mobile Asian Americans. Asian Americans, as Yen Le Espiritu points out, have been more likely to donate money to campaigns than other groups, and Asian American politicians have parlayed those resources into success even when they have run in overwhelmingly non-Asian states or districts.

Ethnic Studies have played an important role for the Asian American movement, perhaps an even more important role than in the African American or Latino American movements. Indeed, the demand for Asian American Studies was the principal goal of the Movement's first major battles, the San Francisco State and California-Berkeley strikes. Students also staged a three-day takeover of a hall at the City University of New York in 1971 to force the establishment of Asian American Studies Programs. William We suggests that the initial willingness of colleges and universities to set up Asian American studies programs lasted only until about 1973, and many Asian American programs disappeared in the late 1970s and 1980s. Yet, he points out, there was a noticeable revival in the 1980s, producing new programs at M.I.T. and new courses and programs at a number of other East Coast colleges. The dramatic increase in Asian American student enrollments fueled this resurgence of interest in schools all across the nation. Like

Latino and Black Studies professors, Asian American Studies scholars have sought to "raise the ethnic consciousness and self awareness of Asian American students" and to challenge perceived assimilationist or mono-cultural biases in the teaching of what America has been or should be. Such efforts, as for many Latino programs, have also helped shape a panethnic Asian American entity by linking together the experiences of Chinese, Korean, Japanese, or other groups by, as one Asian American writer has contended, demonstrating "how Amerika screwed [all of] us."

The late 1960s and early 1970s were a watershed for African, Native, Latino, and Asian Americans. The small radical organizations pro-claiming Black, Red, Brown, or Yellow Power foreshadowed broader political mobilization and cultural revivals among blacks, Latinos, and Asian Americans. Politically, the highpoint of this multicultural coali-tion probably came with Jesse Jackson's campaigns for the Democratic presidential nomination in 1984 and 1988, but through the 1980s and into the 1990s, representatives of all three groups continued to battle for cultural recognition by urging adoption of new course requirements or curriculum changes. Most of these efforts met stiff opposition from many whites, however, and in these and other battles over busing, immigra-tion reform, or affirmative action, or through polarizing events like the O. J. Simpson Trial or the Los Angeles race riots, the boundaries between these groups and the white majority became hotly contested battlegrounds.

Such fights helped sharpen the identities and raise the consciousness of many minorities, but they also helped define a new "whiteness" in America. For while Asian, Latino, and African Americans were mobi-lizing over the last thirty-five years, whites were changing, too. In part they changed because of an internal transformation and in part as reac-tion to the newly self-conscious minorities, particularly African Americans. Because of these internal changes and external influences, ethnic and religious identities took on entirely new meanings among white Americans.

The initial response of many white Americans to the tumult of the late 1960s was to join in the celebration of ethnic roots, the assertion of ethnic group solidarity, and the challenge to old assimilationist ideals. The emergence of neighborhood activists like Barbara Mikulski in Baltimore or Stephen Adubato in Newark, the creation of organizations like Geno Baroni's Center for Urban Ethnic Affairs and a sudden flurry of books and articles by writers like Michael Novak or Richard Gambino seemed to herald a "white ethnic revival." Ironically, this revival represented both a resistance to the new challenge of black and minority power and an appropriation of Black Power rhetoric and ideas of ethnic assertion and pride. Most observers believe that the white ethnic revival was but a temporary interlude. Joshua Fishman suggests that by the late 1970s the ethnic boom seemed to have subsided considerably.

While the ethnic revival flashed and then sputtered, a more long-lasting and fundamental revolution appeared to be remaking the meaning of whiteness in America. Over the course of the period from the 1960s to the 1980s, white ethnic neighborhoods would all but disappear in American inner cities and, though "ghosts" of such ethnic residential clusters reappeared in some suburbs during this period, they too proved transient. Perhaps more important, intermarriage rates among white groups skyrocketed. These were not just rates for marriages across ethnic boundaries, which had been steadily rising among most nineteenth- and early twentieth-century European migrant groups since the 1930s and 1940s; these were rates also for marriage across religious boundaries, which had remained low through the 1950s. The "triple melting pot" of Americanizing Protestants, Catholics, and Jews had fully emerged out of the old ethnic identities only in the 1950s, but by the 1960s and 1970s even it seemed to be fading away. While European Americans might still call themselves Irish, Italian, or Russian, and certainly Catholic or Jewish after the 1960s, those identities, even the religious ones, were increasingly freely chosen, not socially or politically determined. The social boundaries separating these groups were now lightly defended and porous.

There were both long- and short-term causes for these dramatic changes. The long-term causes lay in the rising social mobility of white ethnic groups. There is evidence that the older groups, like Irish and German Americans, achieved occupational and educational parity with white native-stock Americans sometime in the early twentieth century, and some newer groups, like Jewish Americans, had even surpassed native-stock Americans by the 1940s. The rise of unions, World War II prosperity, and the GI Bill significantly accelerated upward mobility for white ethnic Americans from the 1930s through the 1950s. By the 1950s and 1960s, Catholics and Jews were cashing in on this occupational progress and moving out of cities to the suburbs in increasing numbers—again, abetted by federal help from FHA and other programs. Such white ethnics had also achieved significant political power, as vital parts of the Democratic Party's New Deal coalition, as well as cultural power, as Jewish studio owners and the Catholic Church (through the Legion of Decency) consolidated their influence over America's film industry.

Yet it was the tumultuous events and movements of the 1960s that catalyzed these long-term trends and all but collapsed the already weakening boundaries separating white ethnics and religious groups. Kennedy's election and martyrdom and the Second Vatican Council's ecumenism, for example, undermined the old mutual enmity between Catholics and Protestants that had been a premise of political and social organization in the urban North since the nineteenth century.

One of the most remarkable and yet often overlooked trends of the last thirty-five years, reflecting these collapsing boundaries, has been the decline of the "Protestant Establishment." This does not mean that an economic elite, much less an elite class, has disappeared in America. Indeed, on the contrary, there is substantial evidence that the richest Americans have become richer and more powerful over the last twenty years as they added significantly to their proportion of the nation's wealth. That elite also remains overwhelmingly white, despite some minor inroads from Asians, Blacks, and Latinos. Yet that elite is by no means still exclusively Protestant. Not only Catholics, but Jews have moved into the corporate elite and have began to fill up the preparatory schools and men's eating clubs that make up its organizational subcommunity. G. William Domhoff, long-time analyst of American elites, suggests that Catholics had penetrated the elite as early as the 1960s and Jews, he noted in 1998, "are [now] not merely 'the most middle class' and the most affluent white immigrant group. They have become full-blooded members of the power elite . . . " Moreover, though much of the elite organizational subculture—the men's eating clubs, preparatory schools, and country clubs—endures or even thrives, there is little or no recognition of the public authority of a social elite now in the United States. Indeed, as David Brooks has recently suggested, members of the new elite themselves do not believe in the social authority of elites.

The elite has changed in America for several reasons. One has been the changing nature of the economy—the rise in recent decades of sectors like computers or communications open to new entrepreneurs and the stagnation of the old, corporate-dominated heavy industries. But the civil rights and antiwar movements set the process in motion in the 1960s. Both encouraged what would become a broadly pervasive skepticism about authority in American culture. The civil rights movement also made it difficult to justify open racial or ethnic exclusion or prejudice at any level for any group, helping Catholic and Jewish Americans into the upper reaches of economy and society.

If, ironically, civil rights helped undermine the legitimacy of ethnic discrimination among upper-class whites, the Black Power, Latino, and Asian American movements also helped prompt racial solidarity among working-class and lower middle-class whites. The new challenge— African, Latino, and Asian Americans fighting for equality in arenas of politics and society that had once been closed to them—encouraged whites to forget ethnic differences and band together to resist perceived threats to jobs, neighborhoods, or simply status. This had been going on for a long time. White resistance to African American competition in employment and housing ignited violence in Chicago, Detroit, and other city neighborhoods in the 1950s. Yet it surfaced more broadly in the 1960s and 1970s, driving groups like lower middle-class Jews and working-class Italians together, in the embrace of a vaguely defined whiteness, in embattled neighborhoods like Canarsie in New York. In the new racial competition of the 1970s and 1980s, white simply made more sense, seemed a more rational and functional identity to Irish or Italian or Polish ethnics as conflicts between whites and racial others eclipsed older ethnic rivalries.

And yet, if the older white ethnic identities ceased to be "rational" or functional, seemed no longer to mean much in contests for power and resources, or even to reflect social realities in terms of group institutional infrastructure and endogamy, they nonetheless did not die. Indeed, white ethnic identities have never thrived as much in American public life as they have in the last thirty years. The politics and protests of the white ethnic revival might have petered out by the middle to late 1970s, but the cultural production of the revival continues to this day. As Marilyn Halter has documented, celebration of racial and ethnic pride has become big business, spawning products from key chains, ethnic cookbooks, and greeting cards to homeland tours and hosts of ethnic festivals. She points out that much of the new ethnic marketing is directed at the multicultural minorities, but a substantial amount of the new ethnic trade targets white ethnic groups like the Jews and Irish. Genealogy, once the preserve of the old Protestant elite, has become a hobby for hundreds of thousands of more common folk. The web site of the National Genealogical Society, for example, lists Irish, Jewish, Italian, Canadian,

Belgian, and Norwegian American genealogical societies or resources as well as links to traditional genealogical groups such as the Daughters of the American Revolution. Like black, Asian, and Latino studies, white ethnic studies programs sprouted up in universities and colleges. As early as 1973, 135 colleges and universities offered courses in the history or culture of one or more of the white ethnic American groups. Irish Studies, for example, has emerged as an academic discipline only within the last forty years. All the major Irish Studies programs at Boston College, Catholic University, the College of St. Thomas, New York University, and Notre Dame have been founded in the last forty years, as has the American Conference for Irish Studies, the national academic organization devoted to the encouragement of scholarship and teaching in Irish Studies. As Lawrence McCaffrey, one of the founders of the Conference, suggested recently, "In American colleges and universities, Irish Studies enjoys a prestige unimaginable forty five years ago."

Perhaps the most striking evidence of this ethnic cultural revival, however, has been the explosion of white ethnic images in American television and movies. Images of Italian Americans, for example, have become far more numerous and prominent in the movies than ever before. Films featuring Italian Americans since the 1960s have included *The Godfather* and its two sequels; *Rocky* and its four sequels; *First Blood*, featuring the character "John Rambo," and its two sequels; *Mean Streets*; *Raging Bull*; *Goodfellas*; *Moonstruck*; and *Saturday Night Fever*. All of these films were spectacular financial successes, or critically acclaimed, or both. Five of the films—*Rocky*, *The Godfather*, *Saturday Night Fever*, *Rambo: First Blood*, and *Rocky IV*—were ranked among the top fifty money-making films of all time at one time or another in the 1980s. In 1988, *Moonstruck* finished ninth among the top-grossing films of the year; *Rambo III* was thirteenth. In 1990 *The Godfather Part III*, *Rocky V*, and *Goodfellas* were all among the top fifty grossing films.

Some of the profits from these movies were as unexpected as they were huge. *Rocky* was made on a shoestring, $1 million, but grossed more than $56 million at the box office. A year later *Saturday Night Fever*, made quickly and cheaply to cash in on the disco-dancing craze, earned over $70 million. Since 1972, three films about Italian Americans—*The Godfather*, *The Godfather Part II*, and *Rocky*—have won Academy Awards for best picture. Little wonder, then, that Richard Alba has pointed out that Italian Americans have become "Hollywood's favorite ethnic group" in the last thirty years.

Italian Americans were not the only ethnics to enjoy a new prominence in American movies and television. Depictions of Jews, for example, had been surprisingly rare in the movies before the 1960s. Indeed, Lester Friedman notes that the number of films about Jews actually fell to an all-time low in the 1950s. Before the tumult of the 1960s, Jewish studio owners and producers worried about the public's response to Jewish characters, but in the postassimilation age, Jews and other ethnics became much more marketable. In the 1960s, Friedman points out, more films were made about Jews than in any other decade in the history of motion pictures.

In many cases, the new depictions of ethnics still traded on older stereotypes—Italian gangsters and Irish cops, for example. Yet most depictions were more complex than they had been before. Friedman suggests that the new wave of films about Jews presented "an unparalleled range of Jewish characters," and even many of the Italian American criminal characters featured on screen seemed to provoke public fascination, even sympathy, in the new era. Mary Waters reports from her surveys in the 1980s that people of mixed ancestry, with English or German as well as Italian forefathers, for example, invariably identified as Italian. They saw, she said, "Italian as a good ancestry to have . . . because they [Italians] have good food and a warm family life."

If white ethnics seemed more visible, more celebrated after the 1960s than ever before, most social scientists nonetheless dismiss the new interest in white ethnic identities as little more than a consumer fad. Joanne Nagel argues that symbolic white ethnic identities hardly have the same meaning for white ethnics as the "mandatory ethnicity" imposed on African, Asian, or Latino Americans. Mary Waters agrees, contending that for white ethnics "ethnicity is not something that influences their lives unless they want it to" and that it "cannot be the same as an identity that results from and is nurtured by societal exclusion and rejection." Marilyn Halter and Joshua Fishman take the new white ethnic identifications more seriously but agree that such allegiances do not mean the same as they once did, when they represented real political and economic interests and identifications were forged in competition for power and resources. Halter locates the new ethnic identifications in "a search for recognizable or familiar points of reference in a cold, impersonal, and fragmented world . . . a longing to feel included."

Such explanations may underestimate the importance of white ethnic identities and overlook the critical, if new, ways in which white ethnic identities serve their members' interests. To claim loyalty to their specific ethnic group may not have helped or hindered the upward mobility of Irish Americans or Italian Americans after the 1960s, for example. Yet understanding themselves as part of a broad tradition of nineteenth- and twentieth-century European immigrants may, in fact, have been very useful to third- or fourth-generation Irish or Italians in the late twentieth century. Matthew Jacobson uses the term *Ellis Island Whiteness* to define such people's identities. Ellis Island whites are not just people from a specific European nation but all the people who share a story of immigrant flight from Europe to America in the nineteenth and twentieth centuries. It does not matter whether it is an Irish story or an Italian or Jewish one, only that it is part of the same great epic of nineteenth- and twentieth-century European immigration to America. In the thirty years since the 1960s, Ellis Island Whiteness, grounded in this heroic story, has served the interests of such people well. As Jacobson suggests, their story of immigration, discrimination, and ultimate success has provided them a rhetorical weapon to help fend off African American or other minority claims for power or resources. First, it absolves white ethnics from responsibility for the establishment of America's oppressive racial regime because they arrived long after that regime was instituted through slavery. More important, this myth of a white ethnic triumph over poverty and against prejudice also offers a rebuttal to black or other minority demands for special government redress for sufferings of discrimination. Ellis Island Whiteness, however, also helped white ethnics make successful claims for full acceptance on their own terms to places in the highest ranks of American society. In the 1950s, ambitious white ethnics believed that they had to hide their backgrounds and conform to the cultural dictates of a Protestant establishment if they wished to gain acceptance by the WASP elite; such tensions were a commonplace, for example, for the Irish American characters in the writer John O'Hara's novels. If white ethnics had continued to hold that belief in the 1960s and after, the old Protestant Establishment might not have collapsed so swiftly. Yet in the 1970s and 1980s, white ethnics no longer thought such conformity necessary. They now claimed a heritage as good as any other, and a series of national commemorations from the nation's Bicentennial in 1976 through the Centennial of the Statue of Liberty in 1986 confirmed their claim by establishing the Ellis Island epic as one of the foundational stories of the nation. The renovation of Ellis Island in the early 1990s and its elevation to the status of a national icon, rivaling or even surpassing Plymouth Rock or Jamestown in popularity, capped this rise of Ellis Island Whiteness. In Jacobson's terms, Ellis Island Whiteness had routed Mayflower Whiteness.

The emergence of these new multicultural and white ethnic identities provoked several issues, which became important points of conflict between whites and minorities, especially African Americans, over the course of the 1970s and 1980s. Such issues did not erupt outside of the political process but were enmeshed in it. The two major political parties tried to capitalize on these issues throughout the era in order to gain political advantage. Generally, the Republicans played upon them to try to pry whites from both North and South out of the Democratic Party and make the GOP the nation's majority party. In this effort they had some success—at least initially—rolling up big election victories behind Richard Nixon and Ronald Reagan. Political competition over these issues, however, did more than disrupt the partisan balance, it helped exacerbate ethnic tensions, sharpen group identities, and charge boundaries.

The first such issue was school busing—busing children from one neighborhood to another in order to racially integrate local schools. The Supreme Court decisions at the end of the 1960s and the beginning of the 1970s helped shift the battlegrounds of school integration from self-consciously legislated school segregation in the South to the segregation of schools in the North, reflecting residential segregation that school departments permitted or even encouraged. Court-ordered desegregation in Detroit, and particularly in Boston, encountered fierce, often violent, resistance from whites in the early and mid-1970s. Busing controversies, however, extended beyond a few cities to become critical issues in national politics as George Wallace and later Richard Nixon took up opposition to it. Nationally, polls found that three quarters of whites surveyed opposed busing throughout the 1970s.

While the struggle over busing rose to a climax in the 1970s, a new conflict over immigration began brewing in that decade. Few of the older anti-immigration groups like the Daughters of the American Revolution played a critical role in the new anti-immigration fights, and there seemed to be less interest in overturning the 1965 immigration reform law's repeal of the older racist quotas, than on enforcing the restrictions of that and subsequent laws more rigorously. In particular, the movement sought to limit, and perhaps even roll back, the tide of illegal or undocumented aliens who had come to the United States in such great numbers since the mid-1960s. Opponents of illegal immigrants lodged a wide range of grievances against them, but one of the most popular was the suggestion that illegal immigrants were costing taxpayers in welfare, public schooling, and public supported health services. As early as 1975, the state of Texas tried to bar undocumented children from attending local schools. More seriously, in 1994, California voters passed a referendum, Proposition 187, to deny public services to illegal aliens. Courts overturned such laws, but the size of the majority for the California referendum, 59 percent to 41 percent, suggested the power of anti-immigrant feelings in the state at that time. Most legislative efforts to restrict or roll back illegal immigration focused not on the existence of public services for illegal immigrants but on employment of them. Again, as early as 1971, states like California passed laws to punish employers who hired illegals. Throughout the seventies and eighties Congress considered several bills that would have sanctioned employers but passed none of them. Sentiment, however, was strong enough to push the legislation through one or the other of the chambers throughout that period. From 1982 to 1985, congressional efforts focused on the Simpson-Mazzoli Bill, named after Republican Senator Alan Simpson and Democratic Congressman Romano Mazzoli. A version of this bill, a compromise mix of employer sanctions with amnesty for illegals who were longtime residents of the nation, passed as the Immigration Reform and Control Act of 1986.

Though most critics of illegal immigration were not overtly racist or opposed to immigration per se, the campaign against illegal immigrants exacerbated ethnic tensions. As David Reimers notes, the new nativism's focus on illegals may have funneled a broader disquiet with increasing immigration onto the most vulnerable target. Given that illegal immigrants were overwhelmingly (though by no means exclusively) Latino or Asian, the conflicts over them fed and fed off racial and ethnic tensions. Moreover, some of the more vociferous critics of immigration, like the political commentator and presidential candidate Patrick Buchanan, trod very close to the old racism when they openly questioned the ability of newer immigrants to assimilate into American society.

Struggles over affirmative action began as early as the 1960s and have lasted to the present. The phrase affirmative action may have appeared first in an executive order issued by John F. Kennedy in 1961, but the first meaningful argument in behalf of the concept came in Lyndon Johnson's famous speech at Howard University in 1965. "It is not enough," Johnson said, "just to open the gates of opportunity . . . we seek . . . not just equality as a right and theory, but equality as a fact and result." Johnson later issued an executive order of his own, Order no. 11246, authorizing new federal agencies and empowering old ones to create minority hiring requirements for the government and for businesses with government contracts. Ironically, however, it was the Nixon administration's Philadelphia Plan, requiring Philadelphia construction firms under federal contract to meet specific goals for minority hiring, that became the most important first step in implementing the executive order. By 1971, the Supreme Court had agreed to the basic factor underlying the affirmative action concept: that statistics reflecting disproportionately few minority employees may prove discrimination even when overt evidence of discrimination could not be found.

By then, however, affirmative action had also become controversial. Though the Nixon Administration had introduced the Philadelphia Plan in 1969, within a few years President Nixon began to court the growing ranks of affirmative action's opponents. White workers and students claiming reverse discrimination continued to bring suits against governments, businesses, or universities in the courts, despite the Supreme Court's earlier decision. The most celebrated case was Alan Bakke's claim against the University of California at Davis Medical School. Bakke argued that he was a stronger applicant than some of the minority students accepted by the School. While the court agreed with Bakke in this instance it did not overturn affirmative action programs in general as a means of overcoming discrimination against minorities. Nevertheless, affirmative action has remained controversial. Ronald Reagan attacked it in his first press conference, and his administration led an open assault on Executive Order 11246. More recently, conservatives in California placed the issue of affirmative action on the state ballot in 1996 and won their battle, thereby preventing the state or its agencies from employing affirmative action policies.

A host of other issues, incidents, and events have emerged or erupted over the last thirty years that have marked off and reinforced the racial and ethnic boundaries of the new multicultural era. The educational curriculum has been one particularly hotly contested battleground. Probably the most broadly divisive question in cultural contests over education has been the issue of the primacy of the English language. In the face of extensive immigration, several older-stock white organizations have sought to reaffirm the nation's commitment to

English as the nation's official language. Some states have responded to the pressure by passing resolutions confirming the official status of English. Most battles over language have centered on the practical issues of languages in schools and, in particular, bilingual education programs. Californians, taking advantage of their easy referendum process, voted to dismantle those programs in 1998, but the issue has been controversial throughout the Southwest, particularly in metropolitan areas with large immigrant populations. Less long-lasting, but indicative of the cultural tensions emerging over school curricula, was the controversy over Ebonics, "Black English" or "African American Vernacular English" as linguists describe it. That controversy erupted when the Oakland School Board encouraged its teachers to begin with an understanding of the African American vernacular to teach students standard English. Critics saw it as a kind of African American bilingual program—or worse, as an indulgence of improper English.

Beyond the fights over language, there were also struggles over history standards and new social studies curricula, such as the proposed New York State Social Studies curriculum in 1991. These conflicts ran all the way up the educational hierarchy and across the country, provoking battles at California-Berkeley and San Francisco State, Cornell, and California State-Northridge over courses and academic programs from the 1960s through the 1990s.

Many of these battles in the culture wars took place in rarefied academic circles and may have seemed distant to ordinary Americans, but there was plentiful evidence of more pervasive ethnic and racial polarization. Small riots broke out periodically in cities across the country from the seventies to the nineties, and turf fights in white or minority neighborhoods were common. Lynching also continued: as late as 1980, twelve lynchings of blacks by white mobs or vigilantes were reported in Mississippi alone.

In the 1990s race seemed as important as it had ever been in the United States. Three incidents in that decade underlined and reinforced the stubborn persistence of racial and ethnic animosity. In 1992 Los Angeles policemen arrested an African American man, Rodney King, for a driving violation. A videotape of the arrest showed that some of the officers mauled King while apprehending him, but a jury in the largely white and conservative Simi Valley suburb of Los Angeles found them not guilty of police brutality. On April 29, 1992, shortly after the verdict became known publicly, minority neighborhoods in Los Angeles exploded in angry violence over the verdict. When the violence sub-sided, fifty-eight people were dead, more than thirteen thousand were arrested, and more than one thousand buildings were destroyed. About two years after the King riot, Nicole Brown Simpson, former wife of O. J. Simpson, and her friend Ronald Goldman were found dead at Nicole Simpson's home in a Los Angeles suburb. O. J. Simpson, a leg-endary football player and television and film personality, was charged with the crime. Combining sex, celebrity, and violence, the trial drew unprecedented attention. The case, however, was no mere media bally-hoo; it had serious racial overtones and became both a stark reflection of the depth of racial division and an aggravation of that animosity. Polls revealed not only public interest among both blacks and whites but almost diametrically opposed opinions between the races about Simpson's guilt. The Simpson case raised once again the persistent issue of white police prejudice in the testimony of policeman Mark Fuhrman, who led the investigation of Simpson. More important, the case's alleged black male violence against a white woman told a story that lay at the heart of the oldest and darkest fears of white Americans' racial imagination. In the midst of Simpson's trial, Lewis Farrakhan, former Nation of Islam minister outspoken in his condemnations of whites (particularly Jews), called for a million black men to march on Washington on October 16, 1995, in order to "recommit and renew our determination to do God's will and seek justice, freedom, and empow-erment for our people." A million men did not come, but hundreds of thousands did. Here again, opinion surveys revealed a sharp racial split: blacks applauded the Million Man March, but whites, suspicious of Farrakhan's militant and racially hostile rhetoric, were skeptical.

As recently as the mid-1990s, then, racial division seemed as in-tractable as it had ever been in America. Indeed, shortly after the Rodney King riot in Los Angeles, a *Time* magazine reporter lamented, "It had not exactly been unknown that race relations were worsening. . . . But not until last week did many whites and blacks realize how deep an abyss had been opening at their feet." American discussions of race had become so bitter and charged that the Clinton administration launched not one but two initiatives to encourage racial understanding: the National Endowment for the Humanities' National Conversation on American Pluralism and Identity and the President's Committee on Race.

But what was the real state of American ethnic and racial relations at the end of the millennium? The language of a multicultural America, composed of an undifferentiated white (if shrinking) majority and African, Asian, and Latino American minorities, has become common-place in talking about race and ethnicity in America. But does it adequately describe the reality of America's racial and ethnic identities, boundaries, and cultures?

For African Americans, it appears that racial identities remain cen-tral and racial boundaries remain charged. African Americans still lag economically behind whites. Indeed, after some success in closing the income gap with whites over a roughly thirty-year period from World War II to the early 1970s, black progress seemed to slow through the 1970s and much of the 1980s. Some scholars suggest that it may even have halted or slipped backward. Andrew Hacker points out, for exam-ple, that median white family income rose by nearly 9 percent between 1970 and 1990, but black median income grew but 2 percent. Similarly, average black male earnings relative to whites rose from a ratio of $450 to $1,000 in 1939 to one of $654 to $1,000 in 1969, but, from 1969 to 1989, it rose to only $716 to $1,000.

As Hacker and others note, however, such statistics can mask more complicated economic changes in the black community. African American middle classes expanded significantly in the 1970s and 1980s, but the ranks of impoverished blacks did not decline substantially. The persistent economic difficulties of unskilled black workers—compli-cated by an economy that offered fewer blue-collar opportunities and by problems of drugs, violence, and family rupture—remained an impor-tant source of division between blacks and whites in America. African Americans had an interest in maintaining or expanding welfare pro-grams as well as government-funded programs aimed at alleviating poverty. Many whites, particularly working-class whites, who had once backed New Deal welfare programs, now came to see government pro-grams as black programs.

Yet even the black and white middle classes did not necessarily share the same interest. Scholars, like the general public, disagree over the efficacy of affirmative action programs, but it is true that a dispropor-tionate number of African Americans, and middle-class African Americans in particular, have found jobs in local, state, or federal gov-ernments. As Hacker points out, African Americans held 20 percent of the jobs in the Postal Service and made up the same proportion of the Armed Services, about double their percentage of the total population. Police officer was one of the fastest growing occupations for blacks between 1970 and 1990, rising by almost 300 percent. Even higher up the economic scale, the government is an important employer for African Americans; one third of all black lawyers and almost one third of all black scientists worked for the government in 1990. This means that the black middle class has a heavy stake in maintaining or expanding governments and insuring—through affirmative action, strict antidiscrimination, or old-fashioned political patronage—that such governments hire African Americans.

This distinct black economic interest undergirds a distinct black politics. African Americans have made up a powerful and visible voting bloc in the American electorate for the entire thirty-five-year period from 1965 to the present. Black support for the Democratic Party, begun with Franklin Roosevelt's New Deal and confirmed by Johnson's civil rights legislation, has rarely fallen below two-thirds in presidential elections, and even many congressional elections, in the last three decades. Most African Americans clearly believe that such solidarity is critical to defend and advance their interests, whether in electing sympathetic white Democrats to the presidency or their own as congressmen or mayors. Such political solidarity, however, also continues to sustain the group, reinforce identity, and charge its boundaries.

It is difficult to tell how long such identities and boundaries will endure, for there have been some noticeable trends in recent years that appear to have undermined black solidarity. The rising tide of immigration from the Caribbean and more recently Africa, for example, has brought thousands of African or African-descent people to the United States. By 1990 there were nearly one and a half million foreign-born blacks in the United States, and they constituted nearly a quarter of the black population in New York. Such immigrants bring their own perspectives on race and race identity to the United States. As Mary Waters has reported, many West Indian black immigrants have tried to distance themselves from American blacks, viewing American blacks as lazy and obsessed with racial slights. These West Indians believed that they enjoyed higher status in America as members of their own immigrant peoples than as members of a black racial group and thus insisted on identification with their Caribbean homelands rather than with Black America. As black immigration increases, it appears to open a potential fissure in Black racial solidarity in America. There are also trends toward racial integration that may be sapping black solidarity. There is some evidence, for example, that the economic boom at the end of the 1990s began to pull members of all races in, even the poorest blacks and minorities of urban ghettoes, and promised to recast African American conceptions of the economic interests of their race. There has also been a rising trend in intermarriage across the black and white boundary. As late as the 1950s, southern states officially banned such marriages altogether. The 1960s swept away such laws, and the sexual revolution of the decade and its emphasis on individual sexual and romantic fulfillment not only helped reinforce civil rights but inspired tolerance in opening up romantic and sexual relations across racial lines. Thus the number of black-white marriages has tripled since 1970. African Americans have also begun to break into the government elite and become national heroes—Martin Luther King, for example, and popular culture icons such as Michael Jordan.

Still race, at least as defined in black and white terms, continues to matter in America, and it is likely to matter for a long time. Black immigrants, for example, may insist on their separate ethnic identities, but, as Waters points out, the "overwhelming pressure" of the broader culture appears to force a significant proportion of their children to merge into an African American melting pot, identify as African Americans, and take up African American culture. Waters found that only a minority of the American-born children of black immigrants identified with their parents' ethnic group, and most of them were the children of successful middle-class immigrant parents. A larger proportion of the children of black immigrants found that the structure of race relations and white perceptions in the United States lumped them with native black Americans, and they accepted that racial designation. They thus rejected their parents' ethnicity along with their disdain for African American culture. These second-generation blacks eagerly took up black youth culture from "Black English" to rap and hip-hop music.

Moreover, there have been clear limits to the extent of black social integration even over the last ten years. Black residential segregation has dropped only slightly over the last decade, despite the economic boom. As professor John Yinger told the *New York Times* in the summer of 2001, "One of the surprising things about black-white segregation over the years is that it has been, and remains, so much higher than other kinds." Similarly, for all the powerful and pervasive influence of the civil rights and sexual revolutions, marriages between blacks and whites still account for less than 10 percent of all marriages among black males.

Certain trends among whites have also suggested that the boundary between blacks and whites could remain tense for many years. Particularly striking has been the weakening of alliances that once crossed the racial border. Union decline has sapped the strength of class coalitions across racial boundaries. Yet racial tension and conflict may not be as much a result as a cause of the decline of class feeling and union strength. As Bruce Nelson has recently argued, over the last thirty years, white workers have often strongly resisted black challenges to seniority systems or to white monopolies of skilled positions. Thomas Edsall and others have also charted dramatic shifts of white blue-collar workers from Democrats to conservative Republicans over a whole range of social issues, but particularly over race, in the 1980s. More recently, scholars such as Thomas Sugrue, Nelson, and others, cite evidence of white worker resistance to African American integration of jobs and neighborhoods back to the earliest years of the civil rights era, in the 1940s and 1950s, casting doubt on how viable working-class alliances across racial lines have ever been. Whatever the potential for working-class alliances across racial lines may have been in the past, the possibility of such cross-race, class coalitions has seemed more distant in recent years.

Not only did working class alliances across racial lines break down in the new era of race relations, but cooperation between blacks and their longtime white allies, American Jews, also seemed to founder. The apparent demise of alliances between blacks and Jews has seemed a particularly telling example of the new hardening of racial boundaries. Jews had played a prominent role in supporting black civil rights back into the early twentieth century. Jews had helped found the NAACP and the Urban League and over time had played an increasingly important role in sustaining both organizations. From that time through the great civil rights struggles of the 1960s, Jews played an unusually significant role in black struggles. Such efforts reflected an historic Jewish commitment to protecting minority rights, a commitment rising both out of the values of Jewish culture and the practical consideration of Jewish vulnerability as a small non-Christian minority in a largely Christian and sometimes anti-Semitic American society.

Yet even as Jews and blacks fought together in civil rights struggles, strains appeared in their relationship. In the 1950s and 1960s, blacks and Latinos crowding into clothing manufacturing, for example, bridled at the Jewish monopoly of union leadership in these trades and the failure of those leaders to work aggressively for the new minority work-ers' needs for better pay and working conditions. The turning point in black-Jewish relations, however, came in 1968, in the Brooklyn neigh-borhood of Ocean Hill-Brownsville. In an experiment aimed at improving the education of poor African American children, the city, drawing on Ford Foundation funding, sought to increase local input and control of the schools in that black neighborhood. The experiment turned into a two-year war pitting black activists against the school-teachers and their union, the United Federation of Teachers. Many of the teachers and the union's leadership were Jewish, and the battle dis-solved into a bitter wrangle of charges and countercharges of racism and anti-Semitism. Ocean Hill-Brownsville was the first broadly visible revelation of the new strains in black-Jewish relations, but in succeed-ing years there would be many more. Some Jewish organizations would line up against black ones over legal challenges to racial affirmative action plans, such as the DeFunis case in 1974 and the Bakke case in 1978. These cases were, Cheryl Greenberg notes, "the first time black and Jewish organizations had publicly and formally positioned them-selves on opposite sides of a civil rights question." Meanwhile, some popular black leaders, most notably the Nation of Islam minister, Lewis Farrakhan, spoke openly and heatedly of alleged longtime Jewish exploitation of blacks extending as far back as the slave trade. Black and Jewish leaders also clashed over foreign policy, most notably over Israel and its treatment of Palestinian Arabs.

The growing divisions between blacks and Jews appeared to grow out of increasing divergences of perceived interests. Jews had, by and large, been successful in American life and became even more so after the 1960s as the old Protestant elite collapsed and new industries emerged. Despite suffering discrimination and stereotyping, Jews, Cheryl Greenberg suggests, understood their success as vindication of America's potential to work best as a race-blind meritocracy, rewarding individu-als, not groups. Trying to win power or success through assertion of group solidarity and group claims, such as affirmative action allotments, Jews believed, only threatened to set a dangerous precedent that could easily be exploited to establish the privileges of some groups over others. Such notions clashed with many African Americans' sense of how the United States had worked—or better, had not worked—for them in the past, as well as their conviction that they had to assert group claims to expect any measurable change in their people's status.

Clashes of black and Jewish interests did not take place only over affirmative action. Everyday encounters between Jewish teachers or social workers and black students or clients exacerbated the conflicts too. There were also conflicts over neighborhood turf. Jews, as Gerald Gamm and others have noted, were more likely to move quickly out of racially changing neighborhoods than Catholic ethnics, who more often dug in and resisted the influx of new minorities. Still, particularly in the outer borough neighborhoods of New York City, where many lower middle- and working-class Jews had settled, movement out of old neighborhoods was not easy, and clashes over territory provoked mutual hostility between blacks and Jews. "Physical closeness to blacks," Jonathan Rieder argued in his book on the New York neighborhood of Canarsie, "widened the chasm" between Jews and Italians on one side and African Americans on the other.

Yet blacks and Jews clashed not just because of conflicting interests, but also because of changing understandings of what constituted a minority in American life. As Greenberg suggests, the new multiculturalism set in motion by Black Power "putting race first as it does, removes Jews from the outsider community that they helped to legitimize. Instead, Jews have become Euro-Americans with their cultures and contributions subsumed under that broad heading (and their victimization by other Europeans thereby effaced). Now outsiders are racial minorities, African Americans, Asian Americans, native Americans and Hispanics." This is not simply a rhetorical redefinition. Jews' easy upward mobility into the highest ranks of the American elite made Jews look "settled and safe," in short, no different from other whites, to blacks and many other minorities. Indeed, some African Americans and other minorities have seen Jewish opposition to affirmative action and other minority causes as evidence of a Jewish retreat from their civil rights traditions and identification with their new white-skin privilege.

Yet as Greenberg contends, "most Jews do not see themselves privileged as simply white people . . . instead they view themselves as outsiders . . . an insecure minority with a separate culture and a set of beliefs and values." And, as important, they are a people with a history of suffering oppression. Jewish American remembrances of the Holocaust, the Nazi slaughter of over six million European Jews, would have occurred whatever the state of their relations with other minorities or whatever the changes in their own status. Yet the pattern of the remembering, particularly its timing—emerging in the late 1960s and early 1970s—suggests that it must have been influenced by the cultural and social strains and by the confusion that Jewish people were trying to work through as they moved from the outside to the inside. It suggests the dilemma of American Jews in the late twentieth century: on the one hand, a people reminded of their vulnerabilities by the recent horrors visited on their European cousins; on the other hand, a people enjoying the greatest economic and social success in their American history as many of them moved into the highest ranks of the American economy.

Such invocations of the Holocaust, like the Ellis Island narratives, could be dismissed as mere rhetorical strategies for masking Jewish and white ethnics' new white privilege, not unlike the privilege that whites have long enjoyed in the South. Indeed, roiling protests over busing in the North, resistance to affirmative action there, the flight of millions of northern white ethnics from the Democratic party to George Wallace, Richard Nixon, and Ronald Reagan—even the sudden popularity of country-western music above the Mason Dixon line—convinced observers as diverse as social scientists Nathan Glazer and Daniel Moynihan, historian Michael Denning, and journalist Peter Applebone that the United States was being "southernized" in the late twentieth century. It appeared that diverse ethnic and religious groups in the North had collapsed into a single white people confronting African Americans and other minorities, i.e., a southern, bipolar pattern of group identity had spread across the nation.

Yet it is not clear that this "southernization" has yet happened or even will happen. In recent years, as states in the South turned increasingly to the Republican Party, states in the northeast, particularly New England, have pivoted in turn in the opposite direction to the Democrats. This has happened for many reasons, but one may be that the charged racial battles of the seventies and eighties—the fights over busing, for example, now seem old and dormant. With the end of the big black migrations, and with declining crime rates, slashed welfare rolls, and rising prosperity, racial relations in the North have quieted. The absence of racial controversies may simply have allowed other issues that divide northern whites from southern, both cultural and economic, to emerge. Still, one wonders whether the Ellis Island whites, who make up such vast proportions of the white populations in northeastern states, have forged a pluralist political culture different from what exists in the South. Most historians of race relations in the North would be skeptical of an assertion that relations between whites and blacks there have been anything but bipolar, or that whites have ever treated blacks as just another ethnic group. But is there a liberal flip side to Ellis Island whiteness traditions? Is there still a lingering sense of being outsiders, perhaps, or a wariness of political and cultural hegemonies that helps make those northeastern states where Ellis Island whites are numerous approach ethnic and racial diversity differently from the way it is approached in the South? Though Jews have achieved great success and have quarreled with blacks in recent decades, they remain among the most, if not the most, liberal voters in the nation on almost all issues, including minority rights. Even Catholics, who were and remain more conservative than Jews on a host of issues, nonetheless remain more liberal and more Democratic than American Protestants, and far more so than evangelical Protestants. It is too early to tell entirely, but in the Northeast, and perhaps the other parts of the United States, white people may still be a different shade of white than white people in other parts of the nation, most notably the South.

Blacks and whites, however, do not necessarily define the new America. Growing populations of Latinos, Asians, and even Native Americans and, as important, the rising self-consciousness of all these new groups has assured that. Yet, at the close of the century, it is still not clear what the future of each of these groups in America will be. Will the new panethnic identities endure and grow stronger or are they too weak to override the diverse national allegiances of their peoples? Furthermore, what will the relationships of these minorities be to whites and blacks—working with African Americans to remake America into a multicultural nation or seeking assimilation into white culture and admission into white privilege?

There is substantial evidence, for example, to suggest that Native Americans will continue to be a vital group. Despite urbanization, many Native Americans remain on reservations, where they provide a core group of strong identifiers and sustain the tribal museums, colleges, and other organizations that are at the heart of the Indian organizational infrastructure. Economic interests help bolster a separate Indian identity as well. Most Native Americans on reservations are still poor in comparison to whites and, as with blacks, this helps to nourish their sense of difference. And like African Americans, Native Americans depend heavily on the federal government to alleviate this poverty. Some reservations have recently increased their wealth by opening gambling casinos, but these too depend on tribal identification and solidarity.

There are, then, many reasons why Native Americans will remain a distinct, bounded people.

Nevertheless, Native American ethnicity is complicated in the late twentieth century. The upsurge of Red Power and pantribal identity did not eliminate tribes. Indeed, tribes are the foundation of Native American ethnicity; they are the only legally sanctioned Indian communities as well as the original touchstones of Indian ethnicity for all Native Americans. Tribal identities probably could not have melted into broader Indian identities, given the communal, political, and economic roles that they play. Tribal allegiances thus persist as a potential source of division among Native Americans. Another source of division that has emerged more recently is the conflict between urban and reservation Indians. During some of the Red Power protests, older Native Americans on reservations sometimes resented urban activists who claimed to speak for them even though, as some reservation residents believed, these activists knew little about their problems.

There is, however, a broader, more fundamental problem looming for American Indian identity and solidarity in the future. The dramatic rise in the Indian population recorded by censuses since 1960 speaks to that problem, for the census figures include hundreds of thousands of people who decided to declare themselves Indians who had not identified themselves in that way in the past. Who is or can be an Indian then? Is it a matter of self-identification, and if so, is being an Indian an identity lightly worn, an ethnic option not forced by circumstance but chosen as a lifestyle? This kind of Indian identification seems more akin to white ethnic symbolic allegiances than to African or even Asian or Latino American racial identities. It appears to have all of the same attractions—a legendary past, romantic homelands, traditional rituals, and evocative values. Indeed, it may offer more than that, for Native Americans are also eligible for affirmative action programs.

Indian leaders are aware and wary of the sudden popularity of Indian identification. They have assailed New Age writers claiming Indian roots like Jamake Hightower, author of *The Primal Mind*. The Association of American Indian and Alaska Native Professors issued a statement in 1993 attacking "ethnic fraud" and the Indian "wannabies," who claim authority to speak as Indians as well as take jobs and apply for grants as Indians. Most such Indian leaders demand that all people claiming to be Indians establish their membership in a tribe through proof of ancestry. Yet the fact that in the last twenty years only half to two-thirds of Native Americans did so suggests the complications of Indian identity and solidarity that have emerged from 1965 to the birth of the twenty-first century. It reveals the variable meanings of being Indian and the varying porousness of the boundaries of those different Indian ethnicities: from a hard core of oppressed tribal people on reservations; to new Indian migrants exploring pantribal identities in cities; to people who had long been integrated into white society and opt for Indian status because it satisfies needs for belonging and tradition.

What does the future hold for the migrant peoples in the multicultural configuration, Asian and Latino Americans? More specifically, what will become of their newly minted panethnic identities? There has been a significant amount of cultural production among both Asian Americans and Latino Americans over the last thirty years. Among Asian Americans, for example, there has been a remarkable burgeoning of ethnic literature written by authors like David Louie, Frank Chin, and Maxine Hong Kingston. Museums in New York, Seattle, and Los Angeles and scholars in Asian American Studies programs have also worked hard to recover and fashion a new Asian American history. Latino American literature, movies, and art have also flourished during the last forty years, suggesting a cultural base for the broader panethnic identity. More important in providing common ground to disparate Latino nationalities is, of course, the Spanish language itself. In this case, Latino ethnicity profits not just from the work of a few cultural activists but from an explosion of profit-driven media outlets seeking to capitalize on the growing Spanish language market here in the United States as well as the even bigger one lying on its doorstep in neighboring countries to the south. As Geoffrey Fox notes, "No other minority now or in the history of the United States has had as extensive an apparatus for maintaining its language." There are, for example, two national Spanish language television networks: Univision, first broadcasting as Spanish International Network in 1969, and Telemundo, which began in 1986. With Spanish-speaking migrants continuing to pour into the country and the prospect of producing programming for huge markets south of the border, neither the Spanish language media behemoth nor the visibility it gives to the language is likely to die soon.

What is difficult to determine is whether such cultural production helps individual Asian and Latino Americans mark off a distinct identity from whites while at the same time finding common ground with members of other nationalities in their panethnic group. There is evidence that American-born members of both groups are more sympa-thetic to such panethnic identities and cultures than immigrants are. But it is not clear how vital such culture is to the everyday life of mem-bers of the new American-born generations or how critical it is to their self-identification. Survey data suggests, for example, that although the vast majority of second- and later-generation Latinos use English, not Spanish, in everyday life, a substantial proportion know and honor Spanish as the ancestral language.

Even if new American-born generations are sympathetic to paneth-nic identities, conflicts among nationalities within the two groups are not likely to disappear soon. Immigrants tend to hold such national loy-alties dear, and now (and probably for a long time in the foreseeable future) they make up substantial proportions of both the Latino and Asian American groups. Moreover, even for later generations, the dif-ferences among the various national groups, reinforced by enduring class and regional differences, simply seem too strong to become irrelevant soon.

Among both Latinos and Asians, members of each group's national-ities have entered the country with very different backgrounds, for very different reasons, and at very different times—with very different subse-quent histories. Some Asian American groups, such as Japanese and Korean Americans, carry long traditions of mutual enmity with them to the United States. Similarly, among Latino Americans, Cubans under-stand themselves to be political exiles from Communism and thus have a history and historical memory very different from those of Mexicans or Puerto Ricans.

Class and regional distinctions reinforce these national differences and exacerbate internal conflict. Among both Latinos and Asians, members of some groups either enter America better equipped than others or have been here long enough to learn the necessary skills that enable them to reap the benefits of the American economy. Japanese and, to a lesser extent, Chinese Americans have generally been very successful at moving up the American economic ladder. Vietnamese and Filipinos have come later than the Japanese and, in most cases, with less education than the Chinese, and thus struggle to move up. Among Latinos, many of the initial Cuban exiles were well educated and middle-class, setting them apart from the mass of their fellow Latinos. Regional divisions also fracture the panethnic groups, particularly Latinos. The three biggest constituent elements—Mexican, Puerto

Rican, and Cuban Americans—all have their own regional heartlands, the Southwest, the Northeast, and south Florida respectively, and mix only in certain limited contexts, such as in Chicago or New York.

National loyalties reinforced by class and regional differences inevitably complicate Asian American or Latino American panethnic organizational efforts. Among Latinos, the two largest groups—Puerto Ricans and Mexicans—have worked together in the same pan-Latino organizations or crusades, but they continue to eye each other warily. Some Puerto Ricans, Fox suggests, "fear that any Hispanic agenda that gets worked out will necessarily be a Mexican American agenda in which the Puerto Ricans' particular concerns will be lost." In 1994, several Puerto Rican organizations, miffed at Chicano indifference to the advancement of a Puerto Rican candidate for the Supreme Court, banded together in an ad hoc coalition, "Boricua First," and issued a statement complaining that "our issues . . . get diluted within a larger Hispanic or Latino agenda." Moreover, neither shares the rabid anti-Communism that dominates the third most powerful Latino group, Cuban Americans. Asian American panethnic efforts suffer from some of the same internal conflicts. Japanese and Chinese Americans dominated the early Asian American movements and resulting pan-Asian organizations, but the dramatic influx of Filipinos and Vietnamese since 1965 has altered the numerical balance of power and raised new issues within the Asian American group. Conflicts between Japanese and Chinese American leaders and Filipino or Vietnamese staff or clients have chronically troubled Asian American social service organizations, for example. Yen Le Espiritu recounts the lament of Filipino community advocates about an Asian American welfare agency in California: "The funding is dominated by the Chinese and Japanese. The director is Japanese and the next person is Chinese. They hire Filipinos, but only for the lower jobs or community workers way down the organizational ladder."

What interests, then, hold these groups together? What Geoffrey Fox asked about Latino Americans could apply equally to the disparate groups of Asian Americans: "Is there an issue important to all Hispanics, rural and urban Mexican Americans, inner city Puerto Ricans, Dade County Cubans, and all the many other Hispanic populations equally? And more important to them than the non-Hispanics? How many such issues are there where they all have common interest?"

Issues that are critical to African Americans, such as affirmative action and government action in behalf of workers and the poor, although subject to debate, remain important to Latino Americans, primarily because the great majority of Latino immigrants remain near the bottom of the American economic hierarchy. Immigration restriction and enforcement laws and Spanish language issues are also critical to many Latino Americans. Nevertheless, Latino Americans have not rallied around a clear cluster of interests into a solid voting bloc. While black support for the Democratic Party ran from two-thirds to four-fifths or more in the 1980s and 1990s, Latino support for the Democrats has never been nearly as large. In the presidential elections of the eighties, the Latino Democratic vote ranged from 55 percent to 66 percent. Moreover, Latinos have displayed little consistency in individual races. In 1986 Latinos voted two to one for a Republican Senatorial candidate in Florida, a little less than two to one for a Democratic candidate for Senate in New York, and 57 percent to 43 percent for a Democratic Senate hopeful in Colorado.

Asian American political preferences and allegiances have, if anything, been even more variable. Many Asian Americans have little interest in the perpetuation of affirmative action programs, at least in colleges and graduate schools. While some wish to maintain solidarity with African and Latino Americans against what they perceive as continuing racism in America, others believe that open admissions at universities will favor Asian American students. Few other issues bind all other Asian Americans together. They have thus displayed few consistent partisan preferences over the last thirty years. Outside of Hawai'i, Yen Le Espiritu concluded in 1992, "as a group, Asian Americans have not aligned themselves with either the Republicans or the Democrats." She points to evidence that Asian Americans split almost evenly between the Democrats and Republicans in the 1984 elections. The *Los Angeles Times* found the same ambivalence among Southern California's Chinese Americans in the 1990s.

What such numbers suggest is not just a question about the internal coherence and solidarity of each group, but a question about the larger group's solidarity as part of an alliance of multicultural others opposed to a white majority. Jesse Jackson's campaign in 1984, the Rainbow Coalition, posited such an alliance of racial and other outsiders. Yet in the fiery passions of Los Angeles, exploding after the Rodney King verdict, the differences and latent hostilities among these multicultural partners became all the more evident as Latinos and Koreans fought openly with African Americans. At a fundamental level, the viability of a multicultural coalition lies ultimately in a shared sense of exclusion, understanding that the boundary between all these groups on one side and whites on the other remains so charged and impassable that it renders tensions among the minorities themselves insignificant.

Such groups have certainly shared that sense of exclusion in the past, but do they still do so in the present, and will they in the future? One answer may be found in evidence of interracial dating and marriage. Rates have risen dramatically since the 1960s and have increased enormously in just the last two decades. In 1980, a Gallup survey found that just 17 percent of the nation's teenagers had dated someone of another race; by 1997, 57 percent had done so. Yet the changing rates also reveal that some racial and ethnic boundaries remain more important than others. Asian-white and Latino-white rates of dating and intermarriage far exceed black-white proportions.

In 1997, ABC Television broadcast a new version of Hammerstein's musical "Cinderella." In 1957, when the show first opened on Broadway, white actors and actresses played all the leading roles. In the new television version, Brandy, a young African American singer, played Cinderella; Roberta Peters, a white actress, was her stepmother; one stepsister was white and one black; the Prince, Paolo Montalban was Filipino American, but his father, played by Victor Garber, was white and his mother, played by Whoopi Goldberg, was black. In one sense this new version of Cinderella seemed a natural embodiment of the multicultural revolution that began in the 1960s. "In the truest form of the word, it is truly a rainbow," Montalban contended. Yet in another sense, the show suggested an America where race and ethnicity were irrelevant, even invisible—where a young black heroine might have a white stepmother and black and white stepsisters and, more remarkably, a young hero would be Asian, with a white father and a black mother. Brandy inadvertently acknowledged as much when she suggested that "when you watch the movie, you forget that everyone is a different race."

Whether this version of Cinderella captures a real present or prefigures a probable future is difficult to tell. Given the evidence of weak political solidarity and the porous boundaries revealed in the dating and marriage data for some Asian and even Latino Americans, race seems likely to decline in significance over the next half century. If the long run of economic growth of the late 1990s returns and opens up sufficient opportunity for all races, softens racial competition, and tempers ethnic rhetoric, then, for the best-educated, upwardly mobile, and longest resident Asian and even Latino Americans, race may indeed become irrelevant. Yet for African Americans, as the political, economic, and intermarriage evidence suggests, race is likely to remain critical into the foreseeable future and the new version of Cinderella still a fantasy.

ANNOTATED BIBLIOGRAPHY

Brooks, David. *Bobos in Paradise: The New Upper Class and How They Got There*. New York: Simon and Schuster, 2000.
    Brooks's book is a wry and skeptical discussion of the emergence of the new American elite in the post 1960s era that is itself disdainful of the pretensions to authority displayed by elites.
Daniels, Roger. *Coming to America: A History of Immigration and Ethnicity in American Life*. New York: Harper Collins, 1990.
    Daniels's history is a comprehensive, basic survey of immigration to the United States that is very useful as an overview or as an introduction to the subject. It is arranged chronologically by immigration era and then by group within each era.
Edsall, Thomas Byrne. *The Impact of Race, Rights, and Taxes on American Politics*. New York: Norton, 1991.
    The Edsall book is a brilliant analysis of how linkages forged over racial, welfare, and taxation issues broke up the old Democratic majority coalition in American politics and helped to lure many blue-collar workers, "Reagan Democrats," into the Republican Party.
Fishman, Joshua, et al. *The Rise and Fall of the Ethnic Revival: Perspectives on Language and Ethnicity*. New York: Mouton, 1985.
    Several authors, including Fishman himself, analyze the impact and durability of the ethnic revival. Fishman's essay traces the shift in the meaning of ethnic identity for white ethnics.
Fox, Geoffrey. *Hispanic Nation: Culture, Politics, and the Constructing of Identity*. Seacaucus, N.J.: Carol, 1996.
    Fox's very readable study traces the origins of Latino or Hispanic panethnicity from the "Brown Power" radicals of the 1960s through the creation of the Spanish-language and television-media empires in the 1980s and 1990s. In doing this, however, Fox also points out the persistence of internal rivalries and regional differences that still divide the group as well as the effects of American popular culture on language retention of new generations of Hispanics that threaten its future.
Glazer, Nathan, and Daniel Patrick Moynihan. *Beyond the Melting Pot: The Negroes, Puerto Ricans, Jews, Italians, and Irish of New York City*. Cambridge: M.I.T. Press, 1970.
    This classic of American ethnic studies wisely detected the surprising durability of white ethnic loyalties in New York City during the 1960s, after most social scientists had declared them long dead. Like many observers of the period, however, they overestimated the potential persistence of religious divisions in American life.

Goldfield, David. *Black, White, and Southern: Race Relations and Southern Culture, 1940 to the Present*. Baton Rouge: Louisiana State University Press, 1990. Goldfield's work is a careful, well-documented and sober recounting of modern racial politics in the South through the civil rights revolution and its aftermath. While acknowledging the revolutionary impact of the civil rights movement, Goldfield also recounts persisting inequalities and conflicts.

Greenberg, Cheryl. "Pluralism and Its Discontents: The Case of Blacks and Jews," in David Biale, Michael Galchinsky, and Susan Heschel, eds. *Insider/Outsider: American Jews and Multiculturalism*. Berkeley: University of California Press, 1998. Greenberg's short essay thoughtfully analyzes recent relations between Jewish and African Americans and the causes of their growing mutual suspicions.

Hacker, Andrew. *Two Nations, Black and White, Separate, Hostile, Unequal*. New York: Scribner's, 1992. Though many have hailed African American progress since the civil rights revolution, Hacker was far less sanguine in the early 1990s, pointing to a wide range of persistent inequalities and enduring sources of tensions.

Halter, Marilyn. *Shopping for Identity: The Marketing of Ethnicity*. New York: Schocken, 2000. Halter's book documents the emergence of ethnic marketing in American industries, from greeting cards to tourism. This marketing, she argues, is directed not only at the "multicultural" racial groups like African and Latino Americans but at white ethnics like Jewish and Irish Americans.

Jacoby, Tamar. *Someone Else's House: America's Unfinished Struggle for Integration*. New York: Basic Books, 1998. Jacoby's book is an exhaustive look at racial politics over the last third of the twentieth century. She decries the emergence of Black Power ideologies and the abandonment of integrationist goals among blacks. The book discusses points of contention, including local control of schools, busing, affirmative action, and Afrocentric curricula, both nationally and in three cities—New York, Detroit, and Atlanta.

Krickus, Richard. *Pursuing the American Dream: White Ethnics and the New Populism*. Bloomington: Indiana University Press, 1976. This is a contemporary account of the "white ethnic revival" of the 1970s that provides a comprehensive survey of the revival's organizations and leaders across the country.

Le Espiritu, Yen. *Asian American Pan-Ethnicity: Bridging Institutions and Identities*. Philadelphia: Temple University Press, 1992. This is a sophisticated examination of the recent emergence of an Asian American panethnic identity among Chinese, Japanese, Filipino, and other ethnic groups descended from immigrants from Asia. It focuses on the evolution of this new group identity through electoral politics, funding of social service agencies, census category definitions, and responses to anti-Asian violence.

Marable, Manning. *Race, Reform and Rebellion: The Second Reconstruction in Black America, 1945–1982*. Jackson: University of Mississippi Press, 1984. In this chronological overview of American racial politics, Marable recognizes the gains of the "Second Reconstruction," but he is critical of white and black leaders for their failure to understand that the central issue was "not the narrow battle for integration or political rights but the effort to achieve economic democracy."

Nagel, Joanne. *American Indian Ethnic Revival: Red Power and the Resurgence of Identity and Culture*. New York: Oxford University Press, 1996.

This sociological study explores the revival of Native American ethnicity through the "Red Power" political movement and the creation of a number of new cultural movements and institutions. Nagel is also concerned with the evolution of a panethnic Indian identity and its relation to tribal identities.

Nelson, Bruce. *Divided We Stand: American Workers and the Struggle for Black Equality*. Princeton: Princeton University Press, 2000.

This book investigates the "intersection of class and race" in twentieth-century American society through a study of white and black longshoremen and steelworkers. Building on previous studies of "whiteness," Nelson argues powerfully for the need to consider "the role of the worker's own agency in building and defending the ramparts of racially based inequality."

Reimers, David. *Still the Golden Door: The Third World Comes to America*. New York: Columbia University Press, 1992.

This is a smart, well-researched, and rich examination of the shift, during the second half of the twentieth century, from Europe as the principal source of American immigration to Latin America, Asia, and Africa. In addition to his thorough treatment of the groups themselves, he examines the making of immigration legislation since World War II.

Rieder, Jonathan. *Canarsie: The Jews and Italians of Brooklyn Against Liberalism*. Cambridge: Harvard University Press, 1985.

This is an exceptionally rich investigation of racial tensions in an outer borough New York neighborhood that carefully and thoroughly explores the attitudes of white Italian and Jewish ethnics towards blacks in the post civil rights era.

Smith, Carolyn, ed. *The 88 Vote—ABC News*. New York: Capital Cities/ABC, 1988.

A compendium of the results of ABC exit poll surveys, not only from the 1988 election but from several elections in the 1980s that break down votes by ethnic identity as well as other demographic categories.

Waters, Mary. "Optional Ethnicities: For Whites Only?" in Silvia Pedraza and Ruben G. Rumbaut, eds. *Origins and Destinies: Immigration, Race, and Ethnicity in America*. Belmont, Cal.: Wadsworth, 1996.

Well known for work on optional ethnicities, Waters reminds us here that white racial attitudes restrict how much Mexican Americans and even African immigrants can invent or choose their group identities.

Wei, William. *The Asian American Movement*. Philadelphia: Temple University Press, 1993.

This is a rich and insightful survey of the emergence of the Asian American protest movement. It takes the reader from early campus battles at San Francisco State and the University of California at Berkeley to the creation of Asian American social-service programs, cultural organizations, and Asian studies programs, as well as a rising Asian American presence in electoral politics. Wei's study analyzes Asian Americans' new energy and organizational proliferation and their simultaneous efforts to forge a panethnic Asian American identity.

Zweigenhaft, Richard, and G. William Domhoff. *Diversity in the Power Elite: Have Women and Minorities Reached the Top?* New Haven: Yale University Press, 1998.

This is Domhoff's most recent analysis of the American elite in a series stretching back to the 1960s. Using a variety of methods to identify elite members, he chronicles the emergence of Jews among the elite, noting the continued underrepresentation of minorities such as Latinos and blacks.

CONCLUSION

All historians would agree that America is a nation of nations. But what does that mean in terms of the issues that have moved and shaped us as a people? Contemporary concerns such as bilingualism, incorporation/assimilation, dual identity, ethnic politics, quotas and affirmative action, residential segregation, and the level of immigration itself resonate with a past that dealt with variations of these modern factors. American history is particularly complex because it is not the history of just one people but of many—some who strived to become one people and some who resisted. And as this book indicates, there was little in this history (from Indian Wars to Civil War and from expansionism to progressivism to Civil Rights) that American pluralism did not affect or by which it was not affected.

This book was conceived as a beginning, a place to start for those seeking knowledge of American history with a particular perspective. The chapter essays are designed to provide a concise overview of the various eras in this history. Annotated bibliographies and bibliographic essays offer important works for further reading and research. Each author picks up common themes that are carried through the book, only increasing in complexity as new immigrants arrive and the nation becomes more diverse. Carol Berkin's essay immediately reveals conflicts with the Native Americans and between Europeans, which encompassed struggles over land and trade as well as culture. Cultural and power struggles are evident throughout American history. Yet there was a good deal of cooperation as well, which reveals another trend in American life. Survival for the colonist, as it would be for a later more diverse United States, also depended on working with and understanding the "others." The themes of cooperation and conflict, acceptance, exclusion, and subjugation (especially with the beginning of slavery) permeate U.S. history—whether it is English and Indians, Anglos and Mexicans, Irish and Yankees, blacks and Jews. Other than the institution of slavery and institutionalized racial segregation, the alliances formed or conflicts fought were temporary—shifting as circumstances changed.

The dominance of English culture, later termed Anglo-conformity, is raised early in the chapters. Graham Hodges contends that Anglicization did not immediately prevail, and certainly not in areas where the English were the smaller population. Other cultures and identities remained and flourished. Subsequent authors, particularly Andrew Heinze and Timothy Meagher, respectively, deal with the Americanization/Anglo-conformity of the early twentieth century and the multiculturalism of the late twentieth century, both of which were directly related to the colonial cultural struggles. Although English became and remains the dominant language, other languages vied for equality at various times and places (e.g., German and Spanish). Recent "English Only" organizations, which worked to make English the official language, reflect concerns over the effects of bilingualism and multicultural influence. Religion as well was a culturally identifying factor, and the colonies saw varied religious observances within their populations. In the mid to late twentieth century, Anglo-American cultural preeminence drew opposition from those who placed a new emphasis on multiculturalism and from the identity and interest-group politics of blacks, Asians, Latinos, and Native Americans. Whether there are benefits or liabilities for national unity in multiculturalism is still a hotly debated topic. Whatever the eventual outcome, it is clear that group recognition and assertion of rights and interests are significant factors in contemporary American life as they have been in the past.

Naturalization is also an issue that weaves through American history. Who was entitled to become a citizen? This concern was raised early and immediately became part of a nativist reaction to the foreign-born. Restrictionism, which was to reach an apogee in the 1920s, first appeared, as Marion Casey writes, in the 1790s. Discussions ensued about who would make a good American citizen and whether the country needed more immigrants. Arguments against immigration were similar to those raised many decades later. The Alien and Sedition Acts (1798) were directed at foreigners in regard to residency requirements for citizenship and at those, especially foreign-born, who disagreed with government policies. Suspicion of foreigners and efforts to limit dissent are evident also with the Espionage and Sedition Acts of 1917–1918 and with the immigration quota laws of the 1920s. But whether it is Harrison Gray Otis or Madison Grant or Pat Buchanan writing, the premise is the same: certain immigrants cannot become good Americans and will eventually undermine the nation. Catholics, the Irish,

Germans, Jews, Italians, Asians, Mexicans and other Latinos, and most recently Arabs have all, at one time or another, been the target of nativist fears. One only need to remember the anti-German-American campaign during World War I or the incarceration of Japanese Americans during World War II to realize this. In the modern era, these fears have been accentuated by the 1965 Immigration Act, which had the effect of shifting the primary sources of immigration to other countries, and the September 11 tragedy. Euro-centric nativists now lashed out at those who were coming, once again, from the "wrong" countries. As China, Mexico, and Korea replaced Italy, Poland, and Germany, and migration from Muslim countries increased as well, a frenzy of criticism and discussion broke out over the new laws and over legal and illegal immigration, resulting in increased fears about America's racial/ethnic future.

As a sense of nation and peoplehood developed, nativism grew stronger and its reasoning more varied. Immigrants were radicals, who would bring foreign ideologies and political violence to our shores; they were disease carriers, who planted virulent strains in our midst; they would outbreed the "real" Americans and replace them with inferior races; they would lower wages for American workers. A number of the authors in the volume (Casey, Topp, Ngai, Heinze, and Meagher) pick up these themes and show their persistence in American life.

It is clear from these essays as well that race has had a significant place in U.S. history, especially as it related to African Americans. It is not just the subjugation of blacks through slavery and Jim Crow laws that reflects the obsession with race, but also the need for certain European immigrants to situate themselves quickly in the racial hierarchy by proclaiming their whiteness. Thomas Guglielmo and Earl Lewis speak particularly to this issue and note the "malleability of race; the ways in which power and politics—rather than biology or genetics— define race." A white classification opened the door to opportunity. It also led eventually, as Meagher and others relate, to a coalescence of European nationalities into a generalized white group, with various ethnic identities subsumed under the white label. At first considered not fully white, or at least less white than Anglo-Saxons, these "in-between peoples" eventually, as Ngai writes, "embraced whiteness as a strategy for economic and social advancement."

While white immigrants worked to clarify their racial classification, blacks, Asians, Indians, and Latinos developed various strategies for coping with America's Manifest-Destiny expansion into Native American and Mexican territory, the treatment of degraded minority workers such as blacks, Chinese, and Mexicans, and the wars and other strategies to eliminate "unacceptable" minorities through violence, draconian legislation, pervasive discrimination, segregation, social ostracism, and assimilation. The questioning of a group's "racial capacity for civilization," as Ngai states in relation to Indians in the 1890s, reflects the country's attitude toward disfavored minorities. Policies that were developed to subjugate blacks and Indians were used on other groups as well. A constant battle with America's exclusionary laws and discriminatory behavior affected land ownership, job opportunity, political recognition, and cultural preservation. This long struggle is noted in all the chapters, with the culmination in the civil rights movement and some attitude change chronicled in the Guglielmo-Lewis and Meagher chapters. But the modern period did not end the controversy over race; contention over busing, affirmative action, open housing, race riots; and income gaps continued.

Although the volume authors delineate some of the problems and conflicts immigration generated, they also provide a chronicle of immigration's importance to the growth and strength of the United States. Each group, whether vilified or immediately accepted, voluntary or involuntary, contributed to the nation. Whether it was blacks working as tenant farmers in the South, the Irish and Chinese building the transcontinental rail lines, or Mexicans in western agriculture, the nation prospered from their labor. Culturally, the contributions of such figures as Irving Berlin, Louis Armstrong, and Will Rogers illustrate the benefits of a diverse population, as do political leaders like Fiorello LaGuardia and intellectual notables such as W. E. B. Du Bois. A group's contribution, however, was oftentimes not related to acceptance. An ambivalence existed, which is still evident in contemporary America. Some politicians, for example, rail against illegal immigrants, bemoan porous borders, and claim that the nation does not need more immigrants; yet they acknowledge not only the role of migrant Mexican farm workers and Chinese garment laborers in maintaining cheap prices for these American products but the unwillingness of many citizens to do this work.

This book's purpose has been to focus on the racial and ethnic aspects of U.S. history and thereby show how intertwined those factors were with the growth and shaping of the country. Although not intended as a fully comprehensive history revealing every detail of this connection, the volume shows clearly the salience of immigration, race, and ethnicity. It also shows that these issues still resonate, still stir controversy and debate.

The questions raised by this history are perennial ones and key issues are worth pointing out as suggestions for further research and discussion topics. Most important is the question, "Who is the American?" How has this person been defined in the country's history, and has that definition changed with time? We want to know how to define assimilation and if retention of old-world culture, including language, precludes becoming an American. Can immigrants have a dual identity? How have strong ethnic ties to the ancestral home affected U.S. foreign policy? What was the rationalization for excluding or subjugating others due to race, religion, ethnicity, and immigrant status, and has that changed over the last four centuries? The role of stereotypes is important in this regard, and their malleability over time requires investigation. We can see, for example, how transformations in Irish images from the nineteenth century to the twentieth illustrate changing portrayals.

Regional variations, as Michael Topp relates, must also be considered in assessing attitudes toward particular groups, and, as in the colonial period, the level of Anglicization or acculturation for these groups. How has American expansionism and the wars we have fought indicated the effect of racial and ethnic concerns?

While many questions remain, and the racial and ethnic configurations of the nation are still developing, the main point is that America has always been and remains a nation of nations.

CONTRIBUTORS

Ronald H. Bayor is Professor of History at Georgia Tech and founding and present editor of the *Journal of American Ethnic History*. His books include *Neighbors in Conflict: The Irish, Germans, Jews, and Italians of New York City, 1929–1941* (1978); *Fiorello LaGuardia: Ethnicity and Reform* (1993); *Race and the Shaping of Twentieth-Century Atlanta* (1996), winner of an Outstanding Book Award from the Gustavus Myers Center for the Study of Human Rights in North America. He is also the coeditor, with Timothy Meagher, of *The New York Irish* (1996), winner of the James S. Donnelly, Sr., Prize of the American Conference for Irish Studies for the best book in Irish or Irish American history and the social sciences (1997).

Carol Berkin is currently Professor of History at The City University of New York Graduate Center and Baruch College, where she teaches American colonial, early Republic, and women's history. Her books include *Jonathan Sewall: Odyssey of an American Loyalist*, which was nominated for the Pulitzer Prize; *First Generations: Women in Colonial America*; two edited volumes, *Women of America: A History* and *Women, War, and Revolution*; and a collection of primary documents, *Women's Voices/Women's Lives: Documents in Early American History*. Her latest book is *A Brilliant Solution: Inventing the American Constitution* (2002).

Marion R. Casey is Assistant Professor of History and Faculty Fellow in Irish American Studies at New York University. She is the author of *The Irish Image in American Popular Culture* (forthcoming, The John Hopkins University Press) and *The Irish American Experience: A History in Documents* (forthcoming, Columbia University Press); essays in *The New York Irish*, Ronald H. Bayor and Timothy J. Meagher, eds. (1996); as well as entries in *The Encyclopedia of New York City*, *The Encyclopedia of American Studies*, and *The Encyclopedia of Ireland*. She also has production credits on the documentary films *From Shore to Shore: Irish Traditional Music in New York* (1993) and *Emigrant Savings Bank, Since 1850, The Spirit of Thrift* (2000).

Thomas Guglielmo is an Assistant Professor in the Department of American Studies at the University of Notre Dame. He is the author of *White On Arrival: Italians, Race, Color, and Power in Chicago, 1890–1945* (Oxford University Press, 2003).

Andrew R. Heinze is Professor of History and Director of the Swig Judaic Studies Program at the University of San Francisco. He is the author of *Adapting to Abundance: Jewish Immigrants, Mass Consumption, and the Search for American Identity* (1990), and his recent articles on ethnicity, immigration, and race have appeared in the *Journal of American History*, the *American Quarterly*, *Religion and American Culture*, and *American Jewish History*. He has recently completed a book called *Jews and the American Soul: How Jewish Thinkers Changed American Ideas of Human Nature in the 20th Century* (Princeton University Press, 2004).

Graham Russell Hodges is Professor of History at Colgate University. He is the author of numerous books and articles, including *New York City Cartmen, 1667–1850* (1986) and *Root and Branch: African Americans in New York and East Jersey, 1613–1863* (1999).

Earl Lewis is Professor of History and Afroamerican and African Studies, Vice Provost for Academic Affairs—Graduate Studies, and Dean of the Graduate School at the University of Michigan. He is the author, coauthor, and editor of five books and, with Robin D. G. Kelly, general editor of an eleven-volume history of African Americans for young adults. The author of many articles and reviews, he is, or has been, a member of several editorial boards and boards of directors, including The Council of Graduate Schools and the Graduate Record Exam, or GRE.

Timothy J. Meagher is Curator of American Catholic History Collections and teaches Irish American and American immigration history at Catholic University. He was Director of the Center for Irish Studies at the University. Meagher has edited the collection of essays *From Paddy to Studs: Irish American Communities at the Turn of the Century*, and co-edited with Ronald H. Bayor the collection *The New York Irish*. The latter won the James S. Donnelly Sr. Prize for the best book in Irish or Irish American history and the social sciences offered by the American Conference for Irish Studies (1997). Meagher's book *Inventing Irish America: Generation, Class, and Ethnic Identity in a New England City, 1880 to 1928* was published in the spring of 2001. He is currently writing *A Guide to Irish American History* for Columbia University Press. He has also written several essays and articles on Irish American and American Catholic history.

Mae M. Ngai is Assistant Professor of U.S. History at the University of Chicago, where she teaches Asian American and comparative immigration history. She is author of "The Architecture of Race in American Immigration Law: A Re-examination of the Immigration Act of 1924," *Journal of American History* (June 1999); "Legacies of Exclusion: Illegal Chinese Immigration During the Cold War Years," *Journal of American Ethnic History* (Fall 1998); "The Strange Career of the Illegal Alien: Immigration Restriction and U.S. Deportation Policy, 1921–1965," *Law and History Review* (Spring 2003); and *Illegal Aliens and Alien Citizens: Immigration Restriction, Race, and Nation, 1924–1965* (Princeton University Press, forthcoming 2004).

Michael M. Topp is an Associate Professor of History at the University of Texas, El Paso. He is the author of *Those Without a Country: The Political Culture of Italian American Syndicalists* (2001) and of *"That Agony Is Our Triumph"*: *A Documentary History of the Sacco-Vanzetti Trial* (forthcoming, Bedford/St. Martin's Press). He has also written several essays dealing with issues of race, gender, and transnationalism.

INDEX